ESSENTIALS OF VISUAL
COMMUNICATION

ESSENTIALS OF VISUAL
COMMUNICATION

Bo Bergström

Laurence King Publishing

To Lena

Published in 2008 by
Laurence King Publishing Ltd
361–373 City Road
London EC1V 1LR
United Kingdom
Tel: +44 20 7841 6900
Fax: +44 20 7841 6910
e-mail: enquiries@laurenceking.co.uk
www.laurenceking.co.uk

A catalogue record for this book is available from the
British Library.

ISBN 13: 978-1-85669-577-0
ISBN 10: 1-85669-577-8

Printed in China

Designed by Mark Holt and Charlie Smith
Picture consultant: Faye Dowling

CONTENTS

FOREWORD

Essentials of Visual Communication is a comprehensive survey of the building of messages in the various branches of the media. It focuses on news, advertising and visual profiling, where professional subeditors, art directors and graphic designers all work. These professions have a major responsibility for creating today's visual culture, and are the leading characters in this book.

The book's mission is to make clear the purpose of visual communication – its context and effect, as well as its social impact. It crosses borders between subject areas and professions, and its structure is based on the conviction that taking an aerial view over the whole communication process will always benefit the final result. Such a view makes it easier to see the role of the individual, so that the conditions for personal achievement, and its final effects, are clear.

In this way strategy and creation are integrated, ensuring that the increasing demand for both co-operation and the development of efficient methods for integrated communication are met. A designer who only sees the form will not assist the message, just like a typographer who only speaks in Bodoni. A specialist will have a weak voice in creating substance, but a more flexible practitioner, who is able to control (or at least have a good insight into) the complete communication process, will be successful, confident in a media world in which security lies in change. This is the conviction that permeates the chapters that follow, and their comprehensive view makes this book unique.

Essentials of Visual Communication includes all the classic requirements for work in the media (newspapers, television and web). But it also describes the shift of power that is taking place from the media to citizens and from the production companies to consumers. Today readers, viewers, web visitors and mobile users demand to be interactive participants in a completely different way from previous generations. Related areas, such as the new conditions for the creation of images, whether photographs, films or illustration, in the era of amateurism and self-production, are also given generous space.

My ambition is to describe the work process in an intelligible, inspiring and personal voice, illustrated with exciting, up-to-date pictures. I have made it my duty to encourage critical reflection and try to warn against pitfalls – communicative of course, but also economical and ethical.

The process starts with choosing the right *narration*, which in turn is dependent on the *strategy* and *analysis* of the *communication goal*. The *message*, which has to be given shape and form, needs *creativity* as an extra resource to create *influence*. The *typography* has to be chosen, *text* has to be written, the *image* has to be decided, keeping in mind the demands of rhetoric. After which, these elements have to be put together into a coherent, relevant and inspiriting unity – a *form*. Some media need *sound* – music and effects. Not to forget the *profile*, which represents the company or organization, while the *paper* has a particular influence, as does the *colour*. The *interplay* between all these makes the message reach out to its audience with emphasis. And *everything* is communicating.

Essentials of Visual Communication addresses those who are studying at colleges and universities, taking classes in visual communication, graphic design, web and multimedia design or creative advertising. Hopefully the book also addresses professionals who want to be inspired and to learn more about the rapidly changing environment to which they belong.

Stockholm is my hometown, and my BA in the history of art, along with degrees in literature and pedagogic research, at the University of Stockholm still inspires me. I am on the board for the Swedish Academy of Verbovisual Information, which strives to achieve efficient interplay between text and image. I have written a small pile of well-regarded and appreciated books and am a member of the Swedish Writers' Union.

My working days are often filled with lectures at universities and colleges both in Sweden and abroad. I am responsible for courses at design schools, for conducting workshops for photographers and journalists and for leading seminars in visual communication for industry.

I have years of experience as creative director for some of the best advertising agencies in Sweden and, as a co-owner of one agency, I have been awarded many prestigious prizes in communication. I have a deep interest in the supply of news – how news is made and conveyed – and have included some of my thoughts on the subject in this book.

Two worlds, universities and the media, are the basis for each chapter in this book, and they are filled with both theory and practice. Theoretical knowledge has to be put into practice, which is why most chapters are constructed something like a three-stage rocket – firstly the theory; secondly the practice; finally the example.

All my experiences are collected in this book. It has been an exciting journey, with many enthusiastic, generous and helpful travelling companions.

Thank you to John Bradley, art editor at the *Financial Times*, who pulled the first strings and has been helpful all along the tour. Thank you to all the photographers and other helping hands, who brighten up pages in the book – Per Adolphson, Sten Åkerblom, Pål Allen, Yara Antilla, Mats Bäcker, Berit Bergström, Hans Bjurling, Lars Bohman, Peter Cederholm, William Easton, Bruno Ehrs, Ingeborg Ekblom, Bengt af Geijerstam, Peter Harron, Bo Herlin, Tomas Jönsson, Christina Knight, Yasin Lekorchi, Frederik Lieberath, Maria Miesenberger, Gert Z. Nordström, Mikael Öun, Sandra Praun, Åke Sandström, Nino Strohecker, Anders Tempelman, Kenneth Westerlund and Elisabeth Zeilon. And also thank you to the people involved from Laurence King Publishing – Laurence King, Jo Lightfoot, Helen Evans, Lesley Henderson and John Jervis (with skilled external contributors) for their co-operation.

But the greatest debt of gratitude I owe my beloved wife, Lena, my skilled companion, my keen sounding board, my worst critic, my most devoted supporter, and consequently this book is dedicated to her, who else?

Bo Bergström
Stockholm and London, 2008.

1/
SCARED OF
SEEING

ABOVE / The opening scene of the classic Surrealist film, *Un Chien Andalou* (1929), directed and written by Luis Buñuel and Salvador Dalí, opens our eyes to what fascinates us, but also to what frightens us.

It's evening and darkness is slowly falling. The phone rings and a young man introduces himself, explaining that he's one of the leaders of the Swedish Association of Visually Impaired Youth. He has a request which is, to say the least, strange. He is asking me to lecture to a group of blind people on visual communication. Pictures for the blind? For a minute I think it must be some kind of cynical practical joke.

But it isn't a joke. There's no mistaking his seriousness as he describes the purpose of the association, which works towards a society in which blind young people are accepted as equal citizens, and thus are as active and able to participate as fully as their sighted friends.

One week later and I'm standing in front of around 20 young people, all of whom have been blind since birth. I don't have any of the technical aids, such as videos and Powerpoint slides, that would usually reinforce the key points of my lecture. Words, and words alone, convey my opinions and experience to my listeners. I talk about visual communication in general, and about photography, colour and design in particular, and try to explain the concepts. I attempt, as far as I can, to explain what a picture actually is: something light against something dark, a sharp edge and a fuzzy shape.

Am I getting my thoughts and ideas across? Can people understand when they can't see? Seeing and understanding pictures are often symbiotic. As is the language used to describe them – do you see?

Pausing for breath, I run my eye over the lecture theatre. Everyone is listening intently but suddenly something breaks their concentration. A girl picks up a camera to preserve the encounter forever. Maybe she will capture me in a photograph, but who will look at me, and what will I look like? The incident knocks me off balance.

I get going again, though, and talk about the demanding visual environment we live in. I try to describe not only our concern at never getting any respite from the images which bombard us, but also the hunger for visual impressions we paradoxically feel. Maybe it's as difficult for blind people to imagine our visual environment as it is for those of us who can see to imagine a non-visual one of Siberian bleakness and Kafka-esque echoing corridors. Not to mention our painful attempts to imagine the absolute, constant darkness experienced by the fully blind.

Did my lecture achieve its purpose? The idea of the young man on the phone was that I would initiate the blind into the mysteries of visual communication, and get them to understand why a newspaper, an advertisement, a television programme, a commercial or a website look the way they do, what the intentions behind them are and what effects they have. I hope I have given them tools they can use to participate in discussions in the office canteen, where the media is constantly debated and the blind are afraid of being even more left out than they are already. Being an outsider is always tough. Everyone, whether visually impaired or not, will agree there.

A lively discussion follows my lecture, alleviating my fears, at least to some extent.

Then it hits me that we, blind and sighted alike, share a sense of exclusion. Not all of us, and not completely of course, but many people who are not blind feel that they are not at home in the media landscape we live in. Many don't understand it and find it intrusive and annoying.

It can seem as though pictures are our enemies but letters are our friends. It's a lesson we learn as soon as we start school, where logical thought and verbal, linguistic expression are prioritized. Children learn to understand and to interpret verbal means of expression together with adults, but they are never taught to depict the same things using colour and shape. Many people claim that this inhibits our emotional experience and that an upbringing and an education which also included practising artistic means of expression would give us a language of images through which we could express ourselves more effectively. We would also gain a deeper insight into why pictures are created and how to process them critically.

If, instead, a combination of linguistic and figurative means of expression was to be prioritized, we would build a bridge between words and pictures, between sense and emotion, making us more rounded individuals. We would avoid limiting our scope for imagination and self-improvement, giving us a more complete social and cultural life.

But our culture and society rest on 26 firm pillars, the letters of the alphabet, and they're not going to give way that easily.

Most people are afraid of pictures, which slide away from us, and also reveal and expose those who get close. Once bitten, twice shy. Analysing a picture can often say more about the person doing the analysis than about the picture itself, which turns the process of analysis into a kind of self-portrait. Most people would find a photograph that depicts an eye being cut to pieces unbearable to look at, but it might be all in a day's work to a butcher, and to a prospective axe murderer it's pure pornography. On the basis of this argument, we just have to hope that the pictures teach us the value of admitting our secrets and the dangers of hiding them.

But does this visual fear also apply to professional media workers for whom pictures, colour and shape are the very breath of life? Naturally it doesn't apply to those who, through sheer hard work and perseverance, have learned to master the visual elements. But not everyone has got that far yet, and many of us have several rungs on the ladder still to go. I prick up my ears when I hear a photographer voice his fear of pictures once he's turned out the lights in his studio. 'Background paper, props like clothes and shoes, I can talk about them but when it comes to the inner meaning of the picture … no, I can't do that.'

So what's the cure for those who work with visual communication? Knowledge of course, which should cover their specialist function in the communication process and provide a helicopter view of the entire chain from analysis, strategy and narrative to message, image, form and colour. The helicopter view creates more points of contact – 'contact interfaces', if you will – making more people participants in more worlds.

What is to be gained from the communicators becoming more skilful? Firstly, the messages will reach their audience more easily. News and commercial messages are understood, assessed and subjected to detailed consideration, which is necessary in a democracy. This expands our understanding of global mechanisms, lending impetus to cultural and mercantile exchanges. Serious, urgent, direct, human, well-designed messages inspire respect in consumers and act as a platform for critical analysis. The manipulative powers of darkness, which lie in wait around us, are held in check with the help of the light. We all benefit from that. And this is what this book is all about.

BELOW / Knowledge casts light on all the messages that surround us in the media.

2/

STORYTELLING

ABOVE / The bandits silhouetted on the horizon as they approach the defenceless village, in the opening sequence of Akira Kurosawa's *Seven Samurai* (1954).

'We'll take this place next.'

The opening sequence of the Japanese director Akira Kurosawa's film Seven Samurai *plunges the audience straight into the dramatic action. After only a few seconds, we see a marauding gang of bandits about to plunder an idyllic small village.*

This introduction, or *set-up* as dramatists call it, is deeply involving, as a dramatic conflict quickly unfolds: strong against weak, evil against good. Such conflicts lie at the heart of a captivating, dramatic story, and the deeper the conflict, the stronger the audience's identification with the characters is likely to be.

We feel a part of the action when we can relate it to our personal experiences. We have all felt threatened to some degree in charged situations.

It is the set-up that kick-starts the story, and it is the story that is the best way of arousing emotions, and of conveying information and messages. The human brain welcomes a well-structured story, but it is likely to reject a dry, fact-packed report, or a banal detective series on the television that fails to grip the viewer's imagination.

But what is a story? Dramaturges – specialists in dramatic composition – define it as a narrative of integrated events, which involves people, their actions and their struggles. Can we live without stories? Probably not. Rather than 'give me bread', the first thing human beings ever said may well have been 'tell me a story'.

Some people have a particular gift for storytelling, others don't. And why is this? Is it about natural talent? Self-confidence? No, it's knowledge.

ROLE MODELS

We media consumers increasingly search for context and relevance in the splintered world of visual media, where many of us may not feel entirely at home. Actual storytelling, the ability to narrate events and the skill to find the right structure, is therefore crucial for getting through to people. And anyone who can tell a story becomes a role model – it's as simple as that.

There are many role models to look to, from Aristotle to Sergei Eisenstein and Quentin Tarantino. We get to know them at the theatre, in the cinema, when watching television, and of course in art galleries and books. Anyone working with text, pictures and graphic design has a wealth of material to draw on.

DRAMATURGY

But will the audience really be captivated? Isn't it often the case that some seats in the theatre end up empty after the interval?

Well, yes, but the opposite is also true. The secret is the art of storytelling, or dramaturgy, which teaches how to get everyone to listen all the way to the end of the story.

EXPECTATION

The dramatic set-up creates expectation of how things will progress. Every story has its *codes*, i.e., recognizable signs. After a dramatic set-up, the audience expects a drama, and after a humorous opening, a comedy. There is a *preconception* of the play or film's message. And there is great scope to influence a receptive audience.

In Swedish director Lukas Moodysson's film *Lilja 4-ever*, a confused girl runs around an overcast, concrete housing estate. She appears to be being chased and looks battered and bruised. She approaches the railings of a bridge over the motorway and goes up to the railings … What has happened? And what is *going* to happen?

CHANGE

The set-up also heralds change, on two levels in fact: in the actual story and in the audience's consciousness.

The characters in the story face conflict and choices that will change them. Someone will become a victor, someone a loser. A good story mustn't stand still – the audience must always be asking itself what's coming next.

At the same time, the viewer also faces a change. We will never be the same after sharing a story, since the feelings generated change us to some extent, as with stories from a concentration camp, or epoch-making art exhibitions. The audience shifts from uninvolved to involved, from ignorance to knowledge.

The goal of moving and changing their audience unites the dramatist, the dramaturge and the filmmaker with all those who work with text and with images to convey news and commercial

---

BELOW / At the beginning of Lukas Moodysson's film, *Lilja 4-ever* (2002), a young girl is seen going up to the railings of a bridge across a busy motorway. The audience holds its breath – will she jump?

messages. Such storytellers also share the difficulty that people do not always want to change. Change scares many people, but a set-up that quickly establishes itself as serious and credible will create interest and sympathy among the audience, who will decide to stay with the story to the end. And this makes them receptive to change.

STORYTELLING COMPONENTS

All stories operate on two levels – these are the *action level* and the *narrative level*.

The action level (the formal system) describes *what* happens and the narrative level (the stylistic system) *how* it happens.

The storyteller combines these two elements by drawing on various narrative components, not unlike a composer or conductor making use of the various instruments in a large orchestra. If, like a skilled conductor, the storyteller can create maximum unity by sometimes only using some of them, and then adding several, or possibly all, of the components, he or she can get the audience hooked.

The example below illustrates this approach.

What the audience sees
Person
A grey-haired man
Clothing
Grey suit, white shirt, blue tie
Setting
An office
Props
Rings on his finger, a watch and cuff links
Time
Afternoon

How the audience sees
Picture composition
The man is centred in the picture, and looks right into the camera
Cropping

Close-up
Camera angle
A slight worm's eye view
Lighting
Soft side lighting
Editing
A long scene with two cuts

What and how the audience hears
Sound
Just a clock ticking
Music
Strings with low bass notes
Dialogue
'What was it you wanted?' asks the man

THREE STORYTELLING TECHNIQUES

A story can be told in any number of ways – there are as many stories as there are storytellers – but three main divisions can be seen.

The dramatic storytelling technique
This is closed, with little room for interpretation, and is based on strong identification on the part of the audience, who are almost completely absorbed in the action. Conflict, or a balance which has shifted out of equilibrium, lies at the core of the technique.

The non-dramatic technique
This is an open technique, with plenty of scope for interpretation, and is based on significant participation and interaction from the audience, who almost have to knit together the story themselves. Personal reflections and values become building blocks.

The interactive technique
This occupies a kind of middle ground between the two previous techniques, and draws in the online audience. The storytelling technique is both open and closed, allowing deep interaction and involvement on the part of the audience.

BELOW / A skilled storyteller can employ the components of storytelling like the conductor varies the use of the different instruments in a large orchestra.

  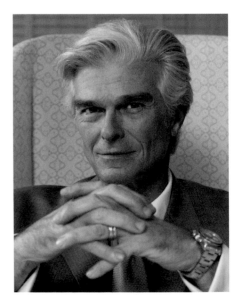

ABOVE / Dramatic storytelling is a closed
environment – rather like a goldfish bowl.
Non-dramatic storytelling is more open –
the wide oceans, inhabited by whales.

DRAMATIC STORYTELLING

The rules of dramatic storytelling were set out way back in history.
According to Aristotle a drama must have a beginning, a middle
and an end. It should also be constructed according to a unity of
time, place and action, i.e., the action must play out in real time
and in a space bound by the limits of the stage.

The various elements of the story must be intertwined, creating a unified plot. At the same time, variation and turning points
must vitalize and create interest in the characters and their
thoughts, drawing the audience further into the story.

The melodrama

To take a huge leap forward in history, nineteenth-century Paris
saw the growth of a form of theatre that would come to have a
major impact on the development of storytelling. Melodrama was
(and is) full of exaggerated gestures, spectacular effects, moments
of horror, tension and, above all, conflict, preferably in sharp contrasts such as good versus evil, beauty versus ugliness. Dramatists
held nothing back, with extreme events such as characters being
buried alive, or tied to railway tracks, and bombs being disarmed
at the last second, and they attracted huge audiences.

Film really found its voice in melodrama (which, unfairly, has a
rather poor reputation). Alfred Hitchcock, Rainer Werner Fassbinder
and Steven Spielberg are good examples of purveyors of dramatic
storytelling, and their work covers everything from social-realist
drama to thrillers.

Eisenstein

In the early twentieth century, the Russian filmmaker Sergei
Eisenstein recognized the importance of conflict, contrast and
struggle for storytelling.

Anyone working in a news studio, an advertising agency or as
a graphic designer can learn a great deal from his work.

He was inspired by Japanese ideograms in which, for example,
the symbol for 'eye' and the symbol for 'water' combine to take on
the meaning 'weep'. Two apparently disparate images create a
third, new image. And so was born the famous Eisenstein montage,
which involves cutting together sequences with changing content
and camera positions to create a dramatic, captivating rhythm.

The classic montage appears in *Battleship Potemkin*, with
innumerable collisions between close shots and long shots of the
attacking military and the civilians under fire.

The montage has an enormous power, which continues to
entrance generation after generation.

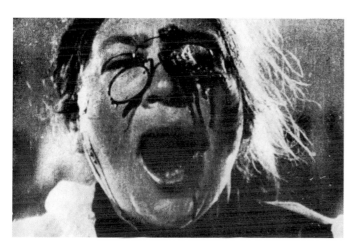

ABOVE / Sergei Eisenstein used his classic
montage technique in *Battleship Potemkin*
in 1925, and this approach is still to be
found everywhere in contemporary media.

THE RULES OF DRAMA

In order to hold the audience spellbound, the director has to introduce a *basic conflict*, with the lead role placed in the position of the *underdog*. The human psyche is such that we almost always side with the underdog (the *protagonist*) and can identify with the situation, as with the farmers in *Seven Samurai*.

Against this protagonist, we have a character in a threatening position of superiority (the *antagonist*) to set the narrative in motion. The bandits in Kurosawa's film fulfil this function, and without them there would be no film worth watching.

Now it's time to leave the samurai and focus on a contemporary story:

A confused girl runs around an overcast concrete housing estate.

The girl is called Lilja. The audience gets to know her through her actions, reactions, appearance and clothing. A *confused* girl *runs around* an overcast *concrete housing estate*. She appears to be *being chased*, looks *battered and bruised* and is far too *underdressed* for the weather.

The set-up

The start of the dramaturgic curve, this lets the audience in on the conflict. It creates a *forward momentum* that draws us in, compelling us to follow the course of events. Lilja approaches the edge of a bridge over the motorway. She goes up to the railings.

The presentation and exposition

Presentation and exposition follow, describing the relationships between the different people and characters (the curve dips

ABOVE & LEFT / TV cameras roll, allowing viewers in millions of living rooms to see reports – often edited using montage techniques – on defenceless people (protagonists), who are being persecuted by military forces (antagonists).

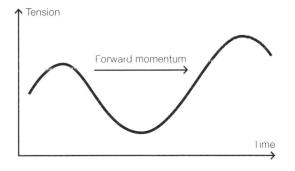

LEFT / The dramaturgic curve.

ABOVE / The contrasting parts of *Lilja 4-ever* provide a forward momentum, leading the audience towards the tragic, dramatic, yet expected ending.

downwards). Flashback to a happy Lilja: the family are planning a trip and looking forward to a new life full of promise.

The rising conflict

The drama is gradually ratcheted up (the curve swings upwards again) as the conflict continues to grow. At the last minute, her mother announces that Lilja will not be going with her to the Land of the Free.

Her mother (antagonist) writes from abroad, renouncing her parental responsibilities. Lilja can't survive for long and starts taking on clients (antagonists), while also being subject to abuse. A pimp (antagonist) then lures her away to an unfamiliar town in a far-off country, where she is shut up in a suburban apartment as a sex slave.

The conflict resolution

This contains the climax of the film, which the audience has been waiting for. Lilja sees jumping from the bridge onto the busy motorway as her only way out.

The fade out

The film concludes gently. Lilja and her old friend from the original concrete estate are playing basketball in slow motion, wearing angel's wings.

CLOSED SYSTEM

The dramaturgic curve is a closed storytelling system, which, in an illusory way, ensures that the audience will interpret the story as the director intended. There must be no scope for departures in interpretation.

Obstacles

A useful way of creating both identification and forward momentum is to weave an obstacle into the action. When someone faces a difficulty, the interest of the audience increases considerably: will the character get through this difficult situation? A man who is fleeing from thieves and bandits keeps trying to start his car, only for the engine to misfire over and over again, until the battery finally dies.

Triangle

Emotionally charged identification on the part of the audience is created by encouraging sympathy with a person in a difficult situation. The character comes into clear focus through the desperate action. A confused young man tries to shut out the ever-present ringing in his ears with pillows and thick rope. In his heart, he knows that the situation is hopeless. He seems to be screaming inaudibly, 'Can't anyone help me?'

Many dramatists suggest that most human relationships can be reduced to a *dramatic triangle*, which is why plays and films are often built around a triangular drama.

It has also been shown that action, and above all dialogue, becomes monotonous with only two parties involved. There needs to be a third party in order for there to be real tension: a *hero*.

THE RESCUER

Someone is threatened by a *persecutor* and becomes a *victim,* desperately seeking someone to come to the rescue. The threatened farmers in Kurosawa's film hire seven samurai, who are paid to help and *save* them from the attacking bandits. So, not one hero, but seven.

Who is the hero, the rescuer *in Lilja 4-ever*? Tragically, it would appear to be death, as jumping from the bridge was her only way out. Or are we, the audience, the great saviours? By absorbing the message of the film and passing it on through discussion and taking a public stand, we can help to combat trafficking and the all-too-common sexual exploitation of poor, young – often kidnapped – women.

The dramatic triangle constantly crops up in visual communication. A TV channel shouts out an ambiguous headline – 'Time for a crackdown' – alongside pictures of a teenage gang standing in a street corner in a suburb of a big city. At first they are only a few but their numbers grow, making them seem a terrifying power in the dark night, with their faces partly hidden behind hoods and a perceived threat from a knife's blade. These teenagers, hanging round estates with little to do, are the persecutors, vandalizing shops and cars and making citizens the victims. The rescuers are the police, who are to put their resources into trying to prevent the crimes. The authorities are also rescuers, who must try and find the underlying reasons (poverty, segregation, etc.) for this behaviour. The journalists behind the feature try to rouse public opinion and explore the full story, looking at changes in society.

Dramatic triangle

BELOW LEFT / The victim is a young man and the persecutor is tinnitus. The rescuer is a medical organization hoping to control the disease through research.

BELOW / In this advert, poverty and addiction are the persecutors, and children growing up in desperate situations are the victims, with the charity (hopefully) as the rescuer.

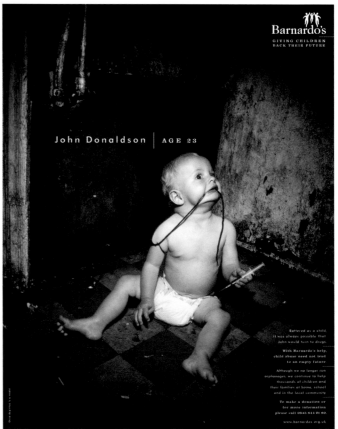

ABOVE / Teenagers (persecutors) are seen as a threat to society (victim) – debate in the media can ensure parents and authorities (rescuers) take responsibility.

RIGHT / Miserable summer weather persecutes us, but an airline, with its seductive adverts, promises to rescue us.

Cold and wet summer weather 'persecutes' holidaymakers, who feel like caravan-bound victims. The last-minute package deal becomes their 'rescuer'.

The rescuer takes us from fear to hope, from anxiety to safety, and presents an alternative plan of action, and thus gets us to act – whether this involves arguing against outlaws or booking a well-deserved trip abroad.

Problems and obstacles are there to be overcome, even for the young man with the pillows and rope. He is a victim of tinnitus, a constant buzzing in his head, present every second of every hour of every day of every year, perhaps for the rest of his life. Other sufferers and their close family feel a responsibility and decide to do something positive. The rescuer is a national association for hearing impairment – their research may prove decisive in getting the noise to stop.

What's going to happen?

It is important that the victim is not in an utterly hopeless situation. Any conflict or struggle cannot be insurmountable. There must be at least a 0.1 per cent chance of the lead character coming out on top. The young man in fact seems to have the power to stand up against his persecutor, in the form of his illness, because there is strength, albeit born of desperation, in his muscles and actions. This strength gets the audience intensely interested in how the drama will unfold, creating that all-important forward momentum. Despite everything, there is a way out.

Paris from just 65€

FIND THE STARTING POINT

Aristotle stated that the story must have a beginning, middle and end, but why tell a story in rigid chronological order?

A television series about the history of football doesn't have to start with tales from nineteenth-century English boarding schools. Why not start in a dark alley of a deprived suburb in a French city, where a small boy learns the finer points of the game by determinedly kicking a poorly inflated ball against a brick wall? The ball seems to love his feet and soon the whole world loves him.

The structure of this book is an example of the same thing. This first chapter is not about strategy and planning, but about storytelling, which is vital for visual communication, and hopefully creates an enticing set-up for the book.

FIND THE DRAMATIC POINT

Dramatization involves creating a limited space, which is naturally not identical to reality but a reinterpretation and distillation of it. In this space, relationships, conflicts and causal context are clear, as in Tarantino's film *Reservoir Dogs*, where a group of gangsters, bloody, on the run and desperate, gather after a botched robbery. Someone must have betrayed them. But who?

In storytelling, there will often be a particular point, an element, an event, that lends itself better than others to dramatization.

In the TV series on football, the director finds the dramatic point in the 2006 World Cup final. Zinedine Zidane, considered the world's top player, head-butts an opponent and is sent off. Spectators, media and television viewers hold their breath. The episode can be used as an introductory image, a vignette or a graphic, bringing together all the other episodes that epitomize the game.

The story behind a good or service is long and detailed. A need arises, an idea is born, a product is created and then mass-produced, packaged, marketed, delivered and used. It hopefully meets the original need – a story in the making, if ever there was one. But where is the dramatic point?

A kitchen designer resists the temptation to explain how satisfied a family was with its new kitchen, instead finding the dramatic point in the rather unexciting delivery, which is skilfully and humorously dramatized. This takes place in the evening darkness, so that the audience are initially led to believe that the fitters are burglars. The heading reads: 'You are on holiday. Two men enter your home. The scene that awaits you is indescribable.'

NON-DRAMATIC STORYTELLING

But surely there are other ways of telling a story? Of course.

Since the early 1970s, people in the film and theatre world have been looking for an alternative to the classic dramatic system, often called *The Hollywood Line*. They spurned the long waiting lists for drama courses, searching instead for a storytelling system that doesn't necessarily have to capture and conquer the audience. What they wanted was to motivate the audience to listen.

The outcome of this search is non-dramatic storytelling, which builds an *open structure* in films, news reports and advertising. This is created from different perspectives, so the audience is required to make its own assessments and complete the picture itself.

Proponents of this approach reject linear storytelling in favour of new, different story arcs that meander and spiral around, often with contradictions and exciting digressions. The linear, dramatic system is often seen as masculine, while the non-dramatic is seen as a feminine form of storytelling.

Non-dramatic storytelling can be traced back to Plato rather than Aristotle, and it inspired the highly personal works of Russian director Andrei Tarkovsky. A good example is Sofia Coppola's low-key comedy *Lost in Translation* about friendship and love cropping up where least expected. Todd Haynes's eccentric film about Bob Dylan, *I'm Not There*, also belongs in this category. It is a kaleidoscopic, evasive film with a dissolved non-linear narrative structure, in which Dylan is portrayed in six different roles (with Cate Blanchett playing one of them) that are woven together.

Another example is an art film, where the artist uses still images to relate gradually how one of the artworks develops. The artist chooses colours, tests and rejects designs, and freely associates around the motif, which is always captivating.

Now to a woman standing by water, who is looking back at us. No wind, no waves. She sweeps a quilt around herself, becoming one with the stillness and atmosphere, enveloped in softness. She may be wishing that this could last forever, but she says nothing. The audience understands that the quilt is wonderfully soft.

Some writers call this technique *the journey* (in contrast to the dramatic *Who wins?* – Sofia Coppola against Clint Eastwood).

BELOW / In the back streets of a deprived suburb, one of the world's top football stars – Zinedine Zidane – grew up. The setting is an ideal start to a TV series on football.

BELOW RIGHT / Zidane is sent off for head-butting an opponent, and can only watch as France lose the 2006 World Cup Final – a strong dramatic point for the TV series.

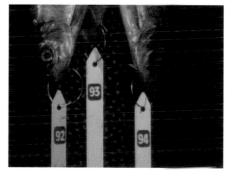

LEFT / A woman in an advert sweeps a quilt around herself – she radiates a sense of well-being in an attractive environment, which encourages us to purchase.

ABOVE / Sofia Coppola's non-dramatic *Lost in Translation* (2003; top); Peter Greenaway's *Drowning by Numbers* (1988; below) is a suggestive hybrid of both storytelling styles.

ABOVE / Tennis legend Björn Borg
successfully generates attention when his
company, besides selling underwear, takes an
unusual approach to campaigning for peace.

INTERACTIVE STORYTELLING

Let us look at an interactive medium (usually a website, but also a CD or a DVD), the purpose of which is to turn the visitors, listeners or viewers into active participants. It is up to them to choose and guide the form and content.

Interactive media will often combine text, pictures, film and sound, thus stimulating the visitor in several ways at the same time, and dramatically increasing the range of experiences open to the visitor and strengthening the impact of the content. This is interactive storytelling.

TWO MAIN GROUPS OF INTERACTIVE STORYTELLING TECHNIQUES

In somewhat undeveloped *one-way storytelling*, the content has a beginning and an end, and there is really only one way for the visitor to go. Despite the huge possibilities of interactivity, this simple storytelling technique is common, for example in e-learning.

In *free storytelling*, which makes better use of the medium's interactive opportunities, there are a whole host of ways in and out. In a number of situations, visitors have various alternatives to choose from, so create their own story. They encounter the content in the order and manner that they decide, often with the help of a search engine that is always available. In principle there are no limits (as in a computer game), particularly when the link options are also unlimited.

Between the one-way and the free approach, there are almost infinite ways of telling a story.

STRUCTURE

This is crucial, as it shows the various parts of the site and their relationship to each other. In order to draw up a suitable structure, a *flow chart* must always be created, which shows how the visitor navigates through the site.

The most common structures are:

Linear
Tree
Web

The first can be classed as one-way (and practically undeveloped), while the other two relate to free storytelling.

Splash page

Sometimes, a splash page appears on the screen before the actual start page is shown, almost forcing its way between the visitor and the forthcoming material. There are both pros and cons to this course of action.

The visitor avoids being plunged straight into the action, with urgent demands to make decisions, and is instead able to approach the start page at his or her own pace. However, many see the splash page as superfluous – extra time and clicks are required to get started.

Linear

The simplest structure is the linear one (the straight line), which takes the visitor from one page to the next in a direct and uncomplicated way, perhaps presenting simple information from an agency (Inland Revenue) or a business (an online bookshop).

The advantage, of course, is that the site is easy to navigate and understand, making it difficult to get lost. The disadvantage is clear: it quickly becomes boring and predictable.

Tree

The (upside-down) tree structure is ideal for most situations. The content can easily be structured in clear groups and sub-groups, although it is important to minimize the hierarchy to avoid confusing the visitor. The rule of thumb is that content should never be further than three clicks away – click: the start page; click: literature; click: a book.

The tree structure is both functional and absorbing, making it ideal for product information as well as more advanced content. A constantly available menu or map should be included, so visitors can always see where they are.

Fans of order may well ask whether there are any disadvantages. Well, the tree structure does have its limitations, particularly compared to the next structure, the web.

Web

The web structure (like a spider's web) is quite advanced, as there is no real first or last page. Everything relates to everything else in an endless web. A word or a picture links to another one on another page, in another part of the world.

Combination

Of course, sometimes the best option is a combination of different structures. An airline may give visitors the opportunity to search for destinations and flights in a tree structure, but when it comes to booking a ticket, the structure is linear.

GAMES

Game-based storytelling, which has constantly been adapted since its original appearance in *Spacewar* in the 1960s, means that the story is cut into fragments, which are spread out to be encountered by the player. Documents, dialogue and short video sequences, which the players discover themselves, are woven together to create a unique story. Games do have certain dramatic limitations in that the game makers hand over control of the pace and direction to the player. However, there is tension (and also

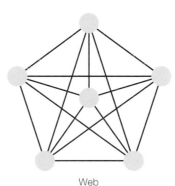

Linear

Tree

Web

enjoyment) to be had, particularly in identifying patterns, solving problems and overcoming dangers.

Many media experts believe that computer games will prove to be the great cultural icons of the twenty-first century, with a significance comparable to that of film in the last century. However, games currently remain a largely undeveloped art form, waiting for skilled storytellers to take them to new heights.

Today, popular films often form the basis of games, with the player having to put a horse's head in the right bed and make sure that Don Corleone gets to the hospital when he has been shot.

BELOW / Getting website design right is vital for a wide range of organizations, from cultural institutions like the Centre Pompidou in Paris to stores like Ikea.

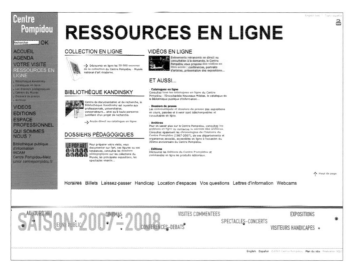

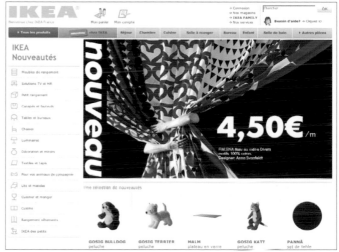

CAPTIVATING STORYTELLING

Whatever the medium and storytelling technique, the important thing is always to get the audience involved in the story. There are numerous methods (or tricks of the trade), as this section shows.

CHOOSE THE RIGHT STORYTELLING PERSPECTIVE

The storytelling perspective is crucial in determining how a story is received, steering both text and picture composition.

It is rarely effective to take an authoritative and expert tone and address 'you down there from us up here'. Such an (almost insulting) perspective is referred to as *vertical*.

The *horizontal* perspective is definitely the preferred option, as it is based on an exchange of shared experiences between the storyteller and the listener, creating trust and respect.

Storytellers can immerse themselves in a role and speak in the third person: 'She realized that the grass had to be cut, so she bought a lawnmower.'

Telling the story in the first person, either singular or plural, brings the storyteller closer to the listener: 'Our lawnmower makes cutting the grass easy.'

The storytelling can also be constructed as an interview or dialogue between different parties: 'Your lawn really needs cutting.' 'Yes, but I haven't got a lawnmower.' 'Borrow mine.'

SURPRISE

The use of surprise is also an extremely potent tool. It can appear in many guises, but the most effective involves the use of shock or humour.

A small boy is poking around in the undergrowth. Suddenly, branches and leaves move apart and a frightening gorilla appears in front of him, but the boy just looks on inquisitively and goes up to the gorilla. Why isn't he afraid? As he moves forward, the boy's nose flattens, as if he was pressing it against a window, which is exactly what he's doing. So what's going on? It's a commercial intended to attract more young visitors to visit the Bronx Zoo in New York.

MISLEAD

There are many ways to make use of clues in stories. One may be a *red herring*, with the audience actually being tricked, for dramatic or humorous effect. In a series of images, expectations are created about what is to come (*protention*), based on what has already happened (*retention*). If the expectations are not met, the relationship between the images and the message is disrupted. What the audience thought was going to happen doesn't, and what happened previously turns out to have meant something completely different. For example, cast your mind back to the mysterious visit by the two men (who the clues suggested were burglars) that turned out to be a visit by two service-minded suppliers, come to fit a new kitchen while the homeowners were away on holiday.

BELOW / This striking poster generates attention and surprise by making a visual link between extremism today and the fascist politics of the 1930s.

BELOW RIGHT / Contrasts captivate and surprise us, raising questions along the way. How did the deer end up in the car park, and what is it trying to tell us?

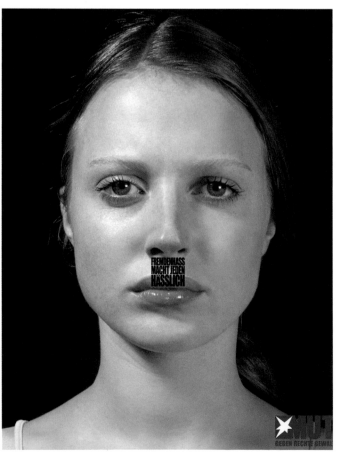

'YOU ARE ON HOLIDAY.
TWO MEN ENTER YOUR HOME.
THE SCENE THAT AWAITS YOU IS
INDESCRIBABLE.'

ABOVE / Interplay between text and
image can often mislead us in a disarming
manner. Here the expected burglary turns
out to be something else entirely.

MODERN STORIES

Storytelling has become an important means of communication, with storytellers employed by companies and organizations looking to communicate their messages packaged as exciting stories. Internally, storytelling is used to unify and manage the company and externally, it is part of the marketing process, perhaps showing how the company was created out of particular events (starting from nothing) and circumstances (a groundbreaking idea).

Some stories need freshening up or replacing. Nokia's success story, of how the company went from manufacturing rubber boots to become the world's leading mobile phone manufacturer, has been told to death.

Of course, it is important to remember that storytelling can also be used to set up a smokescreen and distract attention.

HISTORICAL STORIES

What does Spielberg's 1975 film *Jaws* have in common with the thousand-year-old English heroic poem *Beowulf*? What does Charles Dickens's *David Copperfield* have in common with Harry Potter? They are all part of a storytelling heritage that runs through most ages and cultures.

We fill up our stock of experiences by listening to stories, reading, watching films and plays, in our attempt to understand ourselves in an increasingly fast-paced and frequently alienating world. Our experiences are not unlike bits of script of varying

SUMMARY

'We'll take this place next.'

DRAMATURGY
Dramaturgy means the art of telling a story so captivatingly that the audience have to follow the story right to the end.

All stories exist on two levels. The action level describes *what* happens and the narrative level *how* it happens.

THREE STORYTELLING TECHNIQUES
The dramatic technique is based on *the dramatic triangle*, involving the persecutor, the victim and the rescuer in a tight and closed narrative. Often seen in plays, films, journalism and advertising.

The non-dramatic technique is based on a more open and gentler dialogue with the audience, who are given the opportunity to interpret and evaluate films, news and commercial messages in a freer manner.

The interactive technique is a kind of middle ground between the two previous techniques. A website gives the visitor complete freedom, but of course only within the limitations of interactivity.

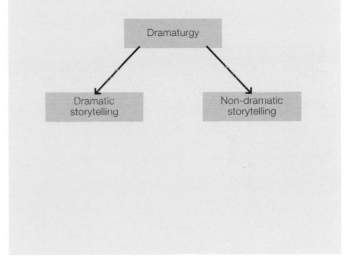

lengths, which we join together. We always return to these stories, which comfort us, like children with their favourite fairy tales ('again, Dad, again!').

This is exemplified by the old *commedia dell'arte* characters, who always performed in a similar way, so the audience quickly got to know the characters' strengths and weaknesses, as well as who was good and who was evil. Or Bruce Springsteen's New Jersey with its asphalt roads, union cards, wrecked cars and driving along the river (with Mary, who got pregnant).

That is why stories are so important, as they have been since time immemorial in every culture. They tend not to differ all that much, being based around just a few archetypes: beating the monster, from rags to riches, the quest for the truth or the treasure, the journey and the homecoming, and others.

All of them are packed with recurring themes such as jealousy, romance and the ever-present fight for survival, as expressed in one of the last lines of *Seven Samurai*: 'Again we have survived.'

3/
WORK

ABOVE / The bus shakes and the train sways, but the words and images in the morning papers still get through.

'Early to bed, early to rise.'

Expectations are high when a newspaper, one of the day's first examples of visual communication, hits a pair of sleepy eyes. Text is read, and pictures looked at, prompting anger or pleasure in response to the stories. Somewhere, perhaps near you, a young man has been attacked. In another part of the world, in a different time zone, a river is threatening to burst its banks.

And then our minds reset themselves. Our thoughts focus on meetings coming up at work, and on traffic jams ahead. In the newspaper editor's office, the front page has to be chosen and designed all over again, while elsewhere companies' goods have to be shifted out of warehouses and services have to meet the needs of customers.

New messages are born and battle for our attention constantly. We were programmed to absorb messages from early infancy. Now we are more concerned with defending ourselves against them, but there is no escape. And these messages change us, at least to a small degree.

FROM A SENDER TO A RECEIVER

The basis of all visual communication is that someone has something to say. A *sender*, be it an individual, a newspaper, a TV channel, a company, organization or public agency has to carefully formulate and shape a *message* which is conveyed to a *receiver*.

The aim of the sender is to exert influence by moving, motivating or informing. The message is tailored to this purpose, and in order for the sender to reach the receiver, a *channel* must be set up between them, a *medium*, such as a newspaper, a poster, a commercial, a website or even a textbook, like this one. The sender expects the message to generate awareness, as well as interest and credibility, and finally to achieve its intended effect (often an action).

The type of message, what the sender knows about the receiver and what the receiver knows about the sender all play significant roles in this process, as do the context of the message and the financial resources available.

The practical work of visual communication comprises three main areas, all of which need to be coordinated in order to achieve a good end result. The *typography* of the text involves the choice and arrangment of typefaces (letters of a particular design) in the headings, introductions, text columns and captions, for example. *Graphics* involve assessing and choosing stills, moving images or illustrations in order to create some sort of interplay with the text. Then in the third phase, *design*, the text and pictures are arranged into an attractive and informative whole, the task of which is to make the message as comprehensible and tempting to the receiver as possible.

MORNING, NOON AND NIGHT

The media form a natural part of our day, bringing us together as people, increasing our understanding of ourselves and others, and making our world more comprehensible.

Many people suggest that the media have a dangerous power to shape culture and society in a way that not even religion or politics can manage. But isn't it the case that we get the media we deserve? The newspaper placards are like mirrors. If they obsess over sex, celebrity, crime and disease, it's because that is what our collective consciousness is fixated on at the time.

THE FUNCTION OF THE MEDIA

The media are very persistent. Wouldn't it be better if we could get away from them, or at least from some of them? Perhaps, but aren't they in fact a kind of extension of ourselves? We can't deny that we have certain limitations. We don't hear what is going on far away, and we can't see beyond our own horizon. Maybe radio is simply a natural (!) development of our hearing and TV of our sight. And what about the web and mobile phones? Well, that's social interaction.

Extension or not, what are the mass media in fact? One of the definitions offered is that they convey information and entertainment with a certain regularity simultaneously and publicly to everyone within a large group. It is also commonly held that they have three important functions:

The *informative* function tells us about the life we are expected to live (all these days rushing past – these days are our lives, you know), what demands are made of us, and what demands *we* can make.

The *social* function, which means that we share experiences with others – in a group discussing the placards outside the newspaper kiosk, squashed on the sofa watching a wildlife programme or chatting in online communities and uploading video clips to file-sharing sites.

And finally there is the *catalytic* (driving) function, which is based on the need for our eyes, ears and brains to be stimulated. Colours, shapes, drama, sentimentality, violence, love – all create feelings. We need an outlet for these feelings.

BELOW / We will never be free from messages – some reach us on mobile phones, others will grab our attention by their sheer size in public spaces.

THE MESSENGER

It is very rare for visual communication to appear simply for its own sake, for cosmetic reasons without any direct purpose. No, text and pictures want something more. A message, banal or life-changing, must be conveyed.

Between the sender and the receiver comes the messenger, who, based on his or her skills and feel for visual codes, plays a key role in whether the message gets across.

Most messengers do not have the free, independent professional role that authors, dramatists and artists enjoy. Instead, they have a service role as the intermediary between their employer and the target of the message. The quality and effect of their work is often determined, unfairly, by the ambition and skills of others.

But in this field there are (or should be) educated people, with extensive *knowledge* peppered with facts, theories and intuition, who know how to apply their *skills*. These professionals have varying amounts of *experience*, based on their observations and the work they have done. They are gifted with the *social competence* to build up relationships and influence. Finally, their instincts are well attuned to *current needs*, *values* and *expectations*, giving them an insight that can be invaluable when it comes to communicating a message through words and images.

BELOW / With his artistic and playful approach, design legend Paul Rand engages us with this famous poster for IBM (1981).

Professionals

The messenger may be a subeditor for a newspaper or TV channel, or a creative director or art director at an advertising agency, responsible for producing a visual design on behalf of a client.

The messenger may also be a designer, working on logos, brochures, posters or other printed material, a director or editor at a production company for film and TV advertising, or a web designer putting together new sites. Professionals who work in close partnership with those mentioned above include the editor and the copywriter.

Production

In the next stage, typesetters, printers, bookbinders and film labs are responsible for the technical production. These people ensure that everything is produced in line with the client's intentions.

All the work that precedes actual printing is usually called *prepress*. Technology is advancing rapidly, which means that certain stages of the production chain are now dealt with entirely or in part by the designer on the computer.

Suppliers

Photographers, cameramen and illustrators are also part of the production process, as they provide advertising agencies, for example, with photos, film and illustrations.

Clients

These may be a newspaper or TV company. Clients may also be companies, large or small, domestic or foreign, looking to sell their goods and services, and the impact of their investment in advertising can be crucial to the company's survival.

The eclipse syndrome

There is a dangerous trend gaining ground among these professions which can be likened to an eclipse. One professional role overlaps another and gradually takes over completely. The relay race of professions, all working in turn on the technical elements and the content to ensure that the message reaches the receiver, has got much shorter.

Many typesetters and repro companies no longer exist, their work having been taken over by the designer sitting in front of a computer screen.

The editor-in-chief of a newspaper may now send out one reporter equipped with a digital camera: one more press photographer out of a job.

A TV channel uses staff with modern cameras that don't just take stills but can also take film sequences, record sound, thus eliminating the need for a photographer, film cameraman, sound technician and interviewer. Four jobs are cut to one.

The head of advertising produces his or her own websites using computer programs that offer simple design solutions. Graphic designers and ad agencies lose commissions.

In this drama, the amateur with a camera phone or a simple digital camera and a burning ambition to get his or her pictures published is a dangerous character. More about this later.

THREE PERSPECTIVES

All these professionals (threatened or not) look at visual communication from different perspectives. The sender, client, editor-in-chief, advertising manager and reporter work from a *perspective of intention*, where analysis, goal and message are key points.

The messenger, the subeditor, the art director, the graphic designer and the web designer work from a *perspective of proximity*, involving text, images and context (the interplay between the verbal and the visual).

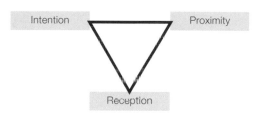

LEFT / The three perspectives on visual communication, from the viewpoint of the sender (intention), the messenger (proximity) and the receiver (reception).

ABOVE / A typical morning meeting at the office of a daily newspaper – war or peace, rain or sunshine?

And finally, the receiver reacts from a *perspective of reception*, which covers perception, feeling and interpretation. This triangular drama features in every section and chapter of this book.

THE DAILY NEWSPAPER AS A WORKPLACE

Let's step into the world of the newspaper office, a modern workplace with its own ancient traditions. Our daily newspapers grew out of the handwritten newsletters of the Romans, which were official messages set up in public places. Later, in the Middle Ages, travelling monks carried news from place to place, and in the sixteenth century a primitive postal service was born.

The advent of the printing press hurried things along somewhat, but it took until the mid-seventeenth century for Strasbourg, London and Paris to get their first newspapers. In the late nineteenth century, a whole range of important factors drove on development. Rotary presses churned out newspapers, the railway distributed them quickly and reliably, and the telegraph signalled the dawning of modern newsgathering. In the early twentieth century, London was lucky enough to be the first place in the world to have a sensationalist tabloid newspaper, the *Daily Mirror*, and New York saw *The New York World* printed in huge quantities.

Soon, an interested, well-educated and influential readership gained quality broadsheets such as *The Guardian*, *Le Monde*, *Frankfurter Allgemeine Zeitung* and *The New York Times* as their papers of choice.

Readers then and now demand a great deal of their newspaper. The first requirement is to be *public*, i.e., available to everyone, at least in the area in which it is published.

The second is *topicality*, with the newspaper actually containing current news, at local, national and international level.

It must also have *universality*, addressing a number of different and important subjects that are aimed at many different groups of people.

And finally there is the requirement for *periodicity*, which means that the newspaper must come out regularly, creating an ongoing relationship with its readers.

The fourth estate

The newspaper pushes its way into everyone's lives with considerable power and authority. It may not always determine what readers think on various issues, but it does influence *which* issues they should be thinking about. In short, the press sets the agenda, which is why they are referred to as the fourth estate – a term derived from nineteenth-century descriptions of newspapers as an unofficial fourth power in the land, after the official positions of the aristocracy, clergy and commoners in parliament.

Newspaper production

The fascinating thing about a daily newspaper is that it is reborn every day, but there are many key tasks which will always recur. The most important one is to present the *news*, of course, thus setting up a *debate* and shaping *opinion*. Readers want the background to events and clarification of context. The newspaper has to explain yesterday and prepare the reader for tomorrow, breathing life into a publication caught in the space between past and future. The newspaper also has a political stance which must be made clear, and an owner who will want his or her input.

So who brings the newspaper to life?

There are the *reporters* with their various journalistic focuses. The general reporters monitor the overall flow of news, while specialist reporters take care of cultural issues, economic analyses and sports events, large and small.

The *photographers* and *online cameramen* are rarely in the newspaper office, instead being out and about on assignments. *News photographers* are used for the topical articles of the day and *feature photographers* for reflective and analytical articles.

Illustrators provide satirical cartoon commentaries on current events and trends.

Picture editors are responsible for the newspaper's photographic material. Most newspapers have a policy on photography, which lays down general rules for the pictures used, including their form, content and quality. The newspaper's attitude to the manipulation of images is very important. Unfortunately these policies are often vaguely formulated, giving the photographer insufficient guidance.

One important question is often forgotten. Is the image even necessary? Some articles would be absolutely fine without one.

The *subeditor* ensures that all the pages of the newspaper have a uniform and attractive communicative form. As well as being the newspaper's architect, the subeditor is also responsible for ensuring that headlines, introductions and body text maintain high standards of grammar, spelling and factual accuracy.

The *managing editor* is the spider in the web, planning and assigning tasks, and is often also the link between the newsdesk and the paper's other departments, such as advertising and PR.

The *editor* sits at the top of the building (when not being interviewed on TV), managing the overall direction of the paper's news – his or her leadership creates the company's culture, and sets the tone for the quality of the editorial work.

But we shouldn't forget all the intermediaries outside the newspaper, including picture libraries, stringers (journalists loosely attached to the paper) and aspiring freelance writers sending in articles in the hope of catching the managing editor's eye.

What is news?

Sometimes the question seems pointless. There is no doubt that a terrorist attack or revealing pictures of the oppression and torture of prisoners of war are news, top news, that wipes clean previous plans for the front page.

When approaching the news, we readers want answers to the five most important questions in news journalism. *When* did it happen? *Where*? *How* did it happen? *Who* was involved? *Why* did the gigantic tidal wave occur, and why is the snowdrop the first of the spring flowers to appear?

How does a news item come about?

Usually, the newspaper will have a subscription with a news agency (which in turn buys material from other agencies), which will spew out a long line of news on the teleprinter.

But news items also have to be sought out, so journalists have to build up a good network of contacts. People in positions of power, civil servants and police hold a great deal of information – secretly listening in to a police radio frequency may well give the journalist a head start, but such daring has to go hand in hand with caution.

Investigative, critical journalism is naturally most important, as it turns the spotlight on abuses of power, corruption and social inequalities. But often the journalists are obstructed, forcing them to go deep undercover to unearth injustice.

Naturally, the public, whistleblowers, informers and eyewitnesses, with their text messaging, are also key players in news production (and with their photo messages for image production, as we'll see later), along with those who write letters to the editor – it all goes into the pot.

Another means of acquiring news is to keep your eye on everyone else. A subeditor reads and clips out items from competitors' news, while national newspapers often have something that can be given a local angle. And vice versa.

However, there is a danger of the news machine going round in circles, when journalists make news out of old material. This news doesn't arise of its own accord, but is fabricated instead. Whether sanctioned by an editor or coming from outside, through PR and lobbying companies, researchers and the rumour mill, this runs into conflict with the press's strongest competitive edge: offering news seen with their own eyes, heard with their own ears, considered in their own mind and written in their own words.

Rules of the game

Another risk arises when the newspaper owner is in financial difficulty or simply demands greater profit. This often results in a package of savings, which sometimes results in journalists and correspondents being laid off, which then leads to poorer journalism and reporting, and a constant barrage of desperate sensationalism taken completely out of context, sending the quality of the newspaper spiralling downwards.

The media and journalists' own organizations try to combat poor quality and increase confidence in the press. The rules set out are as follows:

Give correct news and check sources
Give the right to reply
Respect personal integrity
Exercise caution with images
Do not judge before a hearing
Be careful with names

However, it is obvious to readers that the press does not always adhere to these rules. Personal integrity, for example, seems to be constantly at risk.

AT THE TV COMPANY

The history of television is short. In the early twentieth century, Scotsman John Logie Baird designed a mechanical system for sending blurry pictures of only 30 lines. His mechanics were turned into electronics by the American Vladimir Zworykin, who developed the crucial cathode ray tube.

Broadcasts were being made during the 1930s, but were stopped during World War II, after which TV really took off in almost every country. It is a young medium, which is already well on the way to merging with the even younger media of the internet and mobile phones.

Professional roles

TV viewers are exposed to a host of talking heads in the news studio, from the news anchor, newsreader or studio reporter to the

ABOVE / As the graphics and music come
to an end, we hear an introduction and the
news anchor focuses on the camera and
on us ...

weather presenter, but behind every head there will be various professionals working away.

At the morning meeting, the *editor* goes through the day's features and sends *reporters* and *cameramen* out on assignment. The reporter conducts interviews and then writes a news item, while the cameraman records images and sound. Then back in the office, the *subeditor* puts everything together to create a news item that will hopefully interest TV viewers.

The *angle* is agreed on at the morning meeting, so that everyone is clear about what the news of the day is and how it should be reported.

As the news broadcast approaches, the *technical director* is there to decide on what shots to broadcast, the *script supervisor* keeps everything and everyone in order, and the *broadcast technician* takes care of the technology. A carefully scheduled running order is set up so that everyone involved can see when the various items are to start and finish. Most of it is pre-programmed, with the technology looking after itself, at least in part.

Behind the scenes there are make-up artists, painters, carpenters, property managers, stand-by prop artists and a runner who makes the coffee.

Production companies

Inserted between the TV programmes are the commercials, much to some people's annoyance, but perhaps to others' delight.

TV *advertising* is produced by production companies, often on behalf of an advertising agency, which in turn has its own client.

Workers at the production company include *directors*, *editors*, *lighting technicians*, *sound technicians*, *stage managers* and *stylists*, many of whom are freelancers.

Everything starts with the *production criteria* – careful planning of the goal, target group and message, undertaken with the client.

Then it is time for the *concept* and *script*, which must be put down on paper, checked and assessed. If they are rejected then, unfortunately, it's back to the drawing board.

Budgeting is the next step. What is this going to cost?

The *presentation* to the client must be as clear and captivating as possible.

A skilled illustrator produces a *storyboard*, a series of sketches on paper or card showing the commercial frame by frame and explaining the sound and dialogue. It is a simple system, but the director has to expect an inexperienced client to ask: 'Is it going to be a cartoon?'

A *video sketch* can sometimes be the best presentation method. However, it is worth remembering that the video sketch is very similar in form to the final film, which may cause the client to fix their opinion, reducing their inclination to approve changes and improvements, as should happen in a good working process: 'But it didn't look like that in the sketch!'

Casting involves searching for suitable actors for roles in the commercial. These may be professionals (like Brad Pitt) hired through agencies, or amateurs (like a courier) who have been found in the street.

Pre-production is about preparing for filming, sorting out the scenography, colours, clothing and make-up.

Filming is a time of tension. Everything has to come together which, after retakes, corrections and the odd call to the fire service, it usually does. Everyone involved is there for the filming.

Post-production is the work that goes on after filming. Once it has been developed, the 35 mm film is transferred to digital video, with a skilled professional adjusting the light and colours during the scanning. Then it is time for the rough cut and the addition of music and sound effects, and sometimes visual effects such as speech bubbles or tables.

It is sensible to make the *final presentation* to the client before the final edit.

And then comes the *copying* of the finished material, so that it can be broadcast to its audience, sitting at home on the sofa.

AT THE ADVERTISING AGENCY

The advertising agency creates advertisements, usually on behalf of clients, as they always have done, but in different ways.

The origin of today's campaigns were simple and straightforward advertisements offering a solution to a problem. Can't get across the prairie quick enough? Buy the new Ford! Want to look like Marilyn Monroe? Buy her figure-hugging dress! Such adverts were sometimes dramatic, sometimes sensitive, and often (even today) highly effective. The time was just after World War II, and the place was the Western World. Consumerism was on the rise. The production of goods and services had boomed, along with their consumption.

During the 1960s and 1970s, there was much criticism of the badgering adverts that resulted, which were considered to create a demand for goods which consumers didn't actually need. In the 1980s and 1990s, the advertising industry started to focus on consumers' *perception* of the companies behind the goods and services. Strong brand building became, and remains, crucial to their survival.

Now a young generation with huge purchasing power is coming through. They are said to be completely uncritical about adverts as long as they are *entertaining.* Soon it will be difficult to tell advertising from entertainment.

Do we need adverts, this promotional information with a clear sender and space paid for in the media? Most people would say that advertising is integral to a successful open market economy, where production and consumption of goods and services keep the global economy turning.

Advertising also plays a crucial role in the survival of the mass media. The vast majority of the media were originally free of advertising, but it was the advertisers with their purchasing power that turned them into mass media. If this advertising revenue were to be taken away, the mass media would suffer a catastrophic breakdown. In other words, advertising supports the mass media, but at the same time makes them extremely sensitive to the vagaries of the economy. In difficult times companies cut back on their advertising costs, which in turn means a loss of income for the mass media.

BELOW / 'Isn't it nice ... when things just ... work?' These words end this famous commercial by Wieden+Kennedy for the Honda Accord. The advert lets the audience appreciate the technical precision of the components, and ends with a final shot of the completed car.

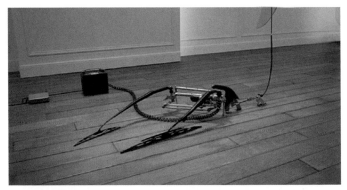

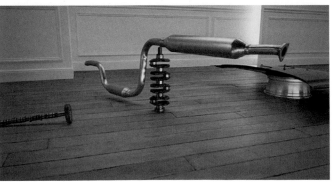

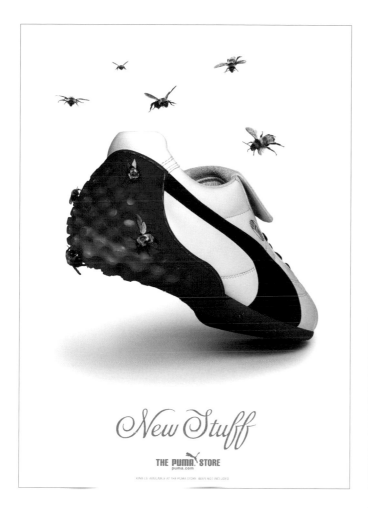

ABOVE / Puma's 'New Stuff' campaign
uses Andrew Zuckerman's enticing
'Creatures' photography to reinforce the
sleek brand concept for their trainers.

The start of the commission

There are many different kinds of worker at an *advertising agency*, but work starts, naturally enough, at the company ordering advertising: the marketing department, in consultation with colleagues, decides to launch a campaign for one of its products. Product development has come up with a new – or partly new – product with distinctive features, and the company envisages huge sales.

There is an expectant air at the company. The *advertising manager*, responsible for purchasing advertising, has been commissioned by the *marketing manager* to contact an advertising agency for a meeting about the planned advertising campaign.

Initial meeting

A team from the advertising agency, which is usually made up of the *project manager*, the *copywriter* and the *art director*, will meet with the advertising manager to plan the work. The project manager keeps hold of all the different threads of the campaign (the finances, the controls, the follow-up, etc.), while the copywriter writes the advertising text and is responsible for the creative concept work, together with the art director who, based on his or her visual expertize, designs the campaign and brings it to life. The task of the *planner* is to create a strategic platform for this creative work. The planner will be a specialist in identifying consumption patterns, ensuring that the right message reaches the required target group, cutting through the ever-increasing media clutter.

At many agencies, this classic team is being broken up: two art directors may be responsible for a joint campaign, or a copywriter and director from a production company might handle a TV spot.

During this initial meeting, it is important for the agency to find out about the company in a *briefing*. Who owns the company? What other stakeholders are there? How is the company perceived in the market? How does the company's self-image chime with what everyone else thinks? What products do they make and who are their competitors? Is there a unique selling point? Who are the consumers and how many of them are there?

The commission

The meeting results in the advertising agency being commissioned to develop a campaign proposal. At the next meeting, the advertising manager expects a carefully considered campaign presentation based on an *advertising plan*, the key points of which are the *goal, target group, medium, message, budget* and *schedule*, along with *evaluation* and *follow-up*.

Second meeting

The proposal drawn up by the team is discussed in depth at a second meeting. The copywriter and art director present in sketch form the concept of the campaign. If it is a major campaign, the *sketches* are often detailed and realistic, sometimes with specially taken photographs. In other contexts, a few line drawings may suffice.

If the campaign proposal relates to TV advertising, a *storyboard* is often used to show the concept, action and message in simple sketches. If the proposal is for a website, it is often accompanied by a *flow chart* roughly setting out the structure of the site.

Production plan

Once the client and the advertising agency have reached agreement, the project manager draws up a detailed production plan and budget (design agencies work in much the same way). A *production manager* goes through a *media agency* to book advertising space or time in the media chosen for the exposure of the message. The copywriter delivers the final advertising text and the art director creates the design that will best convey the message. An *assistant art director*, who helps throughout the working process, takes part by more or less independently testing various ideas in sketch form. An *art buyer* is responsible for contact with photographers and illustrators, and for purchasing their services. Finally the production manager has one of the team in the studio make the material ready for technical production.

The production manager then supervises the technical production, taking responsibility for ensuring that the right material gets to the right supplier at the right time. If printed material is being produced, the following contractors are often employed: *printer, bookbinder* and *distribution company*. Monitoring technical quality is vital, which is why the production manager, often with the art director, will check the printer's *proofs* on-site at the printers to check colours match those on the originals. They will also check *blueprints*, *plotter prints* or *laser prints* to ensure all the text and pictures are present and correct, and the *final proofs*, which are the last chance to make sure everything has been properly reproduced.

If it is a TV commercial, the results of the filming have to be examined. There is a great deal of technology that has to be right, including sound effects and the addition of music. All that remains is a final check with the client before the work is signed off.

External production

Many advertising agencies choose to outsource production and administration to an external production studio, which takes the pressure off the advertising agency (or the company ordering the advertising) and frees up time for the vital creative work.

This is often a *digital advertising studio*, where a customer can go in and order a format adaptation of a specific advert, without even having to talk to an advertising agency.

It is also a place where the advertising agency can place text and pictures, which the supplier can add to, using existing templates, to create the finished product. This method ensures the consistency of typography, design and colour at every stage.

Internal production

Marketing, advertising and information departments also deal with visual communication. Product sheets, folders, brochures, catalogues and sometimes advertising campaigns, websites, videos, newsletters, customer magazines, exhibition stands, annual reports and staff magazines are all examples of what may be produced in-house.

The professions involved include *marketing, advertising* and *information managers*. *Product* and *sales managers*, *exhibition managers* and *webmasters* may also, in one way or another, encounter tasks relating to visual communication.

Many companies and organizations equip an internal production department (often called an *in-house agency*) with advanced technology. The aim is to avoid employing expensive advertising agencies and other suppliers (for some or all productions), making use of internal skills instead. This approach may also generate time savings for the company, as an external advertising agency has long lead times.

AT THE WEB AGENCY

The web agency (in close partnership with the client and based on a needs analysis) develops a strategy, message and design for a *corporate* or *campaign site*. The corporate site is an overall presentation of the company, while the campaign site sells a particular product at its own web address and through *banners* for a limited campaign period.

The web agency also complements the traditional advertising agency, which often lacks competence when it comes to the internet. The web agency must then take onboard the advertising agency's strategy and message formulation, but is often expected to be independently responsible for the web design and, of course, for the technical implementation.

BELOW / This innovative website for the band Arcade Fire makes use of a lot of Flash, evoking its own particular atmosphere.

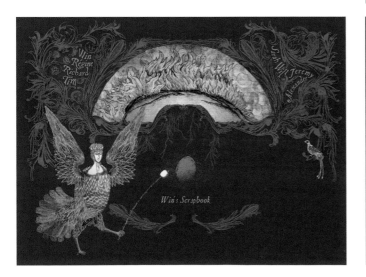

Professional roles

As the boundaries between advertising agencies and web agencies begin to break down, traditional advertising experts (whether art directors, copywriters, project managers, planners or production managers) find themselves working side by side with the web-based professionals.

The *webmaster* has technical responsibility for a site.

The *info designer* sorts and structures facts, text and pictures.

The *web editor* is responsible not only for the text, but also the message, sharing the latter responsibility with others, including the web designer.

At one agency, the *web designer* might be a driving creative force (web art director) with significant responsibility.

The main task of the designer is to create a functional site which is easy to get to, easy to understand and use, invites the right interaction and finally leads to the required result. Sound simple? Or highly demanding?

AT THE DESIGN AGENCY

The graphic designer will have extensive experience and a heavyweight position when it comes to visual communication. In times gone by, they would make such beautiful signs in wood and iron for the shoemakers that customers would pour in. In today's environment, designers are much more likely to deal with an extremely broad range of visual signals, whether on paper, screen and even mobile phones.

The designer works at a *design agency*, either directly for a client company, or as supplier to an advertising agency.

Broad spectrum

Most graphic designers are specialists, designing catalogues and posters for a gallery, magazines and journals for a publisher or a complete visual profile for a company.

For a corporate visual profile, the designer creates a consistent visual look, taking in the *logo*, i.e., the company's name in a

BELOW / A poster from North Design's 'Control Systems' series for G&B Printers, exploring the aesthetics of function while demonstrating their print capabilities.

RIGHT / Packaging provides many different outlets and formats, from Experimental Jetset's cult T-shirts to Stanley Donwood's artwork for Thom Yorke's *The Eraser*.

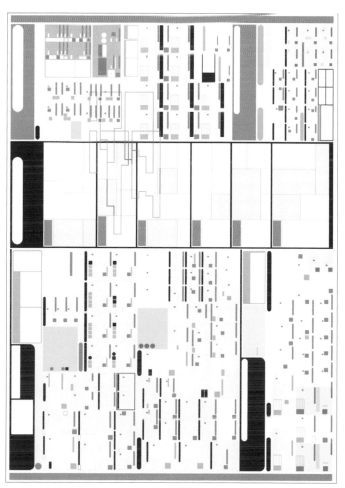

ABOVE & LEFT/ Farrow Design's packaging for food retailer Peyton and Byrne informs, interprets and protects, while also sending desirable signals from the sales outlets.

particular typeface (existing or specially designed) and the *company symbol*, a simple image representing the company's business. The visual profile plays a key role in winning credibility and respect from the world at large.

Other designers specialize in packaging. Cartons, boxes and bags convey messages both in-store and in the consumer's home, i.e., before and after the actual purchase.

The designer must, above all, be able to combine beauty and function, as packaging has to attract buyers and protect the product from damage. The designer is constantly battling to trump the ultimate packaging – it's easy to open and has an instantly recognizable shape and colour. What is it? The banana.

Then there are designers who focus solely on *book design*. They have to be able to distil the content of the book and transfer this to a typographical and visually strong design for both the cover and the interior.

Other designers express, in a suggestive way, a singer, musician or director's feelings and messages on the CD cover to sell an album, or the DVD case to sell a film.

A design agency may also have *illustrators* working in various specialist idioms (ways of creating a drawing for example). A morning newspaper may need bold illustrations for its lead stories and columns, while a trade journal might need an exploded view showing all the parts of a new outboard engine.

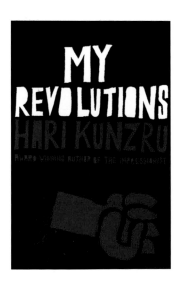

LEFT / Book covers, like these by Jon Gray, have many tasks: to interpret content, create a desire to buy, and send status signals from the bookshelves.

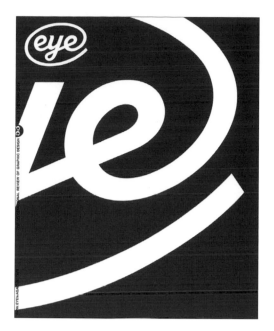

ABOVE / Two magazine covers with
strong arrangements of form and colour –
Eye magazine, published in the UK, and
Re-Magazine from Canada.

AT THE BOOK PUBLISHER
Designers also work in-house at many major book publishers,
dealing with cover designs, layouts and typography (although
there is an increasing tendency for publishers to employ freelance
designers for such work).

However, the designer's expertize also comes into play in the
publisher's marketing and advertising, as author presentations,
information sheets, catalogues, posters and exhibition stands
have to come in an attractive form.

AT THE MAGAZINE PUBLISHER
'How to get the new look!' The magazine racks in the newsagent
and supermarket are always full of new *weeklies*. Many people
find their design (and perhaps their content too) unnecessarily
loud, but there is of course a conscious purpose behind this pop-
ulist and often over-the-top graphic language.

The cover is vital, and you have to have that smiling woman
there, whether you are trying to attract male or female readers. A
dreary male author on the cover would mean a record number of
unsold copies.

'Harold Pinter speaks out about his writer's block.' On the
other hand, *monthly publications* and *magazines* often exude
greater harmony and elegance. And behind this too, there will be
a designer using a carefully chosen visual language.

The *magazine designer* has to be able to unite typographical
knowledge, a flair for images and a journalistic approach. He or
she must be able to handle the weight of the words and the
impact of the photographs, and must display a feel for the captivating rhythm, with all its contrasts, which has to be built up using
recurring headings, images and vignettes.

At every workplace described in this chapter, strategic thinking is required. And that's what the next chapter is all about.

SUMMARY

'Early to bed. Early to rise.'

MESSENGERS
The messenger (a subeditor, designer, art director,
filmmaker, web designer) helps the sender/client to reach
the receiver. The messenger works on a newspaper, TV
channel, an advertising agency, design company or at a
web agency.

SUPPLIERS
Photographers, cameramen and illustrators provide
newspapers, TV channels and advertising agencies with
editorial and commercial material.

CLIENTS
Clients often work on a newspaper or for a TV channel or
in a company's marketing, advertising or PR department.

STRATEGY

4/

ABOVE / In the evening, the narrow
alleys and small squares start to fill up
with masks and sweeping capes. Trade
– and the experience – are in full swing.

'A farewell to meat!'

A very small and unpretentious office just next to St Mark's Square is in a bit of a mess. It's carnival time in Venice and Pierangelo Federici, director of communication and marketing, has just managed to spill coffee on some piles of information material which are to be handed out to interested journalists, sponsors and tourists.

The phones are all ringing at once and Pierangelo is stressed. He's the marketing manager for the carnival and he's got a lot on his plate. His most urgent task is to find space for a graphic designer who is about to turn up, and the tiny desk is needed for folders and sketches. Visual communication is on the agenda.

Carnival, probably from *carne vale* (farewell to meat), precedes Lent and has been celebrated in Venice since the eleventh century. It died out in the late eighteenth century (or possibly was banned by Napoleon) only to be revived in 1979. Costumes were sewn, masks tried on and *commedia dell'arte* plays came into fashion again. Venetians wanted to recreate a fascinating part of their history by encouraging masquerades in squares, on canals and through streets where, protected by a disguise, anything was possible.

'Jumping on the bandwagon wasn't difficult,' as Pierangelo puts it. 'We, that is the town and the tourist office, quickly realized that this was an ideal opportunity to market the city in a new way. In particular it gave us the opportunity to attract visitors in what is the lowest month of the tourism calendar. The streets and the alleys and the tills tend to echo rather emptily in February.'

STRATEGY

Beating the emptiness takes strategic thinking, creating a pattern of decisions and actions in the present to guarantee success in the future.

Those who are responsible for a business have to work their way through an *overall communications strategy* before they can get to the point of grouping together their arguments and starting to think about the text and pictures that will then form their message. This overall strategy encompasses a mission statement, a marketing plan, the branding, communication criteria and a communication plan.

MISSION STATEMENT

To start at the very beginning – a small local newspaper or a global telecommunications company, or perhaps a cultural event such as the Venice Carnival, should all base their operations on a mission statement.

This mission statement explains, preferably briefly, why a company exists. The newspaper wants to report local events, the telecommunications company wants to sell telecommunications systems and mobile phones across the globe and the carnival wants to activate and revitalize local business during a couple of frosty business weeks.

The marketing manager, along with the other members of the management team, have to decide what resources they should allocate and how they will work to achieve the goals in the mission statement.

MARKETING PLAN

The next step is the marketing plan, which covers the following four points with the associated questions:

Analysis of current position:
Where is the company today?
Goals:
What does the company want and where does it want to be?
Marketing strategy:
How is this to be achieved?
Checks, evaluation and follow-up:
What was the result?

Analysis of current position

In this analysis, the mission statement is tested to check that it is in line with the spirit of the times and also with cultural and economic development.

PRODUCTS

These, whether goods or services, must be scrutinized carefully. Is production running as smoothly as possible? Are our consumers happy? Is our product design modern and distinctive? Are sales figures going up or down?

DISTRIBUTION

Efficient distribution is important, and great demand in the market must not be thrown away because the products aren't ready and waiting. Are there any alternative distribution channels? Is online shopping working as well as it should?

COMPETITORS

The company's management should constantly keep a close eye on all competitors. What are they doing at the moment and what will they get up to in the future? We must try to survey their products, distribution channels and marketing activities. Are we better than our competitors? In what way? We need to subject ourselves to a good dose of healthy self-criticism.

And are our competitors really competitors? A strange question you might think. It goes without saying that a crisps manufacturer will see another crisps manufacturer as a competitor for domination of the snack marketplace, fought out on coffee tables and TV screens. But a threat can also be posed by *substitutes*, i.e., other products that could affect crisp consumption volumes – pizza slices, say, or Japanese-style snacks.

Is the carnival in Rio a competitor to Venice? Hardly. However, skiing in the Italian Alps (Courmayeur, for example) is definitely a potential substitute. This realization should be a guiding factor in the marketing.

FINANCIAL CONSIDERATIONS

These must also be analysed and examined in evaluations of the current position.

EXTERNAL FACTORS

Factors such as current trends and new legislation can also influence the conditions in which the business has to operate. It is important to keep your ear to the ground to be able to predict, identify and evaluate changes.

Naturally, any analysis of the current position must be based on research, and it may be a good idea for the company's management to have this carried out by a market research company, as we often don't notice things when we're too close to them. Annual reports and Google can provide us with valuable pieces of the jigsaw puzzle.

SWOT

The current situation can be summarized using a SWOT analysis of Strengths, Weaknesses, Opportunities and Threats.

The first two points focus on the company and the latter two on the world around it, but all should look at the present and the future. This analysis naturally demands both honesty and a self-critical eye (and could also prove beneficial outside the world of business, i.e., before getting married, say).

STRENGTHS

The company's strengths are often easy to identify, and might include a unique product or an unerring feel for trends in the sector. But strengths can also be found where you never dreamed of looking, in the form of specialist skills (language knowledge, for example), which should be exploited.

WEAKNESSES

These are unfortunately always to be found in a company or organization – some are visible, others invisible. They have to be identified, and measures found to tackle them. Talk to the bank about cash-flow problems and to a training company about a lack of service-mindedness.

OPPORTUNITIES

Great opportunities may suddenly present themselves. A large foreign market may open up, or a strong economy may pave the way for expansion.

THREATS

Finally, threats may pop up in the form of new competitors, new legislation or demands to adapt to customs regulations or other restrictions. An economic downturn, predicted by financial analysts, naturally also affects the company.

From his office in Venice, Pierangelo Federici sums up his SWOT analysis as follows: 'Strengths and opportunities are fairly obvious. Our strength lies in the experience we can give people and there are also future opportunities there. The weaknesses and the threats merge together in the form of the intensive expansion and the superficiality we've seen in recent years. It is a difficult balancing act between quality and quantity.'

Goals

The next box in a marketing plan is about goals, which can be general, i.e., *strategic*, or *operational*, i.e., with a more practical focus.

It is important that everyone in the company is well informed and thus motivated to work towards the goals set up. Meaningful and possibly even enjoyable goals unite shareholders and employees, bosses and subordinates.

Marketing

The term 'marketing' refers to the way in which the company uses various *competitive tools*.

The competitive tools available are what world-famous economist Philip Kotler called the *Four Ps*. The company's management has not only developed the *Product* and its quality, design, size, packaging and service, but have also found the *Price*, which will match supply and demand out among consumers (discounts and credit terms also belong here). The product will be sold in a special *Place*, in stores and other sales points, in line with decisions regarding the range, stock and transport. And finally, through *Promotion*, including advertising, salespeople and public relations, it attracts the attention of the consumers.

The differences between marketing and advertising are thus that marketing covers the overall work of getting the products out while advertising is part of the last link in the chain which creates contact with potential customers.

Checks

Finally all that remains is checking, evaluating and following up everything encompassed in the marketing plan. Have the initiatives produced results? Have they met or exceeded expectations? What should be changed immediately (perhaps the product mix) and what should be subjected to long-term analysis and developed (perhaps new markets)?

BRANDING

Despite successful work on the strategy, the marketing manager is worried. The problem is that today most products tend to be confusingly similar and soon it will be impossible to tease out the unique characteristics of individual goods and services. Imitations pop up in an increasingly aggressive flood and are known as *me too* products. 'Take me too, buy me too, read me, taste me … ', they shout, echoing each other from the shelves. And then, of course, it becomes increasingly difficult for consumers to tell them apart.

So how are the consumers able to choose one product over another? Well, the public perception of the company behind the product is crucial. Consumers look for companies with a good reputation who they feel they can trust. In today's tough but uniform commercial media clutter, most people only listen to the companies they respect. It's as simple as that.

A good reputation, trust and respect, there we have the basics of a strong brand.

So what is a brand?

Is it the product, the name or the logo? Yes, but it can also be a registered word, a phrase or even a character. But above all it is a manifestation of the intangible idea of a product. So what does that mean exactly? Well, the product (the good or service) is manufactured in a factory or in a development department, but the brand is born and grows strong (we hope) in the minds of consumers.

Consumers are influenced by all sorts of things. A digital camera, which a young woman learns to use quickly and which, to her delight, takes excellent pictures, naturally creates respect for the camera manufacturer. A greedy managing director revealed in the media to have grabbed a few extra million in bonuses, a brusque call-centre operator or TV ads which make viewers blush also influence consumers. It is the sum total of all these signals that creates the brand and, just like environmental pollution, nothing ever disappears completely, it all hangs around forever, albeit in changing forms.

Carelessness and a poor reputation also affect the company's employees. This means that internal and external factors are connected, so we could say that building a brand takes place on two levels, internally within the organization and externally in the consciousness of consumers.

Commitment

The word 'branding' comes from the practice of burning cattle to keep track of them, which relates to what a *brand manager* in a

---

BELOW / Orla Kiely develops new *products*, to be sold in a *place* – here, their shop on Monmouth Street, London. These products require *promotion* through advertising, and come at a *price* ... all adding up to the *Four Ps*, as defined by Philip Kotler.

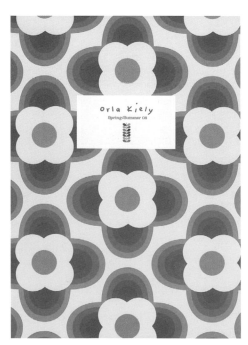

LEFT / Many consumers identify with trendy brands or shops (such as Stash, Maastricht, by Maurice Mentjens) that convey an image that chimes with how they see themselves.

ABOVE / The appealing Smart car concept sprung from cooperation between Swatch and Daimler, and aims to be easy to park, fuel-efficient and environmentally friendly.

company would like to do. Marking a product's territory and creating a feeling of belonging among us consumers. This is known as *commitment,* in the sense that we can be committed to social issues or even to a company and its goods or services.

At the same time a new attitude of *non-commitment* has been identified as growing among many consumers. Many trend analysts claim that we (in parts of the West) no longer feel as committed to our employers, spouses or products. We are demanding change to a greater extent. We do not consume in order to achieve a goal but for the experience, and, above all, we do not live in accordance with the checklists and lifestyle patterns produced by the marketing men and women, but want to switch between various different styles.

There is (claim the trend predictors) even a value-based resistance to belonging to a group, as many people are instead looking to be unique personalities by creating their own combinations of goods and services. The product is the prop for the role we choose to play in life's drama: so the question is no longer 'who am I?' but 'who am I now?'.

COMMUNICATION CRITERIA

So much for the marketing plan and the theory surrounding the brand. Now to some important criteria for communication:

Segmentation
Positioning
Concept
Campaign
Unit

Segmentation

This means choosing part of a market which accounts for a group of consumers with the same values and needs. Consumer needs can vary considerably and it is important to choose different strategies for different groups. Some people only watch the news, others only entertainment. Some prefer carbonated drinks, others still ones.

Positioning

It is important that a company chooses a clear position in a market. Most people have short memories and our internal lists of the various fashion magazines and types of coffee are short. You have to be at the top of people's perception of the particular market place, or *top of mind* as it is called by professionals – a brand leader like *Vogue* or Nescafé.

What tops the list when it comes to carnivals? The carnival in Rio, Mardi Gras in New Orleans or the Venice Carnival? Most people would probably say Rio.

The optimum top-of-mind position occurs when a product – a good or a service – becomes synonymous with and represents an entire product category. For many consumers Google is synonymous with internet searching and Jeep with off-road vehicles, and their competitors have trouble squeezing onto the list.

Concept

Having a concept means designing and formulating a sustainable, long-term and media-neutral theme.

It must be something durable, which everyone inside the company is able to work with for a long period and which won't bore the market rigid within five minutes. Like Volvo, the epitome of safety.

Media-neutrality refers to the criterion that a concept must work in all contexts irrespective of the medium. A concept should not therefore be based on the glugging noise of a beer bottle, which can only be conveyed through sound-based media such as radio, film and the web, but not in a newspaper or on a poster.

ABOVE / A successful campaign will often share similar elements in different media. Lloyds TSB has extended a successful commercial, 'For the Journey' produced by studio aka, into a series including further commercials and print ads, while characters from the adverts appear on information leaflets and the company's website.

Campaign

A campaign will involve a range of activities undertaken in an attempt to dominate the market during a given period. A company rarely has just one ad or TV spot produced, as that alone would not make a very strong impression on the market. No, three are better, or nine. And the effect usually doesn't take long, even if the production costs do go up.

A campaign must tie in with the concept and be able to be managed in several units and in different media in what is known as the *media mix*.

Unit

This is the smallest part (an advert, TV spot or banner) and is the result of work on the segment, concept and campaign. It is this smallest part that does the biggest job: getting the message across.

COMMUNICATION PLAN

The natural next step in communication work is what is known as the communication plan (or the *advertising plan* or *communicative platform*). This answers the question of *how* the advertising manager is to proceed to fulfil the strategy, and will cover the following seven points:

Goal
Target group
Medium
Message
Schedule
Budget
Evaluation/Follow-up

It is important to point out that this process does not necessarily have to take place in chronological order. Each of the phases may merge into and overlap with the next. Work on one question can affect issues which have already been decided and, of course, subsequent ones.

Message, schedule, budget and evaluation/follow-up will be addressed in the next chapter.

GOAL

The goal can be expressed as what is to be *achieved* within a particular *period*.

Formulating goals

The following barrage of questions may help in formulating goals:

What distinguishes our goods and services?
Where is our market? At home or abroad?
What status do the products have? What authority?
Shall we break into a new market?
How can we increase sales? Increase subscriber numbers?
Increase awareness of the products? Change attitudes?
What will the planned measures lead to?
What are the time frames?

The marketing manager and the advertising manager set three important criteria for a goal:

Specific
Communicable
Measurable

Specific

The goal must be sufficiently clearly formulated so that no questions will arise. When the newspaper's editorial team decides to produce a weekend supplement which is to be distributed with Friday's paper with a date for the first issue of 1 March, both the product and time goals have been stated. If a group of employees are to be trained in the use of InDesign before the end of the year, the training and time goals are clear.

Communicable

The goal must be so carefully expressed that messages can be formulated from it, and then formed in their turn, and these messages must naturally be capable of arousing the interest of the receivers the company is interested in.

The company's management should not start working on external communication before they have set out the criteria and goals internally.

Measurable

It must be possible to measure and evaluate the goal. The result of the communication initiative must be able to be set in relation to the goal. Is the weekend supplement out? Can the training group apply their skills in InDesign?

Goals can be *quantitative* or *qualitative*. A quantitative goal is '75 per cent of employees must be aware of the company's mission statement' or 'All of our city's inhabitants must see the productions put on by the city theatre'.

A qualitative goal could be 'Employees must feel faith in the future and high self-confidence'. It goes without saying that this qualitative goal is considerably more difficult to measure, as is the goal that plays should improve theatregoers' quality of life.

Studies

Carrying out an analysis and setting up goals requires evidence and therefore the advertising manager will have studies carried out.

QUANTITATIVE STUDIES

These find out how many people buy and use a certain product and what proportion of the whole market this accounts for.

QUALITATIVE STUDIES

The analysis of what consumers think, and of more abstract issues such as knowledge, preconceptions, emotions, attitudes to a service, occurs in a qualitative study.

PDS

Problem Detection Studies are common. These survey a group's experienced problems with a product. The study is quite easy to carry out because people love complaining.

TARGET GROUP

A company's target group constitutes the group of people whom the advertising manager initially wishes this message to reach. Who are they? New questions to try to answer:

Who might need our products?
What problems can our goods and services solve?
Where is the target group?
What response have we had previously?
Who are our customers and why?
Who are not our customers and why?
What media habits do the target group have?

Defining the target group

This is very important as it makes the choice of media easier and provides guidance for the creative work ahead. Important factors include the sex, age, education, income, leisure interests, type of housing and location of the target group. These are called *demographic* variables and give a fairly rough picture of the target group (for instance, women aged 20–40 who are interested in clothes, exercise and culture).

To gain a deeper and clearer picture, the advertising manager must add *psychographic* variables, which can include political viewpoints, environmental awareness, need for security, adaptability and risk aversion. Through this the advertising manager identifies different lifestyles (male owners of hunting cabins interested in bear hunting in Western Colorado).

Some groups will become primary and others secondary. A simple shower system that is primarily intended for use by leisure

BELOW / Bang & Olufsen have found their target group among people who appreciate both their technical solutions and their high standards of design.

sailors may also attract the owners of hunting cabins, who also need to keep clean.

The advertising manager should also think about attempting to reach those individuals who provide the *initiative* for an action or for a purchase. This initiative taker and the person who eventually makes this purchase in practice do not need to be the same individual (for instance, the workplace safety representative, the finance manager – a fire extinguisher). In other instances it may prove highly effective to attempt to reach the person who, in one way or another, can *influence* the individual who will be making the final purchasing decision (the teenage daughter, her parent – a DVD player).

Research

Incredible sums are invested in researching consumers. Of course it is important to hit the right market. Those who carry out market research examine us through a magnifying glass and group us by idealism and materialism. Let's look at some of these groups (the size of which varies from country to country).

One large group is *preservers* who value tradition and spiritual values. Another group is *status hunters,* who crave the right product and the right reputation. *Climbers* chase wealth and influence. *Trendsetters* or *early adopters* are few and far between but are big spenders and thus attractive consumers. They are curious and greatly value change.

BELOW / Using clichés in campaigns can undermine a product's success. PlayStation is presented in a unique way by TBWA\Paris, with a mode of expression different from its competitors, aided by the powerful photography by Dimitri Daniloff.

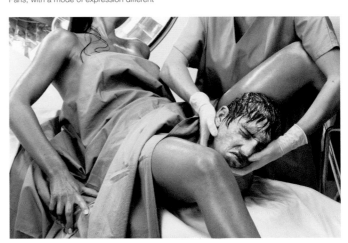

The market for men is currently going through an exciting stage. The modern man spends more on clothes and traditional female products such as skin creams and cleansing products than before. It is completely okay to be a *metrosexual* and put money and energy into one's appearance.

Blunt or pointed

It is important to remember that the larger the target group the advertising manager focuses on, the blunter and more general the message tends to be. Cardinal rule number one is: never choose the general public as your target group.

A smaller target group will allow a more pointed and more creative message.

Stereotypes

It is often claimed that the importance of defining the target group has been exaggerated. All the studies and research tend to create stereotypical descriptions of people. Not all pensioners, to take just one example, always behave like old fogeys. Some, with great enthusiasm and curiosity, will adopt new ideas and standards which might in fact horrify a younger and possibly prematurely fossilized generation.

Start by using yourself as a model instead, say the editors, advertising managers and designers. Start out from your own strengths and weaknesses, don't speculate too much about the personality and character of the receiver. The most personal is actually often the most universally applicable.

MEDIUM

Once the advertising manager is clear about the goal and the target group he or she will focus on, the next task is to choose the medium. Once more some fundamental questions are crucial:

When and where can the target group be influenced?
In what situation?
When the fridge is empty or in the middle of a TV film?
What do they read? And what do they watch?
What are their experiences of the media?
Can our goods and services be experienced in different ways in
    different media? In what ways?
What would life be without questions?

MAIN MEDIA

The most common main media, which can be used either individually or in combination, are listed below. Most of them carry news, advertising and entertainment, but some are only used to convey commercial messages.

Daily papers
Popular press
Trade press
TV
Web
Cinema
Radio
Outdoor
Direct mail

DAILY PAPERS

Many people can't imagine starting the day without a morning paper, which often becomes a friend for life. In Washington people read *The Washington Post*, in Berlin *Die Zeit* and in Calcutta *The Indian Express*. Most people choose a paper in the same way that they choose their friends – on the basis of its opinions, political viewpoint and sense of humour – and the readers often don't like it when editors mess about with the pages.

But newspaper reading is in decline and a once proud medium is showing signs of crumbling. During the 1800s, industrialization led to a strong press and newspaper reading became widespread. At that time the press were alone in the news arena but today they face strong competition from a growing number of new mass media. These include free newspapers, which have gained a fast-growing market, demonstrating that the word 'free' is becoming an increasingly important concept.

The media moguls are convinced that the great days of newsprint (dead wood products) are over and that digital media are taking over.

Electronic paper already exists. This electronic plastic paper is made of thin screens which act like paper and can be folded and rolled up. It consists of a layer of film between two plastic sheets and contains a thin network of electrodes in which positive and negative micro-capsules in liquid build up the texts and pictures. E-paper is loaded with articles the reader wants to read from the computer and then all the reader has to do is settle down comfortably and use a little button in each of the corners to browse through what will probably be the newspaper of tomorrow.

But society's inertia triumphs. Trend predictors might have underestimated the power of the fundamental functions of the daily newspaper, as it is part of our daily conversations and still inspires great trust in the general public. Predictors have certainly also overestimated people's willingness to change their habits and make the switch to new things. The daily paper is deeply embedded in the everyday habits of most people.

It seems as though the readers will keep their old media as long as their replacements are not good enough, comfortable enough or trustworthy enough. Those born in the 1980s and 1990s take digitization as a matter of course, which means that the technology shift is already here.

The daily press is divided into *broadsheets* and *tabloids*. We'll start by looking at the former.

Broadsheets

The term broadsheet is used to refer to the more serious or upmarket end of the newspaper market, as such papers are usually printed in large formats (often around 56 x 43 cm [22 x 17 in]). However, many are now adopting more compact sizes. The broadsheets can be a good medium for advertising – food retailers have an enormous market at their fingertips, as do travel agencies, who seduce us with promises of sun and sand in distant lands. But broadsheet newspapers are also an expensive medium if the advertising manager is looking to reach very large groups, and there may well be problems with the relatively poor print quality.

Tabloids

As everyone knows, you can't really trust the editorial content of the often silicon-enhanced tabloid press. These tabloids are in the front line of journalism and have, for better or worse, won battle after battle in recent decades, pushing the boundaries of journalism, raising the standard for narrative, proximity, cheek, speed and campaigning. This, however, is seen as having gone hand in hand with a decline in moral and ethical standards and a disregard for 'good taste'.

The tabloid press is also good for advertising, being a means of reaching a large and diverse market for general consumer goods.

POPULAR PRESS

The huge volume of magazines that makes up the popular press satisfies needs and entertains half the nation. They are read at the consumer's leisure, often several times, and print quality is high.

Alongside the top-selling popular weekly magazines full of gossip and celebrities are magazines that come out regularly with a particular type of specialized content, such as art or literature. There are also magazines whose content is mixed, combining fashion and interior design, for example.

New magazines are published all the time. Some are one-shots, test products or precisely niched sister products to existing publications; others are supplements to newspapers.

TRADE PRESS

Geared towards professionals in the field in question, the trade press is usually divided into *horizontal* and *vertical* publications.

Horizontal refers to publications that are geared towards a wide readership spanning several sectors. These readers might be interested in economics and therefore choose a business magazine like *The Economist*. Vertical publications seek their readers within a single sector, e.g., the design publication *Eye*.

Both categories are excellent advertising media. They have interested and committed readers, good print, are read regularly, and often have many readers per publication, and what's more, they are also often saved to flick through at a later date.

TV

'The modern version of the campfire which the family gathers around to listen to stories.' 'A kind of pipeline for messages straight into the living room.' Opinions vary, but it is clear that no one is completely unaffected by television.

Television is a complete news medium and can, like no other medium, offer a meeting place for processing traumas which affect a huge number of people (9/11, Madrid, the tsunami, London, Hurricane Katrina and global warming).

But there is naturally a danger in so many people gaining their impressions primarily from television and, as the number of channels grows, viewers may choose only the particular channel that confirms their own world view.

Public service television and radio channels (often known as state broadcasters) attempt to combat this trend. The BBC is the largest public service broadcaster, with a phenomenally wide range of programmes.

Previously advertisers could almost reach whole nations with the help of a few television channels. Niche channels are now growing in number instead, attracting what are known as 'light viewers', who choose channels according to their lifestyle and do not let television viewing dominate their evening. These narrow channels may focus on business, sport or culture, which is good for advertisers, as they can easily find the right target group for their products.

Of all the advertising media (besides the web), television comes closest to a personal encounter. It is an extremely visual medium, which makes it easy and rewarding to use, not only to demonstrate a new product but also to surprise. Television advertising can convey feelings in a completely different way from other media. When at its best, combining images, film, sound effects, music and voiceover can be magical.

BELOW / Terrifying and critical events can be shown on the television screen – for instance, the return of Benazir Bhutto to Pakistan before her death.

Television commercials, often 30 seconds long, are placed in *blocks* or *breaks*. A block is a group of ads between programmes, while breaks are spots inserted in the middle of the programme, interrupting it. Attention tends to be slightly lower in a block than in a break. It's important to be placed at the start or the end as viewers' attention is still high at the beginning and returns towards the end, knowing that the programme they were watching is about to return.

The context is important. Violent episodes in series and films do the adverts no favours. They can disturb viewers, forcing them to process strong feelings, which reduces the impact and retention of the advertising message.

Zapping (using the remote control to switch to another channel when the ad spots and the trailers come on) is naturally a big problem for advertisers. But many television viewers aren't satisfied with just switching channel when the ads appear. No, they want to avoid adverts completely and instead choose to watch user-defined TV on the web. Or they buy a DVR (digital video recorder), a hard disk DVD with a timeshift function, which starts when a programme starts. This means they can then watch their favourite programme with a slight time delay and skip all the advertising.

Product placement

What can companies do against this fast-forwarding resistance movement?

Product placement may save the day, as it doesn't signal advertising as clearly as the ad breaks do. Product placement, mainly of goods, is carried out in three ways. Firstly, the audience *see* them in a home or as part of a public environment. Secondly, they are presented with the help of the spoken word; the name of the product is *said* in dialogue. (James Bond: 'It is Omega'). Thirdly, the product is *used* in different situations, such as shaving, putting on make-up, driving.

But television viewers seem to get bored of unjustified close-ups of Motorola mobile phones. It is thought that excessive product placement will soon have had its day. It is quite a clumsy and over-obvious way of advertising, although the history of advertising celebrates successful campaigns. It is said that 60 years ago Humphrey Bogart raised smoking to an artistic and financial height by chain-smoking his way through the film *Casablanca*. The film is said to have been more significant than anything else in the history of tobacco for getting people to start smoking. But everything has its price and as we know, Bogart died of lung cancer.

Programming

If product placement is now ceasing to work, what can viewers look forward to in the future? Companies have to get their adverts to make their way down new hidden paths, where there are no road signs to herald the arrival of special offers. The solution is programming (or *AFP*, *advertiser funded programming*), which means delivering entire programmes. The companies produce programmes in which their products take on a more or less central and clear role. The programmes have no ad breaks; the programmes themselves *are* ads – *Room Service*, an interior decoration programme, is in fact financed and produced by a company which sells paint and builders' products. We have a similar development ahead of us in the press ('advertorials' are features combining advertising with editorial content), radio and even in books – not to mention blogs, which can be disguised advertising and PR.

What more do we media consumers have ahead of us? Maybe really big companies with worldwide sales will start their own TV channels and start to broadcast news, entertainment and children's programmes. The American greetings card company Hallmark already has a long tradition in this area. The company's

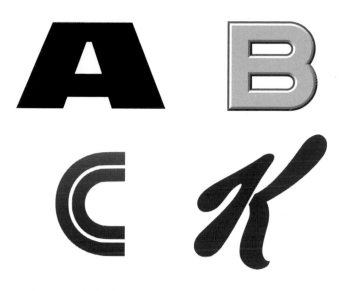

ABOVE / Large multinational companies may even begin to dominate the school alphabet ...

film channel of the same name is part of a TV package that can be seen across the globe.

Or soon maybe we'll walk into a classroom in a village school and see a strange poster on the wall, showing the alphabet. On closer inspection we see that some letters look odd, to say the least. The A looks like the initial letter in the Air France logo. And the B seems to come from Bayer, the C from CNN and the K from a Kellogg's packet. A new generation is learning to read.

TV 2.0

One thing is clear, however, and that is that our media habits change fast. Viewers take the step from passivity to activity when selecting from among the content available and participating in creating it.

This participation, which can be called *communication-TV* or *co-creation*, takes place when the viewers provide a TV programme with text and pictures, or they upload a video clip to a newspaper's web TV site. This is TV 2.0, the second generation of television.

WORLD WIDE WEB

The interactive media also play an important role in passing on news, information, education, marketing and advertising.

CD-ROMs and DVDs

These contain large amounts of information on a small thin disk – for example, museum guides and reference books, which provide information in an educational and suggestive manner. Much of a large company's internal education takes place using these disks. They can also be used for company presentations and product catalogues.

Commercial use will naturally increase too. The popularity of computer games and role-playing games is rocketing. Might they even take over from novels and films?

The web

Here we're looking at the most interesting interactive medium, the *World Wide Web*, which means communicating over the worldwide network of computers, the *internet*. The internet was originally a giant network linking all the information of the US defence department. The idea was to use it in the event of a world war.

In 1995 the whole world woke up to this medium, which proved to be the fastest way of conveying information across the globe. The web is now an important part of a completely different war, for technology and especially for the favour and consumption of the citizens of the world.

Differences

The big difference compared with other mass media is that the web is global, open and up-to-date. The web is not limited by geography – oceans or rocky mountains are no barrier – and it is therefore really a *global* medium. The visitor can read both *The Observer* and *Le Monde* over breakfast.

The small printers in northern Italy can display itself and sell its services to its customers in Verona, Cairo and Perth. The web is *global.*

The web is also always *open*. No irritating voicemail or closed switchboards bother customers who want to order books from amazon.com and iPods from apple.com (although it might take a while before they get them delivered).

And it is *real time*, as fast changes and updates are possible (although a lot of web junk is still out there, like all the space junk circling around the earth).

The web makes it possible to shop nationally and globally with fewer or no intermediaries. Consumers become stronger and have more of an opportunity to influence prices and the goods and services on offer, to make comparisons and create interactive contacts. Knowledge will also be accessible to far more people than just those who have managed to get into a college or university, thanks to the web.

Fast

In the global village things move fast. In Denmark a caricature of Mohammed is printed in a newspaper and, thanks to the latest technology in camera phones and computers, it quickly spreads across the world and several of the country's embassies are burned down in protest. *Flash mobs* are what arise from demonstrations spread via the net.

New media technology has clear advantages, but it is sometimes argued that there are disadvantages too. With the printing presses came religious wars in Europe, with film and radio came fascism, with mobile phones come fragmentation and the growth of myths. Selective information is distorted and spreads in seconds across the world. In countries with government-controlled media and without free debate there is a risk that mutual understanding between different groups will shrink rather than increase.

Websites

In the global village there seems to be little space or time left for regular social interaction. So where in the village does contact take place? On a website, which mainly consists of a start page with a number of sub-pages, which are all connected through internal links. The website can also contain links to other sites – external links.

A *corporate site* presents the company's products and focus. A *campaign site* is almost always more attractive in that it is linked to a particular activity (like sponsoring a sailing boat) or campaign (e.g., the launch of a new magazine).

The web is an excellent advertising medium, which can constitute an entire campaign on its own, such as the launch of a new car model, where the site can cover everything that happens at a car dealer's, comparing models, checking interiors … though maybe not the test drive.

The contact between company and customer partly takes place at *function-based* sites, where the visitor can easily carry out services (order a car in silver metallic paint and special trim or bid for an early Warhol at Christie's) and partly at intensive *experience-oriented* sites (wander round the Guggenheim in Bilbao).

A website is also an ideal supplement to a wide-ranging television advertising campaign as a place for providing in-depth information and answering questions. More and more advertisers are putting more and more resources into web advertising, which is a growing commercial force. Many people think it won't be many years before internet advertising takes over from television advertising, the effectiveness of which is increasingly being questioned. The internet has many advantages but it is its measurability which makes it superior to all the other media. Every click on a banner or link from a search engine is recorded; it's even possible to monitor how many clicks result in a purchase.

Search engines are becoming a medium for advertising based on the search term. Someone with a broken washing machine and access to Google searches on white goods and sponsored links advertising attractive products appear next to the list of hits.

Banners

Visitors will find banners (the name for small-ads on the web) advertising various goods and services everywhere, including in the online versions of newspapers. The advertisements can be found in every sector. They blink and grovel temptingly to grab attention (sometimes to no avail). *Interactive banners* do not become active until the visitor clicks on them.

Public portals

These are the broad marketplaces, often built up around a search service. Several offer free surfing, email, news, a gallery of e-shops and much more besides.

VERTICALS

These are geared towards specific purposes and special interest groups such as opera lovers or fans of old Vespas from the 1950s.

COMMERCIAL PORTALS

These deal with B2B, business to business, which means that a steel company delivers parts for a fridge.

INTRANET

Many companies use an intranet, which is designed for and restricted to their own staff and internal communication.

EXTRANETS

These reveal some information, for example to particular customers and suppliers, who access the site via a login.

Online newspapers

The vast majority of print newspapers also have online versions which are attracting more and more readers, while cross-referencing between print, screen and mobile phones is becoming increasingly common. This is called multi-channel publication.

Online newspapers are developing into web TV and mobile TV, using video clips in news reporting and advertising. The aim is to fill the news reporting with lots of links so that the readers themselves can create a total picture of an event (the web clearly interacts *with* its readers rather than talking *to* them).

Online newspapers also offer monitoring services (RSS), which provide readers with constant updates. If they give a keyword ('space') they'll immediately be sent emails with links as soon as an article on the topic appears ('the countdown has started').

ABOVE / Online newspapers and blogs no longer speak at the readers but with them, creating a dialogue and altering approaches to the presentation of news.

Blogs

Journalists often write their own blogs about specific subjects, for which there isn't always room in the print or online editions of their papers. Blogs are chronological texts on the journalists' own web-sites. There are many different types but the most common are:

Private
describing everyday events.
Geeky
creating a narrow forum for a special interest.
Political agitation
focusing on particular issues such as government corruption or what should be on the world heritage list.
Journalistic
looking to reach a large audience and focused on any subject at all, from protecting the rainforests to combating terrorism.

Often the blogs grow into their own online newspapers where we meet a new journalist, a *sojo* (solo journalist), who doesn't sit incarcerated in the newspaper office, but can easily head out into the world with a laptop, mobile, camera or video camera. These reports can then be read across the world.

But not everyone appreciates blogs. The number of blogs is increasing all the time, encouraging freedom of speech, which is breaking the information monopoly in countries with state-controlled media. The authorities respond by blocking the sites and arresting their owners. In such situations things look bleak for free speech, even if the bloggers fight back by quickly changing IP addresses.

New times, new medium

The only thing that is certain about the future is that it will bring change. The younger generations stake it out by asking questions that can be difficult for old, hard-bitten newshounds at the desk and battle-scarred anchors under the studio lights to answer.

Why should we read print newspapers, when all we have to do is turn the computer on?

Why should we go to a record shop, when we can download all the music we like?

Why should we wait for broadcasters to show television series and films, when we can download these too or can watch them on the web?

Why should we read newspaper reviews, when we can chat with people who share our taste and opinions?

Web 2.0

The web is constantly developing and version 2.0 is now here. This means many things, including the fact that updating and developing programs gives the visitor the impression that the sites have become more user-friendly and are now better adapted to different needs. You don't need to be a technology nerd to build your own site or to put your songs on MySpace and your video clips on YouTube.

MySpace is a social networking site, which unsigned artists have used to bring their music to a wider audience. The site soon became so popular that even established artists started to use it, with the result that the line between fans and stars can become blurred. On YouTube (owned by Google) people can view their

ABOVE / If a strong contact can be made in the hectic city environment – whether New York (left) or Kuala Lumpur (right) – walls and pavements can still prove to be effective spaces for conveying messages.

own clips and those of other people, attracting large numbers of visitors every day.

Self-production is becoming increasingly common in advertising too. A shipping line launched a web campaign in which it encouraged visitors to send in video clips of themselves dancing. The idea became the hottest dance floor in the Baltic and its aim was to maximize the number of visitors to the site. The best clip won a trip to New York. Visitors have thus become art directors and copywriters.

CINEMA
The auditorium lighting slowly dims. The murmuring dies down. Expectations are running high for the film ahead, but expectations about the future of the medium are low as the advertisers are slowly but surely leaving the building. The audience has been getting smaller every year, because there are now other ways of watching films. The key target group has long been people aged 25–35 and it is precisely this group which is leaving the cinemas for downloads.

RADIO
This is an excellent news medium, because a radio reporter with all the technology on his or her back can quickly be on the spot to describe events and carry out interviews. It is an easily accessible medium, as the listener can be cooking dinner or ironing shirts at the same time, and when you're on your own the radio provides perfect company.

This is the disadvantage of radio as an advertising medium, as it often isn't more than a constant background noise. At the same time a really good radio spot can entertain, frighten and above all create strong images in the listener's head. Radio advertising can therefore be an excellent complement and extension to a television campaign.

It is a relatively cheap advertising medium. And many listeners admit that they would rather listen to the radio ads than irritating radio presenters.

OUTDOOR
This media group includes fixed and moving objects.

The big *fixed* billboards decorate the walls of buildings in the towns and the hills along main roads through the countryside. Many see them as environmental pollution and as undesirable commercialization of public space which belongs to everyone; others are entertained by the frequently amusing messages on large screens.

The old, pasted posters will soon be a thing of the past. They are being replaced by moving sequences on huge digital screens which are linked together in a network controlled by a central computer. The advertising messages on the underground, for example (and on commuter trains and in taxis too) can be changed every 14 days or every 15 seconds.

The *moving* objects can be on buses, which offer geographical flexibility during the day from one target group within the city centre to another in the suburbs, which the advertising managers naturally have to bear in mind. This demands extremely short messages that can be quickly absorbed and processed. Quite a challenge.

DIRECT MAIL
Direct advertising is possibly the most hated medium, as many people detest the huge pile of loud, gaudy material that lands almost daily on the doormat.

The advertisers see things differently. A flexible and selective medium, which can be tailored to almost any target group whatsoever and can, for example, be filled with surprising and exciting product demonstrations.

HOW ARE MEDIA CHOSEN?

To reach families, the advertising manager chooses advertising in the major morning newspapers, combined with advertising on a television channel.

Hundreds of hopeful fishermen spend their spare time down by the river which runs through a big city. This is where the small company that sells fishing equipment will set up their small handwritten notice.

A complicated technical product (a new video camera with advanced technology) will find the best reception for its message in the trade press. Outdoor advertising won't do for a comprehensive insurance service (a creative pension), which cannot be described in a single sentence and a single picture. Television advertising combined with a campaign website is a better choice.

Four key concepts

REACH
This concept refers to how many people the company can reach with a particular medium in a residential area, for example.

FREQUENCY
This covers how often it happens. A daily paper influences the target group every day, while a company that sells swimming costumes only wants to get its message across just before summer.

IMPACT
The communicative strength and the effect of the message on the target market is called impact. A tabloid newspaper, for example, has greater force than an organization's newsletter.

TIME
Advertising must adapt to seasonal needs. A series of articles about fishing is ideal ahead of the summer holidays, but a campaign for thick quilted jackets is unlikely to be a great success in the heat of August. It's also important to be ahead of your competitors, e.g., with a travel brochure, and thus get the chance to be considered first.

You have to choose

As we all know, you can't have everything you want in the world. An advertising manager who concentrates on one of the four key concepts must forgo the others. Creating a spectacular, audience-grabbing activity, like Christo and Jeanne-Claude's gigantic art installation of saffron-coloured pieces of fabric in Central Park in New York, will have a huge impact, but poor reach. High frequency will be achieved through a large number of small ads in the daily press, but the side effect will unfortunately be a weak impact.

High frequency often means intensive repetition of a certain unit, advert or TV spot. This is completely okay if the ad is a strong one (even if the target group becomes a bit tired of it) but a word of warning: a weak advertisement is weak even the second time and the third, and in the end the target group will end up losing interest and maybe even get annoyed. In that case it's better instead to take the resources spent on repeating it and put them into new and different creative units which get the message across better.

To get the message across, of course, you first need to decide on your message, which is what the next chapter is all about.

BELOW / The artists Christo and Jeanne-Claude achieved a major impact with their installation in Central Park, New York, *The Gates* (2005), but the reach for the glowing saffron-coloured artwork was limited to those in the city only

SUMMARY

'A farewell to meat.'

OVERALL STRATEGY
Primarily covers the marketing plan which incorporates:
Analysis of current position: where is the company today?
Goals: what and where does it want to be?
Marketing strategy: how is this to be achieved?
Checks, evaluation and follow up: what was the result?

BRAND
The brand refers to the outside world's experiences of, and assumptions about, a company and its products.

COMMUNICATION CRITERIA
Segmentation: choosing part of a market and working on that.
Positioning: choosing a clear position in the market and in the minds of consumers.
Concept: formulating and working according to a long-term, media-neutral theme.
Campaign: creating an idea for several units in different media.
Unit: formulating and designing an idea for an individual unit: a programme, an advert, a TV spot.

COMMUNICATION PLAN/ADVERTISING PLAN
Goal: can be either quantitative or qualitative.
Target group: the group of consumers the company wants to reach.
Medium: press, television, web.
Message
Schedule
Budget
Evaluation/follow-up
These four last points are addressed in the next chapter.

DRINK DRIVING
ENDS HERE.

PEDESTRIAN COUNCIL OF AUSTRALIA

5/

MESSAGES

ABOVE / A message, whether in the news, advertising, or the football stadium, needs to be strong enough to cut through the clutter, even if delivered in a mere whisper.

'Whisper ... '

The key to success is to rise above the clutter. The louder we shout, the more clutter we drown out. Any market trader knows that, and clearly the people in the mass media are well aware of it too.

However, the more the mass media shout, the more clutter will be generated, until eventually it all becomes too much. The receivers begin to listen without hearing, to watch without seeing, and are influenced without feeling. At this point, stronger vocal cords no longer provide any help. What is needed is a message that is strong enough to cut through all this clutter, even with the merest whisper.

Formulating and designing the message is therefore crucial. All the strategic work will go down the drain if the message is unable to get through.

The goal, the target group and the medium have all been sorted out. Now it's time for the message, and we'll start from the very beginning.

MESSAGES

A key building block is the *needs of the target group*, which are usually defined as an inherent demand to meet a certain deficiency, to avoid something or to gain possession of something. We all have to eat and drink to survive, we need a roof over our heads and our sexuality is constantly demanding satisfaction. These fundamental, concrete, physical needs form the first level in the *hierarchy of needs* published by behavioural scientist Abraham Maslow in 1954. The other levels of need, which we move up and down through our entire lives, are safety, belonging, esteem and self-actualization (the top of the pyramid).

In our commercial world, the goods and services of companies have to coincide with these needs, which is why advertising managers and their messengers try to allude to these needs and use their messages to promise that their products will satisfy them. A bed manufacturer naturally alludes to our need for sleep, while a whole host of clothing labels play on sexuality to tempt us into making a purchase. Our need for security is considerable, as insurance and credit card companies well know. The need to belong is

Maslow's hierarchy of needs

exploited by the breweries, who show us suitable places to drink (the beach, the campfire, the bar) as well as the mobile phone operators behind text messaging services. Esteem and self-actualization are targeted by the management training company (become a better boss) and the Venice Carnival (find yourself in the city on the water). The newspapers open up our minds to the world and TV programmes give us fresh experiences and entertainment.

There are, however, more people ready to meet these needs than there are actual needs. The competition is fierce and companies are always trying to create or awaken a latent need. It's not that easy, as they are deeply rooted in our very being, but there's no doubt that a new product can trigger desires even if the satisfaction relates to something on the outer limit of what might be considered a need. After all we are only human, and the list of our inadequacies is endless.

If the advertising manager knows that there is a need (say, to travel) that applies to many people, and has a product (carnival holidays) which meets this need, then the target is found (middle-aged couples, whose children have flown the nest, with considerable disposable income). If the target group is well known, he or she will also be familiar with their media habits, and be able to choose the right medium to reach them (a daily newspaper's travel pages, or why not the entertainment section?). And when they have been reached, it is vital to make the fulfilment of the need as clear as possible (through attractive carnival pictures).

ARGUMENTATION TECHNIQUE

Arguments are reasons, statements, trains of thought used by one person to convince or persuade another. If the sender fails in this objective, the remedy is to hone the argument, not, as many think (and has already been mentioned), to raise your voice.

Delimitation

The first stage in developing an argument is delimitation: drawing a line between what is to be included and what isn't. It's as simple as that. A story that flows aimlessly on and on will never reach its audience – the sender has to know where to stop, based on sound judgement and an instinct for what is relevant. Beware too many facts and too little context, too much included and too little omitted. A website for the Venice Carnival should be full of mystery, costumes and gondolas, not stocky glassblowers from Murano or striking art installations from the Biennale.

Structure

There has to be a structure, a design and pattern to the text and pictures, to highlight the message. What will the carnival set-up look like? Who will narrate and from which perspective? Can Casanova be the person to welcome everyone, thus setting the tone? Or should his manservant select and lay out his master's carnival clothes for the evening's festivities? Is an all-seeing voiceover cut

with interviews exciting, or is a dialogue between a gondolier and a carnival-goer the best way of attracting visitors to the sinking city?

The web designer's two quite rigid structures, *linear* and *tree*, or the free *web* can also be applied in this context (they work for all types of visual communication).

The simple linear structure is ideal for articles, ads, posters and films, which can be planned chronologically (airport, motorboat, hotel) or alphabetically (Arrival, Boat, Casanova).

The deeper and more developed tree structure is great for brochures and websites, and can be planned thematically (Travel, Hotels, Costumes) with sub-groups (Travel: air, train, boat. Hotels: youth hostel, standard, luxury. Costumes: female, male, child).

Geographical organization may mean that San Marco has the sub-groups hotels, costumes and events, as does Rialto. Organization according to interests (music, gala dinners, dance shows) is also common. Things can even be organized according to place of origin: Venetians, Italian tourists, foreigners.

However, the web structure almost entirely lacks the facility for such organization and is most often reserved for more freely constructed sites (depicting the whirl of seduction in Venice, perhaps).

Argument

Now the sender has an insight into the receiver's needs, as well as a delimitation and structure to apply as the basis of the message. Time, then, for the actual argument that will convince the receiver.

There are main arguments (a helmet reduces the risk of head injuries in a cycling accident) and supporting arguments, which help the main argument to convince the receiver (head injuries are very common in cycling accidents).

Each type of argument can be boosted by the rhetorical instruments used by skilled speakers. These include *ethos*, or credibility (head injuries often have serious consequences, says the doctor), *logos*, or logic (250 people without helmets injured this year) and *pathos*, or emotion (it might be you next time).

BELOW / Achieving self-actualization is the highest goal for most people, both as a person and as a professional.

ABOVE / Finding arguments to persuade us to wear a helmet when mountain biking is not difficult – the task becomes much harder for cyclists in the city.

The receiver is said to be convinced by rational arguments, but logic is no more important in decision-making than emotion, and (attempted) objective arguments are no more relevant than subjective ones. The receiver will often happily make a decision based on irrational impulses such as desire, fantasy and curiosity.

But how? In simple terms, the receiver first identifies with and then adopts a position on something which he or she finds better than something else (I prefer wearing a helmet in order to avoid injury). But it doesn't end there. Based on the position taken, he or she sorts and assesses personal counter-arguments and those of others (they look stupid – but they do seem to be becoming more fashionable in Barcelona). It becomes a battle between the pros and cons, and it can go either way, although the first spontaneous position will have the slight upper hand. Once the receiver has chosen sides, he or she starts to reject all the cons. He or she filters out any opposition and consolidates a position and a decision.

ONE-SIDED OR TWO-SIDED?

One-sided argumentation involves the sender only highlighting the advantages, which is a very common approach (and no one loses any sleep over such a lack of morals). But the risk is that the receiver sees too much promotion of the bicycle with the most gears and the newspaper with the most readers.

Two-sided argumentation is less common, and involves expressing the advantages and disadvantages – basically the sender also provides the counter-arguments. This shouts honesty and directness, which is appreciated (as long as it is not just a case of playing to the gallery). Buy quality, cry once.

MORE THAN ONE ARGUMENT?

The optimum message is based on one main argument. But if there are more, i.e., several supporting arguments, what order of presentation will achieve the best impact?

The rule of thumb is to start with the strongest, and keep the second strongest until last, with the weakest arguments in between. It is also common to sum up or repeat the strong main argument at the end, for example in the last paragraph of the text or in a pay-off or a tag line by the logo. Ryanair: fly cheaper.

WHO DRAWS THE CONCLUSION?

It has to be clear who should draw the conclusion: the sender or the receiver. The rule of thumb here is to let the receiver draw their own conclusions. It is important to make the receiver feel involved and proactive, leading them to work out the message for themselves. Accompanying a picture of a chilli, the sender says, 'Cut down on your heating bills, choose our hot'n'spicy wok!' 'A-ha,' says the receiver.

ADVERTISING MESSAGES

The delimitation and structure have been carefully defined, the arguments are equally well honed and the preliminary work has been done. Now it's time for the message, which links sender and receiver and is usually defined as the content of a particular communication. In a less abstract way, it can be described as one person wanting another to think something, know something and, in the end, do something.

Let's start with a number of questions which advertising managers and advertising agencies need to answer:

What problems can our products solve?
What feelings can our goods generate?
What needs can our services meet?
What dreams can they realize?
How can we present and clarify their features?

Through drama, fear, passion, enthusiasm?
Rationally, emotionally?
What promises will we make the target group?
Can we keep these promises? How?

Exhaustive answers to these questions offer guidance in choosing the type of message. There are four types that are seen as ideal for advertising:

Instrumental
Relational
Testifying
Comparative

INSTRUMENTAL MESSAGES

We are constantly surrounded by instrumental messages, based on a problem which we receivers are presumed to be wrestling with. The product's properties can solve the problem, making it a useful *instrument*.

The key is to clearly *highlight* the problem (repeated break-ins) or need (making yourself understood in Tokyo) or allow for a wish to be fulfilled (to escape the asphalt jungle of the city).

The sender has to create as much drama as possible using negative motifs in text and pictures, so that the receiver identifies with the message and recalls a frightening experience or worrying personal shortcoming. The greater the problem, the greater the desire for relief and solutions.

BELOW / Polluted water is an extremely dangerous threat to many. On World Water Day the United Nations highlighted the problem in an offbeat way, encouraging us to see our own role in the problem by embellishing bins with handles, straws and slices of lemon. The solution is knowledge and changes in attitude.

BOTTOM / A serious problem solved – BMW Night Vision is an innovative system aimed at reducing the dangers posed by cars to humans and animals in the dark.

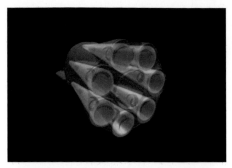

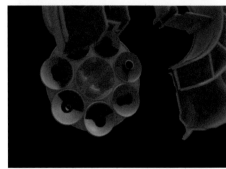

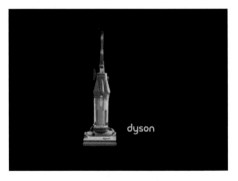

ABOVE / Instrumental messages promise to
solve problems: scraps of food don't stand
a chance, the vacuum cleaner won't lose
suction so will remove dust like no other.

The arguments that build up these messages should be rational, and the storytelling technique should be closed, so that there is actually only one way of interpretation. The messages have to relate to the dramatic storytelling technique (protagonist and antagonist) and to the dramatic triangle, with a persecutor, a victim and a rescuer battling it out.

In this context, the problem plays the role of persecutor and the receiver feels for and identifies with the victim. The goods or service then becomes the rescuer, as when the young man with the pillows and the rope and the tinnitus buzzing in his ears gets the chance of relief or salvation thanks to an association for hearing impairment receiving research funding (see page 20).

USP

Instrumental messages are perfect for products which have a unique property which sets them apart from the rest (called a USP – Unique Selling Proposition – or even better, the selling difference), like a burglar alarm that is impossible to bypass, a language course that uses an original method of teaching, or an estate agent with an eye for the right property.

A strong and effective instrumental message might suggest that the receiver can avoid a hazardous situation, for instance a car accident. Driving in the dark is dangerous both for the person driving the car and for those who are out for a late-night stroll. When visibility is poor, the driver can't see pedestrians or animals. The solution, which turns night into the safety of day, is an innovation from BMW called Night Vision. The car has been equipped with a special video camera that is mounted in the windscreen and the picture is shown on a display in front of the driver – not a bad USP.

Such messages should, in summary, promise or convey the following:

Problem solving (stain remover)
Problem avoidance (low-fat margarine)
Financial gain (pension)
Innovation (hologram TV)

These instrumental messages have a sense of a competition and a goal. Who will win? The persecutor? Or perhaps the victim, the young man with the pillows and the rope.

The messages can be seen as important, but unfortunately are often perceived as exaggerated and contrived, which is why it is important to make them straightforward, honest and rational. They have to speak a clear advertising language, with no pretence to be something they are not, but there is no need to exclude humour or personality in this context.

RELATIONAL MESSAGES

Standing in stark contrast to instrumental messages, relational messages aim to prove that a particular product provides a positive and heightened experience, well-being or group membership. They create a *relationship* between the goods or service and the consumer and want to get us to dream about something (as opposed to the instrumental messages, which want us to wake up).

BELOW / Relational messages promise a sense of well-being. An online newspaper will give intellectual stimulation and chocolate fulfils a profound emotional need.

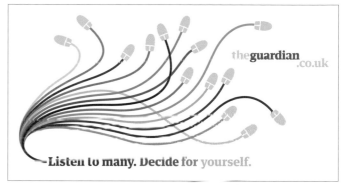

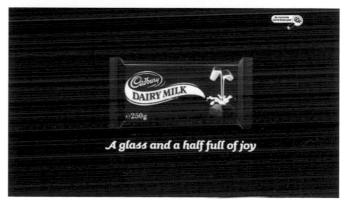

The arguments should be emotional and the non-dramatic storytelling technique, with its open system to promote inclusion and participation, should be selected.

The messages must also be open to wide interpretation and require something of the receiver. The young woman on the yacht with the soft quilt around her allows us to do the interpreting: summer, pleasant, warm, sensual …

ESP
Relational messages are ideal for products that lack unique, concrete properties that set them apart, instead offering an ESP – an Emotional Selling Proposition – or, even better, the selling feeling.

Coffee heightens the experience of a visit to the countryside. A wonderful walk along the beach, fresh air and then a coffee. It is difficult for an advertising manager to say that a particular coffee tastes better than that of its competitors, which is why he or she employs this emotional message.

Faced with a strong relational message, receivers will do everything to put themselves in the *desirable* context, such as a romantic dinner with an exquisite wine – not a bad ESP.

These messages should, in summary, promise or convey the following:

Sensory reward (mineral water)
Intellectual stimulation (books)
A desirable lifestyle (branded clothes)
Social approval (environmentally friendly car)

The relational messages have a sense of contact, partnership and consideration – the seductive trip on a yacht – in contrast to the more competitively focused instrumental messages.

These messages can be seen as important, but also as banal. However, the gap between the product and the receiver is often closed in an alluring way. It is much easier to give in than to fight it, which is perhaps where critics of advertising get some of their ammunition.

TESTIFYING MESSAGES
Whether we are facing an everyday or life-changing decision, we need support from someone we trust. In advertising, the sender can use a testifying person to support the receiver through the agony of choice regarding goods or services.

The managing director who, with integrity and gravitas, can convince the customers about quality targets and product benefits, can play a pivotal role in the communications of a company or organization. Other endorsements may come from a trustworthy professor or journalist, or very often from a celebrity such as a sports star, a performer or actor.

However, a testifying figure need not always be famous. Often advertising managers have ordinary people, preferably consumers, appearing in documentary images and assertive text to create genuineness and credibility in their messages.

ETSP
A number of companies are involved in the battle to protect animals and forests on our vulnerable planet. Telecom companies, for example, make a contribution to the UN by providing telephones during natural disasters and human catastrophes. These ethical values complement USPs and ESPs with an ETSP – an Ethical Selling Proposition.

COMPARATIVE MESSAGES
Comparing your own product with that of a competitor is effective, but the sender must be able to see clear differences. Product

ABOVE / We will believe people we trust. If Tiger Woods testifies to the quality of a product, we believe him, and are more likely to spend money on the item or service.

benefits, prices, delivery times and financing are some of the most common arguments used in comparative advertising, which, by its very nature, is usually rational and instrumental.

As distinctive product features are becoming increasingly rare and consumers are faced with identical goods and services, the number of logical comparative messages is falling, in favour of relational messages.

DO ADVERTISING MESSAGES GET THROUGH?
Do these things get results? Of course, otherwise we wouldn't see one big advertising campaign after another in the mass media

around us. Consumers appreciate humour, an important insight, drama, personal commitment, new knowledge, a splash of artistry or a touch of poetry.

However, consumers are often asking themselves what the advertising manager and the messenger really mean. Among all the errors and mistakes, which create confusion, they mainly zero in on self-absorption, unrealistic self-image and poor industry knowledge, along with inflexible adherence to the target group definition and particular communication theories. We'll start with the self.

Self-absorption

Receivers are encountering more and more self-absorbed messages that can only leave them feeling that companies are in no way interested in anything other than themselves.

The concert hall will soon, in its own opinion, be staging the world's finest concert and the estate agency has, in its own view, the city's widest range of quality apartments. Messages can often be perceived as 'ME, ME, ME'. Advertising managers may well seem only to be talking about themselves, and in a self important way. They are busy patting themselves on the back, when receivers would rather be properly informed so that they can make an educated choice.

Unrealistic self-image

In order to develop a good message, the advertising manager must not only fight the tendency towards self-absorption, but also one of clinging to an unrealistic self-image, which is a common and dangerous disease. Many companies build up an unrealistic and complacent image of themselves in relation to the world around them.

Perhaps things need to be seen through the eyes of an outsider – an external consultant, say, or a new board member – so that the company can be presented in a clear and honest way. Distance often brings clarity.

Is the Venice Carnival really full of mystery, limitless possibilities and excitement? Is this just the tourism chief's wishful thinking? And what if it rains or the sun breaks through the cloud?

Poor industry knowledge

In addition to battling self-absorption and an unrealistic self-image, the company's advertising manager also has to realize what they really have to offer consumers. Some advertising departments don't understand the industry and market they are working in.

Let's look at a computer company that has long been battling to make any headway. Messages are not reaching their target despite excellent technical products – eventually the penny drops and the advertising manager declares:

'We aren't selling computer technology. We're selling the benefit of this technology, and that's all the target group is interested in. Obviously they're not reacting to our technical messages. If we don't know what we're doing and selling, how can the receiver understand the message?'

In other words, senders must make it clear to themselves and to the receivers what business they are in. The advertising manager has realized that the computer company works in the simplification industry, and that must be made clear in the messages to consumers. A practical, simple product should be presented practically and simply.

What does Guinness really sell? Beer, of course. Ireland, perhaps. But isn't it really friendship that they are selling and that we are buying? Friendship and community in the local pub. The 'cheers' industry!

Jean Paul GAULTIER "CLASSIQUE"

LE PARFUM DES FEMMES PAR JEAN PAUL GAULTIER

ABOVE / Jean-Paul Gaultier is selling perfume, but we are buying something else – dreams and hopes perhaps.

What does cosmetics company Clinique sell? 'In our factories we make lipstick, in the stores we sell hope.'

Conversation

It sounds as if, in all communication, the sender must focus on the receiver. All the experts agree, or at least almost all. But let's take a closer look at the relationship between sender and receiver.

Our society is awash with an incredible number of conversations. Some are personal and can be heard in the home or at work between colleagues.

Others are public and take place on the street corner and in the marketplace, but above all in the media. They relate to politics, economics, culture and much more besides, and these conversations and many others are awarded high status, in contrast to commercial conversations.

This is really quite remarkable, as products are a vital part of our lives. Some are necessary, many solve problems, some provide us with relaxation and well-being. The car can take us where the bus doesn't go, and the yogurt gives us a good start to the day.

Perhaps the conversation makes too great an incursion into our lives, with the uninvited guest badgering us incessantly morning, noon and night. Author John Berger believes that advertising robs us of our love for ourselves (by portraying us in an impoverished state) and then gives it back for the price of a purchase. Beauty comes from within … your wallet.

RIGHT / Barbara Kruger, *Untitled (I shop therefore I am)*, 1987. 111 x 113 in (282 x 287 cm). Photographic silkscreen / vinyl. Courtesy Mary Boone Gallery, New York.

Artist Barbara Kruger goes one step further when she points out that while purchasing creates great anxiety, it is a necessary public duty. I shop therefore I am. We humans no longer prove our existence through thought – *cogito ergo sum,* I think therefore I am – as philosophers have always believed, but evidently do so at the checkout.

The tyranny of the receiver

Let's examine this more closely. All communication takes place on the receiver's terms, in theory, so the sender should consider the receiver carefully, so that messages can get through. However, surveys often give a highly generalized view and when the sender adapts and makes assumptions accordingly, it often rings false. The receiver isn't influenced in any way.

So what is the solution? Maybe the focus on the receiver is far too intense? Isn't there a risk of the sender losing any sense of self? Clearly, senders shouldn't try to think entirely from other people's points of view, but use their own brains. Senders can be so exclusively focused on what they think the receiver wants to hear that they end up censoring themselves. No wonder the messages become monotonous, when the key to any successful story has been lost: *the desire to tell it.*

The sender has constantly been chanting the mantra: 'Who is the receiver? Put the receiver at the centre!' The mantra should really be: 'Who are we? What do we want to say? How do we want to say it?'

The answer is to resist the tyranny of the receiver; let your insight and love of storytelling shine through. A good story, as personal and exciting as a great play, film or novel, always comes across.

'Donate money, and we'll stop playing,' promise soldiers of the Salvation Army from a newspaper ad – a fresh message of self-irony that raises a smile and above all generates sympathy.

Basic and incisive

Now it gets complicated. One classic theory suggests that you should focus on the receiver and another (less classic) says to focus on the sender.

The former seeks to cut out all the navel gazing and instead look at the receivers and their problems (which the product can solve), their needs (which the goods can satisfy) or their dreams (which the service can realize).

The latter sticks out its neck and asks the sender to break the tyranny of the receiver, i.e., not to tailor the message to a receiver but to base it around the sender. So how do we reconcile these two approaches? Well, the message comprises two elements, the basic message and incisive message. The basic message has to be based on the receiver, while the incisive message takes a different tack, as we'll see later. But we'll start with the basic message.

Basic message

Sidestepping the tyranny of the receiver is impossible when the advertising manager is working on basic messages. Modern survey methods are far too effective to be ignored, as they can map out interests and attitudes. Surveys are therefore crucial in identifying and reaching the right target group.

Surprising, beautiful and melancholic – the Venice Carnival is all of these things. The sender now has a basic message showing how to use promises to reach target groups. Visit the Venice Carnival, full of surprising beauty. However, the receiver may be inclined to see this as a rather mediocre message!

Incisive message

The advertising manager in Venice has to sharpen the message. An incisive message that battles against the tyranny of the receiver is needed. The incisive message comes from the sender and should be bursting with a desire to tell a story, urgency, shrewdness, self-awareness, distance, drama, emotion and surprises. The sender should tell the story he or she wants to tell and do so in the way he or she feels is most suitable. The receiver will soon be singing from the same hymn sheet.

Pierangelo Federici is considering what sets the Venice Carnival apart from others. It's the setting and the mystery – it's dark and cold, perhaps with a light dusting of snow, and capes and masks fill the winding narrow alleys.

What's needed is a strong idea that the wording and image can build on, determining the incisive message. It may promise a solution to a problem or a heightening of emotion. It may promise that consumers will avoid something ('leave the land of fluorescent lights for the shadows of Venice') or gain something desirable ('find yourself among the mystery of Venice'). Pierangelo smiles when, focusing on the latter alternative, he picks up a photograph showing several masked carnival-goers. Text and images will work well together in this incisive message.

Incisive messages comprise two elements, the text and the images. Sometimes the text can convey the basic message, while the image ties the whole thing into an incisive message. 'Eat more wholemeal bread' is accompanied by a picture of a belt around a white loaf, with the bread swelling over the belt like a roll of fat ('you are what you eat').

Conversely, a simple and straightforward image can convey the basic message, while the text turns the whole communication into an incisive message, for instance in the case of a picture of a desirable sports car with the tag line 'Two seats but only one steering wheel'.

Incisive messages can be needed in so many different contexts. The director of the Old Vic theatre in London has a problem with some of the audience forgetting to switch off their mobile phones, causing major irritation. The basic message is: 'Switch off your mobile before the performance'. However, this direct message isn't getting very far. Something else is needed, something more pointed: 'Don't forget to switch your mobile back on after the performance.'

BELOW / If you drink and drive your journey will not end where you expected – an incisive, urgent and effective campaign by ad agency Saatchi & Saatchi in Sydney.

LEFT / This unusual melding of a bicycle and its street environment makes us understand the strength of the lock immediately.

ABOVE / If the brain is tricked, good ideas can result, helping a firm see promotional opportunities for a product, or parents find intellectual stimulation for their children.

IN SUMMARY

The message can be a little blunt sometimes. Its one element, the basic message, may reach its target, but it fails to stick. The incisive message, its other vital element, is like a pin-sharp dart that embeds itself deeply, moving and influencing the receiver.

The basic message focuses on the receiver, but the incisive message must be packed with the sender's own desire to tell a story, making the receiver part of an enthusiastic audience. However, the receiver is also very demanding, and without some point, most things will be incomprehensible, and without insight, boring. Without surprise there is no curiosity and without personality, no interest.

Topical messages

The sender can take advantage of the hot topics of the day, taking a striking episode in a reality show or a government minister being implicated in a scandal as their starting point. Then there is no need to explain everything from the beginning. The sender can simply cut straight to the message, as the receiver is already familiar with the background.

When the newspapers and TV are full of reports on hijacked security vans, a credit card company can point out briefly and concisely, 'Choose the safest way of transporting money.'

Surprising messages

Telling receivers what they already know is a waste of resources. The coffee producer doesn't need to explain how coffee is made by depicting beans in hessian sacks – we already know that.

There are different grades of message: *static* and *dynamic*. The static message gives consumers what they expect, while the dynamic one offers the unexpected, offers more, in fact.

People will be positively surprised if they're promised little but receive more. A phone manufacturer throws in a few extra services in the same way that the florist might slot an extra rose into the bouquet. It will pay for itself in satisfied and loyal customers.

Warning about sex discrimination

The worst cases of sex discrimination in advertising fall into two main categories. The first might have a scantily clad woman holding the product, say, a drill. The other shows that the woman cannot hold the product, because it is too large or heavy, and so has to lie on it, like a ride-on lawnmower. Many might think, with relief, that such examples have been consigned to the past, but that isn't the case. The Hall of Shame constantly gains new members.

Whether or not underwear images tally with reality, they are essentially discriminatory, as they help this perception to establish itself and grow, cementing gender roles.

NEWS MESSAGES

We will now leave commercial messages, which can be used for goods (newspapers or cars) and services (speech therapists or lawyers), and focus on messages in the news, which often have to compete with the commercial messages for the attention of readers and viewers.

Gatekeepers

Bird flu has claimed new victims in more countries while in a suburb of a capital city, cars are being set on fire. Most people see this as the truth, which is hard to refute.

However, events have to be selected, assessed, interpreted, processed and broadcast before they become news. This news work, called *gatekeeping*, clarifies the role of journalists as a filter in the flow of news. They take decisions and open the gate to certain events, allowing them to reach readers and viewers, but just as often they close the gate on other stories.

At a newspaper, the gatekeeper is often an editor or a night editor, and in the TV news studio it's the producer.

Visual gatekeepers

The newspaper or TV subeditor is of course also a gatekeeper. The angle has to be decided, and images have to be chosen and inserted into a particular context that includes headings, intros and other visual elements.

Other visual gatekeepers include picture editors (who select or reject a particular image), image processors (who manipulate the image), reporters (who describe and interpret the image), graphic designers (who turns colour into black and white) and newsreaders (who perhaps unnecessarily pre-warn sensitive viewers).

Is gatekeeping simply biased filtering? The answer has to be no, as responsible gatekeepers not only consciously manipulate images and context, but also safeguard ethics.

Advocates of the free reporting of news naturally want to keep the gates open, but sometimes the lack of pictures can be equally important. In the hours after the terrorist attacks in London there was, unusually, a rare absence of images. TV helicopters had been banned and photographers (including amateurs) kept at arm's length, which meant that London's residents missed the shock effect from New York and Madrid. The terrorists' aim of spreading fear with pictorial evidence spread across the globe thus also failed to a degree.

During the riots in the Paris suburbs, the burning cars on our television screens made a major impression, arousing powerful emotions. To avoid the risk of contributing to more violence and rioting, several of the French television channels chose not to show any of the more excessively brutal images.

The journalists in Paris emphasize their personal and social responsibility and thus adopt one of two main theories which dominate among publicists in the West. The first theory is based on a sense of *responsibility for the consequences* (as in the cases of London and Paris above) while the second highlights *consequence neutrality* and is based on impartially publishing whatever is considered to be true and relevant with no thought for the consequences – this lack of discernment can be dangerous, and have an adverse effect on both groups and individuals.

STAGING

Let us call the journalistic message a 'staging', a suitable term considering the extreme diversity of people involved in the process: correspondents, picture libraries, photographers, reporters and all the gatekeepers.

There are two types of staging, *dramatic* and *non-dramatic*, which of course are closely linked to the storytelling techniques in the second chapter of this book. The former goes against the grain, with stringent restraints, while the latter goes with the grain, kept more loosely in check, but both have the same purpose, to influence media consumers.

DRAMATIC STAGING

American writer William S. Burroughs expressed the preconditions for journalistic work clearly and concisely: *No problem, no story*. Who wants to read that aircraft are taking off and landing on time at the airport outside town? No one. Only when something happens, something dramatic, do the readers and viewers become interested, particularly if there was a narrowly averted accident that could have injured someone close to them.

Conflict

The newspaper offices and news studios are full of conflicts. This means that dramatic conflicts and catastrophes become the main feature, while equally dangerous but less dramatic catastrophes, such as a famine or an AIDS epidemic, end up in a kind of media no man's land. It is as if this emergency lacks the required dramatic date (9/11) when something changes in an instant and the people of the world all hold their breath together.

Conflict-free news is thus often rejected (mainly by TV editors) and the risk of rejection increases when there are no pictures and obtaining them is likely to be problematic. This is reported to have led the International Red Cross to draw up handy advice for creating awareness of its relief efforts. The almost absurd action plan seems to be: invest in good media relations. Provide a concrete death toll. Supply dramatic pictures. Fly in a celebrity.

It is conflict that makes readers sit up and take notice, makes them interested and attracted, and hopefully spurs them into action. At the same time, many believe there are dangers in constantly focusing on opposition rather than unity. Conflicts become a kind of popular entertainment, while unity simply becomes boring, which is why positive news is often very well hidden among all the other new stories. The mayor of New York tries in vain to get the media excited about the fact that the safest city in the US has become even safer.

BELOW / Before we as watchers see the news report, there have already been a number of gatekeepers who, in one way or another, have filtered the text and images.

ABOVE / Somalia 1992. This photograph by Kevin Carter has few components, but nonetheless creates many more in our consciousnesses – death, severe drought, loneliness, defencelessness, waiting.

The present

Dramatic staging lives in the present, and in today's media world, with competing news channels and online news services, the present is a constantly recurring tense. Readers and viewers are meant to find it fascinating and frightening that everything is happening live, nothing is concluded, and that they are at the centre of the action.

Excitedly, the newsreader makes the announcement, 'Reports are now coming in that an unknown individual is indiscriminately driving into tourists in the narrow streets of the old town. The police are on their way to the scene.' And in a live broadcast from another part of the world, the war reporter points to a town behind her that has just been bombed. The film cameras are rolling, everything is happening now.

AIDA

The conflict and the present captivate the receiver, but that is not enough, so AIDA comes to the rescue. It is not about opera, but about not losing your hold on your readers and viewers. AIDA stands for:

Attention
Interest
Desire
Action

The front page of a newspaper: a large photograph shows a small child with a swollen stomach. The child is crawling on the parched and cracked ground, trying to get up. Perhaps, in her confused state, she thinks that somewhere, perhaps nearby, there is someone who can help her with water, someone who can take away the pain in her stomach. But, at first glance, the background of the picture is empty – there is no aid station, no nurse or doctor, but there is a bird. A couple of metres behind the child, a large vulture has landed, conveying a sickeningly clear conviction that there will soon be food here. The *attention* of the newspaper reader has been secured.

The headline, 'Famine disaster in Africa grows', the caption and the body text provide shocking information, which creates a strong *interest*.

The power of the report also creates a *desire* (often contradictory), a wish for *action*, a wish to do something, not simply to sit back and let this terrible scene be ignored. Attitudes are changed (people want to know what is really behind this famine) and the readers may finally follow the newspaper's advice, donating money to charities to alleviate the suffering. There we have AIDA at work.

Creating dramatic interest in the studio

In a newspaper article, the most important information has to come first, with the rest following in descending order of weight. In television, the producer does the reverse. The news item needs to have a beginning, a middle and an end, just like a good story. The three elements must be intimately interrelated, and if anything is then taken away, there is a risk that the whole thing will sink without trace.

The subeditor will open the TV news item with a situational description to arouse the viewer's interest, which is then followed by the main point of the story (the course of events, including some sort of conflict), before closing it with an epilogue, which may well comprise an open question, a general conclusion or a splash of morality.

The dramatic curve

The three overarching elements may well benefit from the application of a dramatic curve. The *set-up* – the dramatic start – highlights the conflict and so creates forward momentum, which means that viewers, full of curiosity, willingly stick with the news item. It is essential to set up an agreement with the viewers about what is going to be shown and how the subject is going to be framed. Like the news of an oil slick that is drifting onto the coast of Brittany: disaster is predicted, with the footage creating fear and disgust.

Then it's time for the *exposition*. Viewers want to know how such a thing could happen. How can so much oil leak out from one tanker? The editor has to document the news, show what the leaking oil looks like and engage the viewers through concrete examples: 'Here in the English Channel the two tankers crashed, there's the hole in the hull where the oil is gushing out! And look, a blackened seagull!'

Then, in the *rising conflict*, the editor should expand the perspective and provide some clarification. What about the condition of the vessels? What were two large oil tankers doing so close to the coast? In other words, documentation before explanation, and concrete examples before abstract reasoning. If the editor starts the other way round with the reasoning, viewers will feel excluded and never really get into the story.

Now the piece reaches a kind of climax, or *conflict resolution*. It is clear that the beaches are being devastated by the oil and that the tourist industry will suffer badly. A council leader is interviewed, and then a representative for the clean-up operation. A summer visitor, standing among sticky lumps of oil, viscous, black, like landmines, also has a say.

Whatever has come before, the report should conclude with a calmer *fade-out* (unless a greater disaster is looming). A seagull, clearly untroubled by the gooey oil, circles up in the sky and the clean-up worker fills a black bag with sticky sand.

In the news item, the beach itself becomes a stage, and how the editor lets people act on this stage is important. A person should enter the frame (preferably from the left) at the beginning of the piece and leave at the end (preferably to the right). In the same way, the editor can also make use of a zoom-in shot of the beach at the start of the news item, and then can zoom out at the end. But not vice versa.

At the same time, the editor should beware of focusing too much on the dramatic structure. Credibility is the ultimate guarantee of the news media's survival, and when creating dramatic interest is allowed to take precedence over the journalism, you're in dangerous territory.

Creating dramatic interest out in the field

A talking head has now left the safety of the studio for a considerably more dangerous location.

The *stand-up* is the foreign correspondent standing in front of the Manhattan skyline, outside a bombed train station in Madrid or on a roof in New Orleans. Microphone in hand, he or she talks straight to camera about what is happening. A demonstration marches past and explosions light up the night sky.

The stand-up sometimes has contact with the home studio, whose anchor asks questions. There is often a short delay between question and answer, as the satellite phone links aren't always terribly quick, but this gives the situation a proper journalistic presence and sense of reality.

LEFT / The dramatic curve is a useful tool to supply news, for instance about a devastating oil spill.

ABOVE / The stand-up will often make a live broadcast from the scene of the action, emphasizing their proximity to events.

NON-DRAMATIC STAGING
Let's now throw off the constraints of dramatic staging and look at non-dramatic staging.

No problem
Where dramatic staging is based on conflict, non-dramatic staging is about gentler contact with readers and viewers. Such staging forces its way into the conflict-based media of newspapers and TV in the form of analytical series of articles, in weekend and special supplements, in debate shows and, of course, in the plethora of magazines, where considered ideas and visions can be aired.

Non-dramatic storytelling creates an *open structure*, which invites the receivers in and makes them feel involved. It is like comparing a punchy billboard headline with an editorial page. The latter allows for explanation, discussion and reflection, alongside the reader, about developments in a poor country in Africa, about the relationship between Christianity and Islam, about global warming. Readers are required to complete the picture themselves and mull over what they are becoming involved in.

The past
While dramatic staging takes place in a live broadcast, non-dramatic staging focuses on the time gone by, the past. A crisis situation is no longer a crisis, having reached a solution and a resolution. A completely different news spotlight is trained on the event, with the light no longer trying to seek out the combatants, but what has happened, what lay behind it, what consequences it will have and what the world can learn. The staging allows subjective storytelling, with memory, meaning and morals.

A group of people invited onto a debate programme are allowed to agree, reach a consensus (without TV viewers nodding off!) and the news that was rejected from a conflict perspective – that the big, safe city of New York has become even safer – is presented and analysed.

DOES THE STAGING HIT HOME?
All around the world, there are thousands of dedicated, ambitious and skilled newsmakers, all of whom are filling their newspapers and their news reports with high quality work, both in terms of its angle and its execution.

Unfortunately, however, there is also the other side of the coin. The circulation and viewing figures feed anxiety in the newsrooms, and to assuage this, the owner stares blindly at the reader surveys and viewer profiles and then does everything to satisfy and retain the audience.

A sensational, flattering, receiver-oriented tabloid journalism is thus gaining ground in many media houses, filled with self-obsessed presenters and writers with big byline photos.

In fact this is also where a truth-seeking, crass, consequence-neutral journalism flourishes, with objectivity as its watchword. This can create dangerous and seductive news reporting as behind it there are always people with opinions.

Subjectivity wins
No one can report like an objective truth machine, as all interpretations of the world around us are subjective. And the future is probably closed to those journalists who succeed in hiding their underlying assumptions and selection principles (on which all journalism is based) but open to those who are able to manage them. Honesty wins.

What journalists have to do is to turn their gaze from the reader and the viewer and look to themselves to decide how a piece of news is best to be conveyed (sender-oriented, as in the incisive messages). The staging (dramatic and non-dramatic) plays a major role in the convincing angle that is chosen for the story – the human interest in the personal reportage (complementing the straight reporting) which attracts readers and viewers to what is relevant.

There is a real art to news staging, and honest, sincere, personal creativity is the very essence of art. As Picasso is reported to have said once, 'I say what I have to say in the way I feel it should be said.'

See how well the basic message of the advertisement matches the justification for the staging in terms of the facts and course of events. At the same time, the incisive message of the ad reflects the personal nerve of news reporting.

LEFT / Non-dramatic staging – as with this interview between Oprah Winfrey and Madonna – is often focused on the past, analysing a situation and its implications.

SCHEDULE AND BUDGET

After messages and staging, it is time to tackle the last three points of the communication plan.

There has to be a detailed schedule for all activities, creating further questions:

When is the best time to carry out the communication measures?
What is the schedule for the series of articles?
When will the advertising start?
When will the website be ready for visitors?
When, and how often, will updates be made? Who is responsible?

And yet more questions, this time budget-related:

How big a budget will be needed to achieve the goals?
What will the consultancy services cost? No, really, how much?
How much will the photographer charge for the photos in the advertising campaign, and how much will the illustrations for the annual report cost?
What will the media costs be? And the technical production?

EVALUATION AND FOLLOW-UP

So there we finally have the article with its dramatic, black and white photographs and the advert with its bold, personal form of address in a newspaper on this, the rainiest Wednesday in living memory. It is every subeditor, art director and graphic designer's dream (or is it a nightmare?) to be able to sit next to a person in their target group on the bus that morning. To overhear how the text and pictures are received, to see whether they attract attention, whether they are read …

Successful

In fact, the messages often get through, taken in by the receiver in the intended way. There are many effective methods of measuring and confirming the effect, with market share measured, attitudes analysed and telephone surveys and subscription figures pored over by satisfied companies.

Unsuccessful

Sometimes, however, the sender fails and there is no reaction. Why? Could the media choice have been misguided? Were the messages not incisive enough?

If the answers are affirmative in this *evaluation*, the whole, or at least parts of the communication initiative have to be amended and improved, which of course costs time and money.

In this context, the following words may offer some solace: instant success is the biggest enemy of genuine success. Success may breed success, but instant success breeds hubris, a difficult and dangerous condition.

Whether the results are positive or negative, the evaluation lays the groundwork for a *follow-up*. What have we learned and how should we proceed? The questions are asked around the table and everyone involved has to do their best to answer.

So we have now been through the whole communication plan, looking at goals, target group, medium, message, schedule, budget, evaluation and follow-up.

In the next chapter, we delve into the inner workings of the brain.

SUMMARY

'Whisper … '

WORKING ON THE MESSAGE
Key cornerstones are *delimitation*, *structure* and *argument*.
The basic message: based on the receiver, whose needs form a foundation.
The incisive message: based on the sender's personality and desire to tell a story, which sharpens text and image.

ADVERTISING MESSAGES
Instrumental messages: promise a solution to a problem.
Relational messages: promise a heightened emotional experience and well-being.

NEWS MESSAGES
Messages in a news context are called staging:
Dramatic staging: conveys news in the present (live broadcasts).
Non-dramatic staging: conveys and analyses news from the past.

SCHEDULE / BUDGET / EVALUATION / FOLLOW-UP
Checking whether the goals set have been achieved and planning future activities.

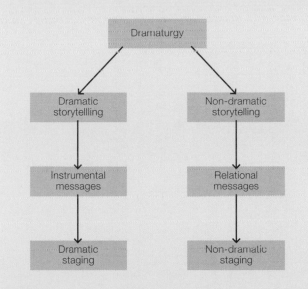

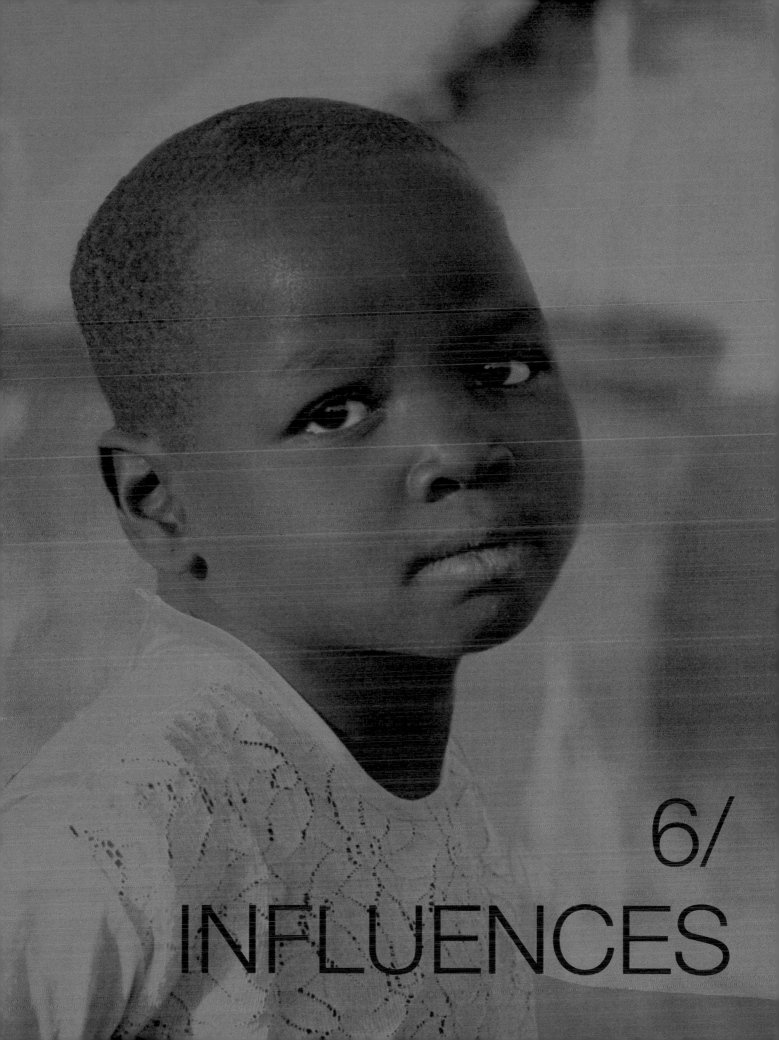

6/
INFLUENCES

ABOVE / Among friends, but who is fastest?

'At last,' she sighs.

The dog breaks free from the lead, which has forced her to wait for quite long enough outside the newsagent's. She looks round and sits, with some difficulty, on the saddle of the old, rusty, ladies' bicycle. She takes a firm grip on the handlebars, and although she can't quite reach the pedals, is soon rolling down the sloping street, dreaming of freedom. 'At last,' she sighs, taking no notice whatsoever of the stunned looks.

As we've seen, every day and hour we are bombarded by messages, creating a world that is information-rich but attention-poor – a case for Robin Hood possibly. How can a sender get a message across?

Things which are far too common, far too everyday, almost trivial, are examples of *redundancy*. Like the dog tied up outside the newsagent's, alongside the rusty ladies' bicycle. Locals hardly notice the dog or the bike.

The opposite, *entropy*, refers to new information, which doesn't match the codes in our visual rules. It can be so incomprehensible that we find it frightening and hostile. What sort of dog is that? It's all going to end in disaster!

Redundancy doesn't grab our attention, entropy threatens us, but somewhere between these two poles, senders and curious receivers coincide, making contact and shaping the outcome. Look, what an amazing dog! It's cycling!

ATTENTION
Effective combinations of text and pictures in interesting, contrasting shapes and colours attract the eye like magnets, and if movement is added – in flowing neon on a wall, for example, or animations in a banner – they attract even more attention.

But strength isn't always the most effective option – in a noisy and smoky jazz club in Paris, the saxophonist explains, 'If I want to make myself heard, I whisper.'

It's the same on television, where attention is often attracted by two things: *silence*, when suddenly the loud voices disappear, and *black and white*, as suddenly the glaring colours vanish.

Relevance
When it comes down to it, attracting attention is quite simple. All the sender has to do is shock the receiver with nudity or blood – cheap yet still effective tricks, if rather desperate.

Catcalling and swearing in church are simple. The real question is what people will think of you afterwards. Another issue is the use you make of the attention gained. Receivers must feel that there is a relevant reason why their attention has been captured by an arrangement of pictures in a newspaper. If they can't find a legitimate context for the powerful image, they feel tricked and no contact is made.

If a photograph of a woman with wounds and bruises appears on the cover of a brochure, and the viewer is told this reason – 'my husband is ill' – communication is initiated and the effect won't be far behind.

Relevance in visual communication can be illustrated by the following formula:

A strong image that creates attention but lacks relevance results in the message having little effect: $1 \times 0 = 0$

A weak image, which is still valid in the context, does not influence the viewer to any great extent either: $0 \times 1 = 0$

However, if the image is strong and the viewers also feel that it has been placed in a relevant context, they will be captured by the message: $1 \times 1 = 1$

So what would be a relevant continuation of the story about the dog getting on the ladies' bicycle and rolling down the street? It might be the prelude to a film about creativity and developing ideas, which highlights the importance of combining things that at first glance appear not to go together at all. Or it could be a commercial message demonstrating the importance of effective bike brakes, so simple that even a dog can use them.

CONSTANT INFLUENCE

We are influenced throughout our lives, from cradle to grave, whether we like it or not. Our parents bring us up, schoolteachers educate us, instructors retrain us, politicians try to get us to understand ideas and issues. Whenever we open the paper or turn on the television, messages are drummed into us, and their influence can't be denied. We respond by changing our opinions, sometimes reluctantly, sometimes willingly.

So what's going on inside our heads in all the twists and turns of our brains? It all starts with our eyes, ears, nose, skin, muscles and intestines receiving and sending countless signals through a sensitive system of nerve fibres to our brains.

Perception

The term 'perception' is used in psychology for conscious and unconscious processes, which transform mental impressions into meaningful information. Our sense of sight is the sense that sends the most signals to the brain. The retina's 130 million visual cells capture rays of light from the outside world, refracted by the lens of the eye, and send them in the form of nerve impulses through the optic nerve to the visual centre in the brain. Here they are put together to form the visual impression that we see.

Sorting takes place in what is known as the *prioritizing function*. Our brains try to create context and meaning out of the visual impressions they receive. But we cannot process everything that bombards our senses so the brain sorts it all out so that we can quickly make sense of our surroundings. We quickly screen out trivial information, while what is interesting and relevant is prioritized and taken further. We also spend time reorganizing the signals by removing things we actually can see, adding things we can't see and changing things which do not fit our preconceived opinions and prejudices.

Many signals are recognized from previous occasions. These form the basis of the way we experience, interpret and understand new, incoming sensory impressions. But we guess and draw conclusions too, sometimes quickly, sometimes slowly, sometimes too hastily.

Existing memories can influence the way we perceive a new signal, making it both positive and relevant. Here the short-term memory is activated, a kind of waiting room for things which will later be stored in the long-term memory. The experience is then stored in this final memory in something which can be compared with an enormous database, which can never be completely filled. The database contains three types of memories. Procedural memory, which retains, for example, the memory of the ability to ride a bike; semantic memory, which deals with purely factual information; and finally, episodic memory, which focuses on events and experiences.

Experience

It is therefore important for the sender to use the message to attempt to affect emotions stored in the receiver's consciousness – an accident, a dream, a lie, a journey, rain, wind, snow – so that the receiver becomes open to influence.

Sometimes this influence is gentle, sometimes powerful. It is often dramatic, and ideally human and personal. The stronger and more unusual (but not frightening) the mental impression, the greater the influence. A cycling dog might be a topic of local conversation for a day, or even a year.

Experiences also tend to live on for some time afterwards. A terrifying war report in a magazine may influence the reading of the

BELOW / It is quite simple to attract attention, but the receiver demands that the means used are relevant, as here in a campaign against domestic abuse.

WHAT DOES IT TAKE TO GET PEOPLE TALKING ABOUT DOMESTIC ABUSE?

A picture of a celebrity with fake bruises may seem like a cheap trick but at least you noticed her. It's the 500,000 plus British women that are abused by their partners every year who go unnoticed. The thing is, real victims rarely show their bruises or emotional scars. But domestic abuse shouldn't be kept quiet. Which is why we want you to ACT now: Admit it's a problem, Call it by its name and then Talk to someone about it. For info or to donate, contact womensaid.org.uk or to give £3 now, text ACT 64424*

women's aid act

mamma, pappa,

barn

I Etiopien har nästan en miljon barn förlorat sin mamma och pappa på grund av aids. Nu måste många av dem själva ta ansvar för det som är kvar av familjen och för att det ska finnas något att äta. De kommer kanske aldrig att kunna gå i skolan och för att överleva kan de tvingas sälja sig själva eller sina syskon. Men det finns hopp. Det finns lösningar. Och framför allt: det finns en enorm kraft hos de drabbade. Det enda som saknas är pengar. Hitta ditt sätt att bidra på unicef.se/aids

RÄDDA AIDSOFFRENS BARN!

SKÄNK 50:– SMS:A UNICEF TILL 72 900

unicef

ABOVE / 'Mother, father, child' – AIDS claims many victims. Those children who survive may have to play a role that they are not capable of.

other articles, while an affecting news item influences the entire night of TV viewing.

What provokes us? Well, it differs from case to case, but the more single-tracked, black and white and fanatical we are in living our lives, the more provoked we are when we are faced with something which is subtle and has several layers of meaning.

Interpretation

Perception and experience lead to interpretation, which involves expressing the meaning of a message either to oneself or on to other people.

The entire process is pervaded by our attitudes, values and experiences, and, not least, by the situation we find ourselves in at the time (nose buried in the newspaper on the bus, for example, or with a friend in front of the TV).

In reaching our interpretation we first make a kind of basic assessment of what we are seeing and experiencing. What is this about? Is it important or unimportant, friend or foe? This rough assessment is soon followed by a more subtle one. We often interpret the message incorrectly, and so the intended message fails to reach its target. The sender may only find this out a long time afterwards, if at all.

FILTER DEFENCE

Not only do we interpret things incorrectly, we also tend to make ourselves impossible to reach. This is actually necessary, as we would collapse if we were to take on board all the messages that persistently and insistently try to reach us during the day. Our human hard disk would crash.

Therefore we have been equipped with a defence mechanism that is more powerful than the prioritizing function. We could call it the *filter defence*, which is linked to our psyche and has strategies on two fronts, one passive and one active.

Selective exposure

This simply means not exposing oneself to certain messages. The receiver does not order any morning papers, maybe watches only one or two television channels (and even then only nature programmes), and zaps past all the commercial messages apart from some car ads.

Selective perception

This involves actively listening to what we want to hear and turning our gaze towards what we want to see. The bird lover hears faint birdsong in the middle of the high street despite all the noise of the city almost drowning it out.

When the double bed begins to fall apart from old age, the family suddenly becomes interested in bed advertisements. Whenever they are watching television they keep seeing adverts for beds between the programmes – how handy that those bed manufacturers just started advertising now, they think.

Humour and irony

But our filters have one, or possibly two, Achilles heels – humour and irony.

What could be more appealing than relieving tension with a laugh? That's why the media are full of jokes, to the joy of receivers ('I've given up smoking. I only smoke when there's something to celebrate. Look – it's snowing, let's celebrate!'). But sometimes the laughter, or that positive reaction on the receiver's part, fails to happen. The deciding factor is whether or not there is a natural link (relevance again) between the humour and the message itself. A joke purely for the sake of it tends not to get you very far.

It's also important to remember that what one person thinks is funny, others might not find that amusing. People living in the city tend to laugh at completely different jokes from those who live in the countryside.

Many people would say that you should never make jokes about religion or other serious matters. The Danish caricatures of the prophet Mohammed aroused unprecedented protests in the Muslim world, leading to significant loss of life as a result. Others, however, laugh at witticisms which make fun of both the Bible and the Koran.

After a couple of rainy weeks in August, the holidaymaker can't stand cursing the weather any longer but has to relieve the pressure by bursting out with 'Great weather, isn't it?'

This is irony and it works by saying one thing while meaning the opposite – reversing the language, in other words. Irony reinforces and deepens the message, which thus becomes sarcastic, disarming, witty.

However, it has to be admitted that irony can be hard to handle in some visual communication, where body language, facial expressions or a knowing wink are not available to provide clues. The problem becomes all too apparent when the person the sender is targeting fails to understand the double message and is merely confused. The assumptions of the sender and the receiver must match.

But the sender should also be aware of the fact that irony can mark distance, while it is humour that can often bring people closer together.

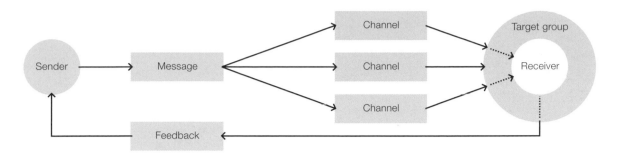

The linear communication model

ABOVE / An attention-grabbing double-take for a *Spider-Man 2* (2004) advert in India. Humour is an effective way to create media buzz and achieve communication.

LINEAR COMMUNICATION MODEL

You could say that a story is the opposite of a filter. Every day we tell stories, chat, reflect, discuss and confide experiences and secrets. We listen, react, laugh and answer questions. This is the simplest form of communication between two friends or a couple of neighbours over the garden fence.

Mass communication

When someone wants their message to reach lots of people, things can start to get more complicated. The editor-in-chief of a newspaper, a marketing manager in a company or an information officer for a government agency all need to reach people properly. This is why they will often use the mass media, which carry news and advertising.

The sender – the newspaper, company or agency – conveys a message to several receivers, who may be a large group of readers, a society of potters, or the majority of the population.

But the message only goes in one direction and the sender therefore has no idea whether the message has reached the receiver, whether it has been understood, or how the receiver has reacted. This mass communication, therefore, is never more than information (monologue) or *one-way communication*.

Two-way communication

The opposite, two-way communication, is something completely different and, according to the theories, only occurs in conversations between a few people. However, in mass communication the editor, the marketing manager or the information officer is able to create something *similar* to two-way communication. To do this, the message has to be designed so that the sender can discover whether the receiver has actually received it. This form of response is called *feedback* or *dialogue*. And it involves getting the receiver to react.

Action

The sender often gets confirmation of the reaction through some kind of action on the receiver's part. The newspaper receives thousands of text messages after encouraging a protest against a political decision. Following an advertising campaign, the company's product manager notices an immediate increase in demand for its products (then rings the factory and asks it to get a move on), and the agency gets replies to a questionnaire geared towards the whole population.

This entire communication process is described in a very simplified *communication model* (above). This model shows that the message often does not reach the entire target group. It is only part of the target group, the receivers, who are reached and it is very important to remember this. The villain of the piece is clutter.

Clutter

Interrupted contact between sender and receiver is caused by clutter. The most common reasons are the following:

TECHNICAL CLUTTER
Poor printing in a newspaper or a web link that doesn't work can both cause technical clutter.

SEMIOTIC CLUTTER
This is generated by unclear intentions and muddled execution in text and images.

COGNITIVE CLUTTER

Limitations on the part of receivers may lead to cognitive clutter, as they may simply not understand the message because of a lack of knowledge or insight.

Clutter affects different parts of the world in different ways. For a woman in Madrid, a man from Rome and a villager just outside Athens, bird flu and the risk of a huge pandemic are a very real threat. To a poor farming family out of media reach, the risk may be completely unknown. In their village, they may still be eating sick birds and the children die painful deaths, one by one.

CIRCULAR COMMUNICATION MODEL

The interactivity that is offered by websites creates the second communication model.

The sender has created a *virtual context*, which consists of a site with a particular aim (for instance, to sell books). It has been filled with specific *content*, and here the sender and the receiver (the visitor) meet in a more direct way compared with other media (the sender displays books, a visitor chooses between them). They act together within the site, almost as in a conversation (the visitor asks questions, the sender answers with reviews, the visitor then orders, the sender posts them off). And so it continues. They exchange roles and two-way communication or interactive communication is the result.

The visitor receives sensory impressions, processes these, reacts and finally *packages* everything. Packaging refers to the bits that are put together (text, pictures, questions, answers, complaints, orders). The site has become the way the visitor wants it (until he or she changes it all again), furnished according to personal taste, appropriately, in strong colours … Over time, the book site becomes a homepage, and the visitor subscribes to news and tips and gets discounts.

The subeditors of online newspapers also talk to their readership. When they notice that many visitors are clicking their way to a particular article in the paper, they can move it to a more prominent place in order to attract even more readers. They can also easily update and develop text and pictures to attract yet more people.

CONTEXT

People have internal and external lives. In our internal lives, we can safely be ourselves, but our external lives are subject to the demands made of us by society. We have to adapt ourselves to the different contexts in which we spend time. We are judged according to how we behave, and we have to adapt to the various contexts in which we move.

Visual communication works in the same way. Everything – the story, the message, letters, text, logos, trademarks, images, design, frames, screens, newspapers, television channels – has an internal life and an external life and appears in a certain context (from the Latin *contexere,* to knit or weave together). Everything has a relationship with itself, the medium, the place and the time. A photograph finds its context in the page of the newspaper but also in the mind of the owner of the paper, in the station newsstand, in the city, in the morning and in relation to the spirit of the time in the early twenty-first century.

Let's concentrate on the external context, to which our texts and images can relate in two ways. They can *blend in* or *stand out*.

To create attention and reach the receiver, the latter is naturally preferable. A man dressed in a fabric in the same pattern as the background blends in and almost completely disappears, like soldiers in desert camouflage or the ray on the seabed.

However, a man in the colourful suit really stands out, as he contrasts strongly with his surroundings. He detaches himself from the background, takes a step out of his setting and becomes very clear to us. By taking some quick steps to the side, almost leaving the picture, he creates even more attention. Like a civilian among soldiers, like a colourful coral fish against the seabed.

The advertisement for Venice stands out in this layout in the same effective way. It differs from the muddled and over-filled newspaper page thanks to its simplicity and its space, which attract attention. The space around the text acts like a mount framing a work of art. The white space around the picture separates it from other things close to the frame, highlighting the shape and message of the work.

The Venice advert also differs in another way. It is about a journey and should be on the paper's travel pages, but is seen here in a completely different context, in the entertainment section. The travel advert is unexpected and will attract attention, as it faces no competition from other travel companies. It is alone, and therefore strong, in this context.

Explaining

It goes without saying that it is important to stand out. But is blending in a total disaster? Not necessarily.

Messages can sometimes be difficult to interpret. When a child asks an adult what a word means, the adult often wants to know the context before he or she can answer. It's the same in visual communication, where the message gets through more easily when the receiver has help from the context. The context explains things.

The slightly damaged character below blends harmoniously into its context and the assumption is that this is a letter. Change the context and it's a number. And the duck is changed into a hare. The context can do a lot more than explain.

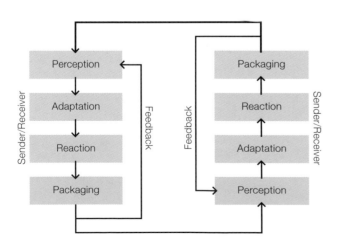

The circular communication model

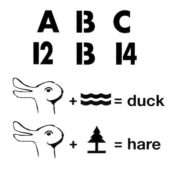

TOP / What sticks out gets us interested. The man disappearing into the background doesn't grab our attention, unlike the other man's contrasting clothes and movement.

ABOVE / Contrasting size, generous use of white space, simplicity, and the few elements employed all make the Venice advertisement stand out.

Reinforcing

As well as explaining, the context can also reinforce a message. Take a ghost story, which isn't remotely spine chilling in daylight, but is very much so when told by a skilled storyteller in an attic in the middle of the night.

And then there are the furniture catalogue's calm images of relaxation, which are surrounded by a stressed, hectic layout. We all long to sink into their chairs after a hard day at the office. Finally, home sweet home.

Changing

By altering context, senders get a strong weapon in their attempts to influence receivers. When a common object – Duchamp's bottle rack – was placed in an art gallery, it became a work of art.

BELOW / A catalogue offers an enticing vision of relaxation after a hectic journey home, while harmless beach photos are consigned to history by changing times.

BOTTOM / Text and images create feelings and thoughts, making us active – an attractive film poster makes us purchase a ticket to the cinema.

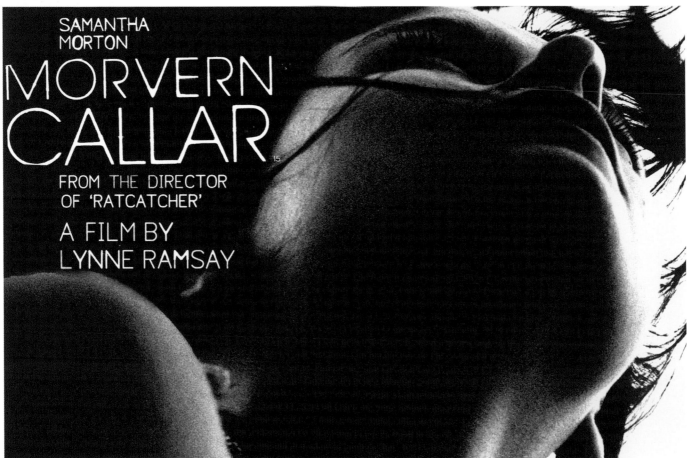

SAMANTHA MORTON

MORVERN CALLAR

FROM THE DIRECTOR OF 'RATCATCHER'

A FILM BY LYNNE RAMSAY

With the help of the context, the sender can achieve a lot. Photograph a car in front of a luxurious house and it turns into a luxury car, put it next to a sports arena and it becomes sporty, while on the Le Mans track, it's a racing car.

The fate of a message is intertwined not only with the context in which it is created but also with the context in which it is encountered. And time changes the way we see images. The recent attention given to paedophilia cases and a cynical, growing flow of child pornography on the internet have changed the way we see pictures of naked children, for example. The once harmless beach holiday snaps in the photo album suddenly take on completely different associations. It feels as though our pictures have been stolen from us. Others have taken them and are using them to satisfy their own needs.

FEEL, THINK, ACT

Influence leads to change. However, there are lots of things that you have to get right. Attention must be secured, the brain set to work and filters bypassed, but there's no doubt that, without feelings and thoughts, the receiver will not be influenced to any great extent. Let's tie it all up and end this chapter with a simple model, the 'Feel, Think, Act' model.

Feel

The article, the advert, the website, quickly arouse a feeling in the receiver. This feeling, which takes the shortest route to the brain, is mainly created with the help of the visual elements, the arrangement of shapes and colours, and the contrast and meaning of the images. Whether they are strictly or playfully arranged, they speak directly to the right side of the receiver's brain.

A feeling for the whole has arisen and there is an idea of the message to a lesser or greater degree. The receiver *has an idea* about something.

Think

Now the receiver's intellect makes a kind of assessment of the message and the receiver has a thought. Is it credible? What is demanded of me? What can I get out of this?

Thoughts quickly take root in the receiver's mind and the text, the verbal communication used, is very important in this context. The receiver *knows* something.

Act

An action is the aim. Attention, relevance, feeling and thought have influenced the receiver to change from passivity to activity. The receiver *does* something.

How did that happen? Maybe there has been a brief conflict between the left and right sides of the brain.

The right side of the brain is a hedonist, an emotional yes-man eager to accept inviting messages. The left side of the brain is logical and rational, and quickly sees the advantages but also the disadvantages – an inveterate nay-sayer.

Maybe there wasn't a conflict, maybe cooperation between the left and the right led to a joint decision. The receiver therefore stretches for the house keys and goes, maybe to a cinema with a friend or just down to a corner shop for some fruit and a magazine.

In the next chapter we go into more depth on a remarkable tool which we need in our attempts to reach the receiver: creativity.

SUMMARY

'At last,' she sighs.

REACHING THE BRAIN
Making sense of external signals requires perception, experience and interpretation.

FILTER DEFENCE
The receiver sets up a filter defence against messages from the media. The main ones are *selective exposure* and *selective perception*.

MASS COMMUNICATION
Communicating with large numbers of people results in *one-way communication*, which entails difficulty in reading or measuring the receiver's reaction.
Two-way communication enables the sender to check and analyse the reaction of the receiver.

ATTENTION
Powerful contrasts in size, movement, colour and shape attract attention.

RELEVANCE
Using blood and nudity to attract attention has a limited effect. The receiver demands *relevance* and needs a valid reason to have been captivated by a visual arrangement.

CONTEXT
An image, an article, an advert have an *internal context* where all the elements interplay with each other. But there is also an *external context* (medium, place and time), which has a crucial impact on the receiver's interpretation.

EMOTIONS AND THOUGHTS
Humour creates emotion, bringing the sender and receiver closer together.
Irony influences the receiver but also creates distance and can make communication more difficult.

FEEL, THINK, ACT
The ideal reaction on the part of receivers:
The feeling gets them to experience something (often conveyed visually).
The thought gets them to find out about something (often conveyed verbally).
The action is the result of the interplay between the visual and the verbal.

CREATIVITY

ABOVE / Good ideas brighten up our lives. Even among commercial messages, which bombard us constantly, a few will break through with their intelligence and their humour – this one, which uses sensors hidden by the bulb, is taken from AbbotMeadVicker's long-running campaign for *The Economist*.

'But out there is where the fruit is.'

Most people sit curled up in their tree, perched on a branch clinging on to the trunk for dear life. That's where it's safe. Out on the branches it's dangerous, it sways about and you could fall off. But that's where the fruit is.

Fruit is vital to the continued existence of the tree, just as ideas are to the development and survival of the company. The future will happen all by itself, but progress has to be created.

Of course there are good ideas and bad ones. The bad ones are like windfall fruit that rot away to nothing. Good ideas, on the other hand, generated with courage and an open mind, lift the entire company. Strategies are refined, products born, consumers delighted. All this leads to good jobs, consumer attention and a good reputation, which in turn lead to more satisfied customers, which leads to better employees, which leads to better customers, which leads to more resources … a positive spiral, in other words.

WHAT IS A GOOD IDEA?

A good idea, maybe hit upon suddenly, is a thought that offers a first overview of a problem, or a starting point for a solution. It often injects something new into a message, giving a lift to the wording and design.

A good idea is also something that the receiver cannot avoid being influenced by, and may consist of a disarming angle in a piece of journalism, a subtle way of combining text and pictures in an advertisement, or a homepage quite unlike anything seen before. The idea may be found in an overall theme or concept, which covers all the company's products, producing a unifying and cohesive effect.

Good ideas have the following characteristics:

They create immediate attention.
They produce an 'a-ha' experience.
They create emotions such as joy, fear, longing and sympathy.
They look simple and clear.
They can be developed and used again and again.

Adverts for the UK magazine *The Economist* grab attention with their use of the magazine's strong red signature colour, of large areas of empty space and of white text. They have been doing so

in roughly the same way for about 20 years, with great success. The magazine is read by people high up on the social ladder and those who aspire to such dizzy heights. The articles focus on economics and political, social and cultural issues.

The level of journalism is high, and that goes for the advertisements too. Praise is not only lavished on the paper in London. Tribute is paid all across the world to its quick-witted humour, packed with ideas, which makes people stop and think. *The Economist* attracts readers with sarcastic but appealing irony.

The basic message is that successful business people read the magazine, and so gain membership of an invisible but exclusive club. Who wouldn't want to be a member?

Photographs are in fact quite rare in the magazine's articles and advertisements, but they are seen and have become more common recently. Alongside the picture of a cigar, the text merely says 'Castro, Clinton, Marx'.

BRAINWORK

Creativity is a misused word, which is applied to practically anything to do with ideas and working on them. It is derived from the Latin *creare*.

Brainwork does not really differ very much from muscle work. The brain is also a muscle, which has to be trained if we are not to lose our mental and creative flexibility. We train our brains every hour of every day, and it all starts back in that first year of life, when we get to grips with a succession of new challenges, from climbing on tables to knocking over vases and eating felt-tips.

Most people would agree that creativity is all about bringing things together and combining things that do not really belong together in different and unexpected ways to create something new and exciting.

This is why it is important to think *laterally*. This kind of thinking gets creators to leave the well-trodden paths and break new ground. You have to go *that way* when everyone else is saying *this way*.

Framework

Visual communication demands a very special form of creativity known as *framework creativity*. You still have to come up with masses of ideas on the right subject, but you have to do it within the parameters of a particular framework. You can't give your imagination free rein and soar off into flights of fancy all of your own, as that will only confuse the receivers.

This given framework does not necessarily need to pose you difficulties. In fact, having total freedom can be very difficult to deal with, and may even cause you anxiety. Restrictions often bring security and can also help, as a framework is needed in order to stand out, to provide something to protest against and a tradition to break. The big challenge is to push the boundaries, not to exceed them.

Look up

It is always a good idea to look up and seek inspiration from new contexts. If the company or its messengers derive their inspiration and references from nothing but their habitual and secure surroundings, there is a risk of inbreeding. This can be termed *group-think*, where everybody thinks the same way, and brings with it a lack of self-criticism, resulting in everyone overestimating their own abilities.

Many people say that as simple a thing as taking a different route to work can help facilitate new ideas. It can give you the opportunity to forge an acquaintance with a lot of new things and to see everyday things in a different light. Cross to the other side of the street, the shady side, and look up at the buildings. What beautiful baroque details there are on those façades, and look, up there they've got a south-facing terrace – I wouldn't mind living there! That gives me an idea …

Sneaking out of the office to melt into the dark of the cinema in the afternoon has led to countless revolutionary ideas, even if your boss might show an irritating lack of understanding.

Travel often offers new perspectives and angles on difficult nuts to crack. Suddenly the stripy tops of the gondoliers in Venice or the romantic melancholy of Lisbon contribute towards an epoch-making idea.

Hocus-pocus?

The street, the cinema, travel? But isn't that a lot of hocus-pocus in order to come up with an idea? The fact is that the real professionals simply sit down and get on with it. They have neither the time to wait for inspiration nor the need for such rituals. They are creative to order and this is what their clients are paying for.

INTERNAL AND EXTERNAL CREATIVITY

Where do ideas come from? There is a dialogue on two levels. One internal, deep in the creator's innermost thoughts, and one external, in cooperation with one or more colleagues.

The internal creative process

The human brain consists of two hemispheres. The left hemisphere is analytical, while the right hemisphere is creative and artistic. The left hemisphere is home to the rational approach and

BELOW / Benetton's campaigns have attracted attention because of their use of images that attack prejudice rather than highlighting their colourful clothes.

BOTTOM / Smith + Foulkes award-winning ad, 'Grrr', inspired by Honda's chief engineer, Kenichi Nagahiro, who refused to make a car unless he could rebuild the diesel engine first.

LEFT & ABOVE / A creative environment can help in the production of advertising campaigns. KesselsKramer are based in a converted church in Amsterdam, where they have created such successful adverts as their 'Action!' series for Diesel.

the right hemisphere the emotional. They talk to each other and an idea is often born when one produces an idea, which the other then carefully tests, until they finally agree.

According to creativity researchers, further inside the brain, where the X-rays can't reach, we have a *self*, which originates the idea, and an *I* which receives it. The 'self' is a clean, clear place in contact with each individual's source of creativity, while the 'I' often blocks creativity. But if the creativity does get through, the flash of genius suddenly just happens.

Often it appears in a state of *flow*, a feeling of being on the right track where everything is going well, that the flow has commandeered all your attention and that everything is taking place in a kind of ecstasy.

The external creative process

The door to the workroom is closed and creative teamwork is about to begin. Two people (or maybe more) are sitting around a table with an assignment in front of them. They might be a sub-editor and a picture editor discussing the pictures for a series of articles, or an art director and a copywriter working on an advert to be shown to a client. Often a graphic designer will be there with a photographer.

Who else might be present? A presenter and a technical director may well be there, working out how the presenter will make an entrance during the big charity gala. Or the copywriter and the director of a commercial leaning over a half-finished storyboard. Or perhaps a web editor and a web designer, working together on an online newspaper.

It is important to point out that creativity is not only required in contexts that involve text, pictures, design and film. Creativity is just as important in the preparatory analytical and strategic phase. The editor-in-chief, the project manager and the product manager must also think laterally and therefore also visit the room.

The practical creative work involves eleven stages or phases that should be passed through.

1. Insight

Work on an idea begins with the insight that a problem must be solved. This may be a solution to a new problem (how are we going to design a new website?), or a new solution to an old problem (how are we going to update and refresh this old site?).

2. Goal

The team must have a clearly defined goal. What is to be achieved? It is also important to clarify who you are creating for – your boss or an external client? And how much time is available and what is the budget?

3. Situation

At the first meeting a complete description of the situation is required, but at a second or third, recapitulation or repetition are needed. Initially, there can be lots of talk and not much work, but this is worth it in the long run.

More questions: how is the result of this meeting related to the assignment in general? Do other functions in the chain, for example ordering procedures or the delivery time, depend on the result?

4. Preparation

In this phase, material is gathered together, questions asked and some small, sketchy suggestions voiced.

But it is important to take it slowly. It has been said that a really creative person is someone who manages to gather together lots of facts and impressions – including ones that conflict as well as agree – without trying to put them in any system or logical order at too early a stage.

5. Openness

It is also important to create an open, informal working climate. Working with other people is easier if the creators know or quickly get to know each other, notice and accept different behaviours, and are not afraid of different points of view. Some people are creative introverts and others creative extroverts. Everyone must feel secure enough in the group to be able to voice unthinkable and even daft ideas.

The openness described above must constantly counter all the objections which are usually thrown up. The four below are the most common:

Direct: *No.*
Hidden: *Yes, but …*
From experience: *We've tried that before.*
Common sense: *But it's actually the case that …*

LEFT / Children's play and imagination inspire communicative solutions that can fascinate both young and old.

6. Priorities
Everyone in the team must be equal and everyone must invest the same amount of energy, concentration and enthusiasm for the result to be successful.

Criticism must be open and constructive, and given at the time and face to face, never afterwards. Criticism should act as a guide for how the team relationship can be improved.

Nor should bad ideas and solutions ever be accepted just to keep a colleague happy.

7. Pauses
On the way, the group should pause occasionally to sum up how far they have got and what conclusions they have reached so far.

Plenty of breaks are required in creative work. Wait until after lunch, or next day or even next week. It can help to get some distance, and you may need time to check a number, track down a picture or draw your own sketch. And useful ideas can turn up while playing table tennis or in the supermarket, or your neighbour might have an interesting angle on the problem.

It's important that the team have agreed on what is required of each person before the next meeting.

8. Tricks of the trade
There are many ways of getting to the big idea. The pressure of the deadline may do it, or the team may bat ideas back and forth, and many go for role play.

Role play is an excellent way of illustrating a problem or the criteria surrounding an assignment. The team take on different roles and act out some scenes to try to determine how, for example, a consumer, an entrepreneur and the head of the consumer watchdog might act in a particular situation.

9. Censorship
This can be internal or external. Internal censorship is self-censorship, which betrays poor self-confidence and is dangerous. Many prisoners are their own prison warders. Of course the group must sift out and reject ideas, but often good ideas are thrown out for no good reason.

External censorship is about restrictive legislation and regulations which the creators have to comply with. Other external censorship derives from the social or moral climates, for example, which have to be considered and adapted to.

10. Respect and lack of respect
Work must be characterized by respect for the different roles involved. The writer is naturally responsible for the verbal aspect and the picture expert for the visual. But does it always have to be that way? Sometimes failing to respect these roles – allowing the writer to freely encroach on the picture expert's field and vice versa – can be liberating. The result can often be surprisingly good, promoting continued creative teamwork.

11. The idea
Three full waste-paper baskets, six cups of coffee and nine dried-up marker pens later, one finally says to the other: 'Hey, what if we did it like this … ?' And there's the new idea, on paper, like a new-born baby.

And like a newborn baby, it needs looking after quickly. The idea must be developed and tested, and is not really a creative solution until it has been accepted by the entire team and the client, and maybe also by colleagues and superiors. It is said that an idea should have wings, but it also needs landing gear. An idea is defined as an untried solution to a problem, and it becomes meaningful only when it is put to practical use.

Much has been said about creative excellence, that fantastic, revolutionary idea that lifts a product into the limelight overnight. But it takes more than creativity – it takes depth, breadth and length. Ideas must be deeply embedded in the company and in all employees at all levels. They must also fit together breadth-wise in every sense (all departments, all places and all countries) and, finally, also in continuity, long into the future (hand in hand with the vision, in other words).

TRICK THE BRAIN

As we all know, good ideas do not come to order and many of us suffer mental blocks, sometimes for a long time. The sheet of paper sits in front of us on the table, irritatingly blank, the clock is ticking, your forehead sweating.

But it is possible to trick the brain into turning on the ideas. Four techniques are described briefly below.

Association

Also known as *brainstorming*, this is when the team tries to come up with as many brainwaves as possible. All new suggestions must be accepted, nothing can disrupt the process. It's about letting go, blue-sky thinking, trial and error, using your imagination and testing limits.

A sifting-out analysis phase should naturally follow this playful but effective process of generating ideas.

Sketching

Here, the creative process is triggered by the hand and by the pencil. The first mark on a piece of paper will always be the most difficult, but once it has been made the team have to reach an opinion on the next one, which in turn will generate new ideas. One leads to another, which is turned into a circle that stands for repetition and following the same track, which is soon pierced by a straight line that challenges the compulsion to repeat.

The most appropriate tool for this is probably the most simple and the most elementary – a pencil (erasers also leave traces) or even a stick in the sand (the surging sea rubs out contours and new pictures are thus created).

Opposites

This method is based on constantly working with opposites and so changing the focus on problems and opportunities. Trying a different perspective, trying to change culture, nature, colour, thinking in metaphors instead …

Can we do two articles instead of one? Throw out the text and fill the space with pictures instead? Shall we start at the end? Where is the least dramatic point? Most people like our product, so let's think about someone who doesn't.

Rhetoric helps too, for and against. Someone, or several people, argue in favour of a particular thing and others against it – relationships and solutions become clear.

A band had a problem. A recording session just wasn't working. Days passed and the producer started to get a panicked look in his eyes. On the last day, the last chance, something radical had to be done. They put the piano into the small recording room for the drums, and dragged the drums out into the big studio. And suddenly it all came together.

Start at the end

This relates to the previous method and is based on the idea that there are two routes to innovation. One is to find solutions to problems and needs; the other is to invent new techniques and patterns of acting and then try to work out places where they could be applied afterwards The latter method is common in the telecommunications industry, for example, where product developers first introduce technical innovations, which might later result in mobile video communication for moklofs (Mobile Kids with Lots of Friends).

ADMIT YOUR FAILURES

The idea seemed good but when the project got going, it turned out not to really work. All those responsible have to admit that they made a mistake but they often compound that mistake by making two more.

Firstly, they analyse their way to one acceptable reason for what went wrong and make do with that, even though there usually tends to be more than one.

Secondly (worse), an unsuccessful project is quickly swept under the carpet as no one wants to have anything to do with it. But there is always the risk that the team will miss drawing any conclusions and learning from the experience. In addition, the nuggets of gold that did exist will be swept under the same carpet and be lost for ever.

FORCE OF HABIT

As we all know, force of habit is very powerful. You only have to flick through the first newspaper you come across. Most messages are designed in almost the same way and it is virtually impossible to distinguish between them.

This means it is important to try to break force of habit. It takes self-confidence to dare to make your way out onto the farthest branch and bring home the fruits hanging from a tree growing in the forest clearing that can only be found by someone who has strayed from the path.

The 26 characters in the next chapter might help.

SUMMARY

'But out there is where the fruit is.'

A GOOD IDEA

A successful idea is characterized by the fact that it captures attention and invokes emotions (joy, desire, sympathy). The idea should be simple and have the capacity for further development.

PRACTICAL CREATIVITY

This involves a number of phases which have to be passed through: insight, goal, situation, preparation, openness, priorities, pauses, tricks of the trade, censorship, respect and lack of respect, and the idea itself.

TRICK THE BRAIN

The following methods can be used to escape a mental block:
Association: brainstorming, where all suggestions are welcome.
Sketching: drawing triggers completely new ideas.
Opposites: trying to come up with ideas using opposites and conflicts.
Start at the end: starting with the idea and working backwards towards the necessary prerequisites.

FORCE OF HABIT

It's important to identify and break force of habit with a message in an innovative form with unpredictable content.

8/
TYPOGRAPHY

ABOVE / Paul Myoda and Julian LaVerdiere's annual *Tribute in Light* memorial preserves the iconography of the twin towers.

'Why 9/11?'

Why did al-Qaeda choose 11 September for its terrorist attack? Was the date random or did it have some religious symbolism? Or was the number 11 supposed to become a graphic representation of the twin towers, so every time we see it we are reminded of the carnage?

VISIBLE TYPOGRAPHY

This brings us on to a discussion of visible or *narrative typography*, an arrangement of letters and numbers which, in one way or another, reveals the sender behind the message, with the purpose of bringing to life the message and strengthening it through the use of type.

Letters can take on different characters. They can be pompous, pretentious, hesitant, tentative, cheeky, affected, harsh, cheap and vulgar. But they can also be open, lucid, clear, elegant, simple and distinguished. Just like people.

Each letter has its own character and personality. A stands for the start, Z for the end and K for Kafka, and it is clear that children learn to read better if a J can sometimes look like an elephant's

trunk. Eminem boosts his career with a reversed letter, just like ABBA did 30 years ago.

Share traders on the NASDAQ in New York often characterize the stock market and its economic fortunes in terms of letters. Thus V is a rapid fall followed by a rapid recovery, while U is a downturn with a period at this lower level before the upturn kicks in. And there is one letter that makes the traders shake in their boots – L. To them, this one little letter means a major, rapid and sustained crash.

INVISIBLE TYPOGRAPHY

The opposite of visible typography is, naturally enough, invisible typography. The designer will create a link between the sender and the receiver – between the author and the reader – without revealing anything of him or herself in so doing. The motto of invisible typography is that silence should be the servant of the content – a good example of this will be well-designed pages in a work of great literature.

The input and imagery of visible typography are banned – images are to be created in the reader's head, rather than appearing on the page.

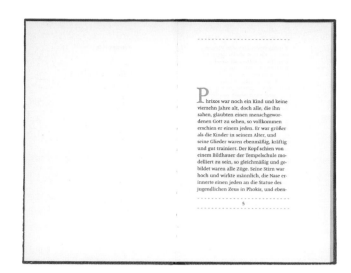

LEFT / Visible typography assists the message – the character of the letters and their arrangement strengthen the message and its possibilities are expanded.

ABOVE / Invisible typography makes a silent link between the author and the reader, with no reinforcements to disturb this contact.

VISIBLE OR INVISIBLE?

The designer should of course choose the most suitable approach in communication terms. Visible is usually best suited to free and expressive contexts and invisible to more literary, informative and educational texts.

It is also possible to have a mixture of both approaches in the same production. A magazine cover might sometimes require an outrageous look, while the articles and reports inside may have to be rather more restrained in appearance to make them attractive to readers.

WHAT IS TYPOGRAPHY?

Typography is about the shapes of letters, their use and the settings in which they appear. For thousands of years letters have, on a daily and hourly basis, conveyed thoughts, feelings, warnings and hopes, packaged in messages from sender to receiver.

Letters are therefore around us at all times. There aren't that many – 26 – but they can be combined into thousands of words, which enable us to develop, but also threaten to overwhelm us.

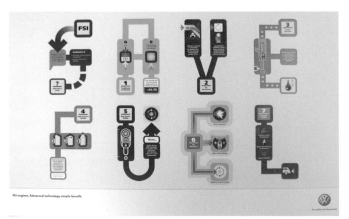

ABOVE / Two inventive approaches to type in order to reinforce a message, one for World Press Freedom Day, and the other for Volkswagen.

RIGHT / Daily papers use both visible and invisible typography. The main section will usually be restrained, while other sections will often be stronger and more visible.

ABCDEFGHILMNOPQRSTVXYZ

O R ABCD

A modern set of Roman capitals (Trajan)

The origin of letters

In order to discover the origin of letters, we must travel back tens of thousands of years. Excavations at various sites around the world have uncovered pictures of animals, suns and moons painted straight on to stone walls in caves and on rocks. Initially, these pictures (ritually) symbolized the objects themselves, but later also came to represent syllables which could be spoken. The Egyptian *hieroglyphs* and Babylonian *cuneiform* were milestones in this revolutionary development.

The first written language to be based entirely on an alphabet and sounds appeared in Phoenicia in the Middle East around 1500 BC. The ancient Greeks then developed the alphabet further, for example introducing vowels, which had not been represented before, and the convention of writing and reading from left to right.

Carved Roman capitals (Via Appia, Rome)

Roman capitals

In their letters, such as those in the forum in Rome at the base of Trajan's Column, the Romans developed the Greek alphabet further, creating what are called Roman capitals, or *capitalis monumentalis* (*capitalis quadrata* when later written with quills).

Letters were first painted on the stone with a broad brush, which was held at a slight angle. The O gives the impression of leaning slightly, due to this *diagonal stress*. Then the letters were carved with a hammer and chisel, before the letter sculptor finished off each stem by placing the chisel horizontally and giving it a tap. This is how the letters got their heels, or *serifs*, which came to play a major role in both their legibility as letters, words or sentences, and their readability when combined to form larger blocks of text.

These monumental and beautiful letters were *upper case* (capitals) based on a system of two lines, one upper and one lower, running from letter to letter and from word to word, as the illustration above shows.

Uncial script (Roman)

Uncial script

The letters were constantly changed and developed, and the need arose for a script that could be written more quickly.

The solution was the Uncial script, which saw the appearance of the first *lower-case* (small) letters. The writing surface also improved, as the type designers of the sixth century dropped rough *papyrus* in favour of *parchment* (animal skin), which was considerably smoother. The coarse writing implement, the *calamus* or reed pen, was also replaced with the much finer *quill*.

Half-uncial script

Certain letters gained increasingly pronounced descenders and ascenders, sticking up and down, creating an alphabet along a more refined four-line system.

Half-uncial script (Insular)

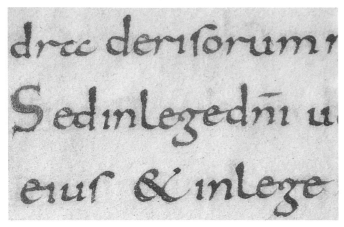

Carolingian minuscule

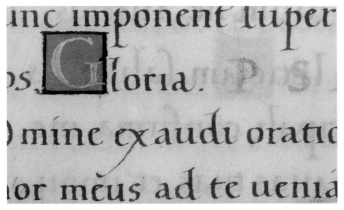

Humanist script

![Gothic script]

Gothic script (42-line Bible)

![Venetian antiqua]

Venetian antiqua

Carolingian minuscule

Charlemagne's kingdoms stretched far and wide by the end of the eighth century. With his coronation as emperor in Rome in 800, Carolingian minuscule, partially developed under his patronage, naturally became the dominant script in western Europe. The letters had both upper and lower cases, but at the time they were rarely used together.

Humanist script

This script was created in the fifteenth century in Renaissance Venice, when type designers learned to draw shapes that were both taller, more slender and more open than anything that had come before. The two cases were used together in the same script for the very first time.

Gothic script

As a consequence of population movements in Europe, Gothic scripts arose where the path of Carolingian minuscule crossed with those of various national scripts. One of the results was the evolution of a script known as textura.

The birth of the printing press reinvented the world of graphic communication, aided by the fact that parchment was being replaced by paper, which had been invented by the Chinese around 1500 years before, but was only now coming into use in central Europe.

The German Johannes Gutenberg is usually credited with the invention of printing in Mainz, a revolution that involved the reproduction of words and sentences with the help of individually cast, moveable types (characters), which could be placed together again and again to create completely new lines each time. These lines were set in columns, which were then inked. A sheet of paper was laid over this type and, to produce an impression, a wine press was then used to force the paper and type together. And out poured not wine, but messages, contained in pamphlets and books.

The 42-line Bible, which was printed in Mainz between around 1450 and 1454 (with 42 lines per page), was Gutenberg's great masterpiece. Gutenberg took the textura script that was in use by contemporary scribes and he then converted this into the first printing type. In Germany, such Gothic styles were used for many purposes up until the end of World War II (and today they have also made something of a comeback for the tattoos of top footballers …).

Gutenberg is often accused of being a separatist. Some academics feel that he expunged the closely integrated interplay between text and pictures that had been such a major part of the art of book-making from the time when monks hand-crafted books. Text and pictures were kept apart, often placed on separate pages in the printed book, which hardly helped people to understand the content.

Now, just over 500 years later, digital technology has finally put things right on this front. On websites and in the graphics of newspapers, we can once again see a close integration of text and pictures, photographs and drawings, whether we like the result or not.

Venetian antiqua

The final phase of the developments towards modern printed letters is down to Nicolas Jenson and Aldus Manutius. Both were book printers in Venice in the latter part of the fifteenth century, and they created the elegant and soft lines of Venetian antiqua (far removed from textura), which signalled the dawn of a new age in printing type. The invention of italic type is often ascribed to Aldus Manutius and his punch-cutter, Francesco Griffo.

ABOVE / Gothic script is over 500 years old, but refuses to be buried. It remains a favourite among tattooists, and fashion designer John Galliano has adopted it as his own.

TYPEFACES

A typeface is a complete alphabet (letters, numbers and characters) in a single design. A font is technically a typeface in a particular size and style, but the term is now commonly used to refer to the typeface itself in a digital context.

Designing a typeface is a long and laborious process. Type designers often start with some of the lower-case letters, such as o, d and n, which contain the details that will then be repeated in the other letters.

Something has happened

We are forced to accept that very few changes have been made to the shape of letters since Gutenberg's time, but in this new millennium everything seems to be subject to a kind of 'ketchup effect', with a great flow of typefaces now reaching professionals and amateurs alike.

Software offers unlimited opportunities that might have Claude Garamond turning in his grave. His letters, designed in Paris in the mid-sixteenth century, became the standard European type for over 100 years. They can now be inclined at every imaginable angle, squashed, expanded, transformed into outlines or shadowed. But up in the heavens, perhaps he is smiling and mumbling longingly, 'If only I, back then, in Paris in 1530 … '

The constituent parts of letters

Learning about the constituent parts of letters makes it easier to recognize the individual characters and the overall personality of each typeface.

Variations of letters

Designers have a whole range of variations of letters at their disposal for creating individuality and impact. This means the letters, numbers and characters may be roman, italic, normal, extended, condensed, semi-bold or bold, all in various type sizes.

cap-height / ascender height / ascender / x-height / baseline / depth of descender / descender / thin / thick / crossbar / bracket / counters / bowl / tail / foot serif / head serif

upper and lower case / small caps / lining figures / non-lining figures

Small capitals (small caps)
Some typefaces contain small caps capital letterforms that are designed to work optically with lower-case letters. They are generally a little higher than the x-height.

Numerals
These can be of two kinds. Numerals of cap height are known as 'lining numerals'. In older typefaces and good contemporary ones, there exist 'non-lining numerals' to balance lower-case letters.

Italics
Sloped letters are known as italics. They may be 'cursive', i.e., with a flow like joined-up writing, or non-cursive, which may appear like a sloped roman.

cursive / sloped roman

TYPE FAMILIES

In our digital age, new typefaces are appearing on a daily basis, so in order to keep some order, they can be split into two traditional main groups and then into families:

Romans
Sans serifs

Romans

These typefaces are characterized by their serifs and the varied rhythm between the thick strokes and fine hairlines, and between the various movements of the stems, bowls and stresses.

They can be divided into three families: *diagonal, transitional* and *vertical romans.*

DIAGONAL ROMANS

Soft and attractive, with rounded serifs and a diagonal stress, diagonal romans have been extremely common in books since the sixteenth century because of their readability. Examples (whose favourite garment is a lambswool cardigan) include the following typefaces: Garamond, Bembo, Berling, Galliard, Goudy, Nordic Antiqua, Sabon and Times.

TRANSITIONAL ROMANS

Designed in the latter part of the eighteenth century, trans romans are characterized by greater contrast (compared with the diagonal romans) between thick strokes and hairlines. The serifs are usually pointed. Trans romans appear in practically all visual application contexts (often in a casual club blazer). Examples include Baskerville, Caledonia, Caslon and Century.

VERTICAL ROMANS

These formal and coolly elegant typefaces were developed in the nineteenth century. They feature a very strong contrast between thick strokes and hairlines, as the type designers took their inspiration from the growth and opportunities offered by copperplate engraving. This gave the letters more delicate lines, thin, horizontal serifs and an upright stress (making them comfortable in tailcoats and long dresses). Examples: Bodoni, Didot, French Antiqua and Walbaum.

Sans serifs

These typefaces have a very distinctive look, because of their lack of serifs. Their design is also very even, with almost no changes in thickness.

Sans serifs were developed in the late nineteenth century, and were later influenced to a great extent by the Functionalism in architecture and design that swept 1920s and 1930s Europe, and which advocated simple, functional forms. These typefaces give a technical and industrial impression, and their simple geometric shapes can create a certain monotony when they are read. They are therefore usually considered to be better suited to headings, text on signs that are to be read at a distance, captions, diagrams and tables, rather than longer body text (they all look good on a well-fitting T-shirt).

Sans serif typefaces are often divided into four families, *grotesque, neo-grotesque, geometric* and *humanist.*

GROTESQUES

Introduced in the early twentieth century, these have a clear movement in their open form, which easily binds letters together into words, helping to make reading easier. Particularly effective in newspaper headlines, they include Trade Gothic, News Gothic, Franklin and Akzidenz.

ABCDEFGHIJKLM
NOPQRSTUVWXYZ
abcdefghijklmnopqr
stuvwxyz123456789

Diagonal roman (Garamond)

ABCDEFGHIJKLM
NOPQRSTUVWXYZ
abcdefghijklmnopqr
stuvwxyz123456789

Transitional roman (Baskerville)

ABCDEFGHIJKLM
NOPQRSTUVWXYZ
abcdefghijklmnopqr
stuvwxyz123456789

Vertical roman (Bodoni)

ABCDEFGHIJKLM
NOPQRSTUVWXYZ
abcdefghijklmnopqr
stuvwxyz123456789

Grotesque sans serif (News Gothic)

ABCDEFGHIJKLM
NOPQRSTUVWXYZ
abcdefghijklmnopqr
stuvwxyz123456789

Neo-grotesque sans serif (Univers)

ABCDEFGHIJKLM NOPQRSTUVWXYZ abcdefghijklmnopqr stuvwxyz123456789

Geometric sans serif (Futura)

ABCDEFGHIJKLM NOPQRSTUVWXYZ abcdefghijklmnopqr stuvwxyz123456789

Humanist sans serif (Gill)

ABCDEFGHIJKLM NOPQRSTUVWXYZ abcdefghijklmnopqr stuvwxyz123456789

Slab serif (Rockwell)

ABCDEFGHIJKLM NOPQRSTUVWXYZ abcdefghijklmnopqr stuvwxyz123456789

Script (Mistral)

Decorative (Dama)

NEO-GROTESQUES
These typefaces originated in 1950s Switzerland, where pared down, pure typography and graphic design dominated. Neogrotesques have a closed movement (like an autobahn with no exits) and are good in headings, but are not always successful as body text. Helvetica, Univers and Folio are strong examples.

GEOMETRICS
As the name suggests, geometrics are designed according to strict ideas of form, and look great on book covers and posters. Examples include Futura (designed by Paul Renner in 1930) and Avant Garde.

HUMANISTS
Softer and less geometric, humanist typefaces have a strong open movement. Gill Sans is by far the best-known example, and was created in 1927 by Eric Gill, a legendary type designer. Frutiger and Kabel are other examples.

COMBINATION
This involves mixing typefaces. Examining the character and shapes of the typefaces, the designer is able to see that certain families are drawn to each other. The cool formality of Bodoni (vertical roman) attracts Futura (geometric) while softness and openness unite Garamond (diagonal roman) with Gill (humanist). But there is nothing to stop the designer from seeking out other more daring combinations.

Combination

Other families
Much more limited in their use, other typeface families include slab serifs, scripts and decorative styles.

SLAB SERIFS
This is a very distinctive family of typefaces that were designed mainly in the late nineteenth century. They are bold, sometimes rather unwieldy in their shape, and are common on vintage posters. The family includes Beton, Clarendon, Egyptienne, Memphis and Rockwell.

SCRIPTS
These typefaces are designed to look like handwriting, and they are mainly used for specialist purposes – for instance on restaurant menus and on smart invitation cards. The typefaces in this family include Basilica, Brophy Script, Citadel, Bankscript, Künstlerscript and Mistral.

DECORATIVE STYLES
Sometimes a reader (or indeed a designer) will stumble across a typeface that is almost impossible to make out. It belongs to a loose and bohemian family that is wild and growing (particularly on the web). The uses of these typefaces are of course limited, although they can be exploited in a logo or form part of a free and playful typographical arrangement on a cover.

Digital typefaces
The sheet of white paper is increasingly being replaced with a bluish glowing surface with a wandering cursor.

The screen is a difficult and demanding surface on which to work, and a great deal of energy is being put into new typefaces. Georgia and Verdana (one roman and one sans serif) are two of the typefaces that are well suited to the screen.

GEORGIA

This is considered by many to be the best roman typeface for the screen because it has robust details, but still gives an airy impression. It works very well at small sizes, the italics are the best of all the screen italics, and it is also striking in larger headings.

ABCDEFGHIJKLM
abcdefghijklm

VERDANA

This is many people's favourite among the sans serifs. Open and broad shapes, which give an even and airy impression, make Verdana equally good in body text and for headings.

ABCDEFGHIJKLM
abcdefghijklm

THE ETERNAL PROBLEM

The web is the visitor's medium. It actually makes no difference how much work the designer has put into a page on a website if the visitor doesn't have the typeface used in the style template.

A visitor's computer settings dictate typography, so designers are left to explain that things didn't turn out the way they intended (unless a PDF file is used, where the typography is locked and looks exactly the same on their screen as it does on the visitor's).

CHOOSING A TYPEFACE

Type marking involves choosing a typeface and a suitable layout. It is a fascinating and difficult job that begins with the following:

Read the text.
Identify its inner structure and logic.
Find some harmony between text and typography.

Reading the manuscript naturally takes time and thought, but is a crucial factor in eventual success. Structure and logic are primarily about how and in which order the thoughts or information embedded in the text are conveyed. If the designer can identify the author's chain of thoughts, then the structure can be broken down into sections, and the hierarchy of headings sorted.

Harmony? The typeface has to fit in with the context, i.e., be true to the spirit of the text.

True to the spirit

In order to capture the spirit of the text, a designer has to analyse the message carefully and find the best way for it to be conveyed. Visible or invisible, dramatic or non-dramatic? Then the key is to try to put yourself in the reader's shoes. In what context will it be read, what experience does the reader have, and what values?

Three typefaces

Most designers cherry-pick a small number of typefaces, which they learn to master completely. They investigate all the expressive possibilities so exhaustively that they eventually know intuitively what size should be used and how upright, italic and bold characters can be combined.

Many designers feel that three typefaces can be used to solve most typographical needs, for example combining Sabon, Didot and News Gothic. But sometimes a designer has to go on the hunt for a specialist typeface to achieve a particular look.

READABILITY

What happens when we read? The eye follows the letters from left to right, again and again, and people, scenes or thoughts that someone else has thought, recently or a thousand years ago, are recreated in our minds. It's a marvel.

But the marvel does not happen on its own. The designer has to use the typography to ensure that the text can be read without difficulty. This requires knowledge, the key element of which is that we read not letters, but word formations. Our eyes scan the letters and send signals to the brain, which puts them together to form words.

The eye progresses in what is known as *saccadic movement* over the lines of text. This means that the eye will stop regularly, fixing on one word, and at the same time reading a few words around it.

The eye progresses in what is known as *saccadic movement* over lines of text. This means that the eye stops regularly, fixes on one word and at the same time reads a few words around it.

Saccadic movement

For the unpractised reader this can prove quite a slow procedure. However, reading will happen at a high speed for habitual readers. When we are reading quickly, the brain is stimulated, which increases our concentration, motivation and understanding. And if we come across an unfamiliar word in the text, the brain will skip elegantly over it, creating comprehension based on the context of the piece. But if we read more slowly, the reading process is understimulated, and this can create gaps in the flow of information.

The easier the designer makes it for the reader's eyes to move over the page, the greater the level of readability will be – the following typographical tools and conditions are crucial to the readability of a text:

Typeface
Lower case and upper case
Type size
Line spacing
Line length
Column set-up
Word spacing
Character spacing
Text against background
Ink and paper
Language, content and the reader

Typeface

The shackles of habit are strong. Experience shows that the greatest readability is achieved when we read a text in typefaces that we are used to. Times and Nimrod are very common typefaces in books, newspapers and advertisements, and are therefore perceived to be easy to read.

ROMAN DESIGN

Both researchers and designers know that the serifs on letters play a key role in reading text (as did the ancient Romans ...). The serifs give the words and lines a kind of track for the eye to read along.

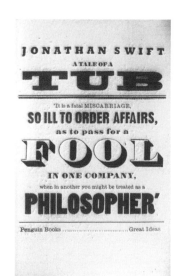

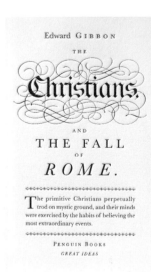

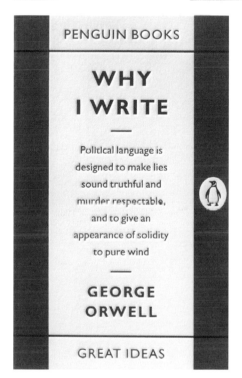

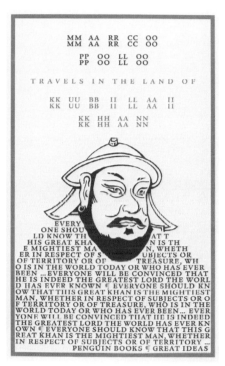

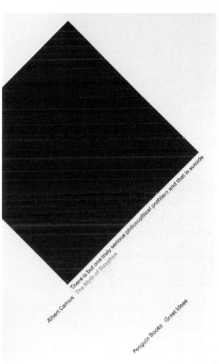

ABOVE / A set of books will usually be uniform in its typography, but the Great Ideas series from Penguin does the opposite, dressing each cover in the lettering or typographic styles appropriate to its time.

It is also thought that the switch between the thick and thin elements gives roman letters clear and individual characters, making it easier for the eye to identify letters and to put together the word formations.

Readability varies among the different roman typefaces. The diagonal and transitional romans (such as Garamond or Caslon) are considered superior in this respect to the vertical romans (for instance Bodoni or Didot).

The reader will usually prefer typefaces that have a diagonal stress to ones that have an upright stress. This diagonal stress reduces the monotony of the type and also gives the eye an extra push along the 'rail' (rather like a string of pearls), while an upright stress tends to hold up the reading process a little (more like a picket fence).

Typeface
Times

Typeface
News Gothic

abcdefghijklm
Garamond

abcdefghijklm
Bodoni

SANS SERIF DESIGN

With their even thickness and geometric design, sans serifs can cause different letters to become confused (particularly the i, j, l and I). The individual characters are less distinctive, making reading harder.

News Gothic   Univers

As mentioned before, some sans serifs are open and some closed, as can be seen in the two letters above. The open shape creates a feeling of movement, which helps the eye to bind the individual letters together into word formations (they extend an open, helping hand). With the closed typefaces, each individual letter feels more closed, with less forward momentum, making words a little more difficult to read.

Individual letters can also affect readability. Gill Sans' lower-case 'a' has a distinctive two-level construction that makes it more legible than Futura's single-level 'a' (which can be confused with an 'o').

Gill Sans   Futura

ON SCREEN

In web design, there are good grounds for choosing sans serifs over romans. Designers feel that the usability of roman typefaces is very limited in smaller sizes, e.g., 13 point and less. The strong, glowing and low-resolution screen burns out the thin strokes and the serifs are converted into oversized lumps that distort the characters, creating a muddled mass of text.

However, Georgia, which was specially designed and adapted with these problems in mind, works very well on screen, as we said before.

Lower case and upper case

The individual character of the lower-case letters, with their descenders and ascenders, makes it easy for the eye to process them into word formations. Upper-case letters, on the other hand, are always at full height, creating no variety of outline. The result is a lack of character, which makes identification more difficult. In upper case, words are read letter by letter, which doesn't promote easy reading. The capital letters can be useful in headlines, book titles and extremely short text, but definitely not in body text.

It's not just designers who have considered the relationship between upper-case and lower-case letters. On an electric hob, a capital H lights up on the panel when the cook has just switched off a ring but it is still very hot – as a warning signal. Once the ring has cooled down a bit, the hob signals this with a lower-case h.

American singer/songwriter Tom Waits has a keen sense of the nuances of letters: 'The large print giveth and the small print taketh away.'

Type size

This is a measure of the letter size, stated either in points or in millimetres. The point concept goes back to a very old typographical measurement system used since the time of lead typesetting. One point (pt) is 0.376 mm (0.015 in).

The distance between the eye and the letter affects legibility and therefore determines the choice of type size. A poster naturally requires larger type than a book.

In newspapers and magazines, where the designer not only has to find a suitable type size for the body text, but also a clear hierarchy between heading, intro, sub-headings and captions, the *golden ratio* may offer some guidance. This classic ratio of proportions has been used for many centuries in various quarters, for example in architecture.

The golden ratio gives the harmonious proportions 3 : 5 : 8 : 13 : 21 : 34 and so on, and has proven extremely useful in visual communication in general, and typography in particular. Based on this number series, the type for a book may be marked up as follows: captions in 8 pt, body text in 13 pt, sub-headings in 21 pt and finally chapter headings in 34 pt.

RIGHT / A classic series of type sizes, following the golden ratio, is used in this typographic arrangement, creating a distinct hierarchy.

34pt – # Chapter heading

13pt – American singer/songwriter Tom Waits has a keen sense of the nuances of letters: 'The large print giveth and the small print taketh away.'

21pt – ## Sub-heading

13pt – American singer/songwriter Tom Waits has a keen sense of the nuances of letters: 'The large print giveth and the small print taketh away.'

8pt – **Caption**

Line spacing

The distance between the lines also affects readability. If the distance is too small, the lines merge into each other, making reading more difficult. On the other hand, if the distance is too large, the eye has difficulty keeping the text together.

Line spacing is given a measurement (also in pt) called body size, representing the distance between the baselines of the rows of text. The measurement 8.5/11 expresses a type size of 8.5 pt and a body size of 11 pt, as in this book. This means that there are 2.5 pt of empty space between the lines.

Most designers agree that a body size one, two or three pt greater than the type size promotes readability. To be honest, the easiest way to determine what works is usually to cast a trained eye over the proofs.

The line spacing should be increased proportionally with the type size up to 14 pt (e.g., 14/16) and after that reduced proportionally, until at 18 pt the line spacing should be equal to the type size (18/18). With even greater type sizes, the line spacing should be further reduced (e.g., 24/20) to avoid creating too much space between the lines.

Line length

Also referred to as column width or measure, line length affects readability. A line should not be longer than around 60 characters, including spaces.

On the web it should be shorter, perhaps 35 to 45 characters per line.

Column set-up

Depending on the required typographical composition, the designer may choose various column set-ups – a choice which has a major impact on readability.

FLUSH LEFT TEXT

This means that the text is set with an even left-hand edge and a ragged right-hand edge. The ragged right-hand edge allows for consistent word spacing and minimizes the number of hyphenations, which makes reading easier. This very common style gives a free and open impression.

However, flush left text sometimes creates a *line arrangement* on the right which may cause problems, as the different lengths of the lines can generate undesirable formations. The most common ones look like a bite, a dent or a ledge.

The designer can make the column look considerably better by adding or removing certain words from the end of the lines or inserting a hyphen. The aim is a pattern that switches between long and short lines. A more advanced solution is to have alternating long, medium and short lines.

| Bite | Dent | Ledge |

FLUSH RIGHT TEXT

This means that the left-hand edge of the column is ragged and its right-hand edge even, which makes for poor readability, as the eye has difficulty finding its way back to the correct line along the uneven left-hand edge. Flush right text is relatively uncommon, but may occur, for example, when a caption is to be closely linked to a picture.

CENTRED TEXT

This is distributed evenly either side of a middle axis, making the whole symmetrical. Centred text should be used judiciously, being best suited for titles and short texts on book covers. In longer texts, readability is seriously compromised, as it creates a rather busy pattern.

JUSTIFIED TEXT

This has each line the same length, making both the left- and right-hand edges even, as in this book. The designer (or computer) varies the distance between the words in each line to fill the width of the column. This is probably the set-up most commonly used, appearing practically everywhere, in books, newspapers, brochures and catalogues.

A justified column of text is economical, as it accommodates a great deal of text (all the lines are filled, down to the last space), requiring shorter columns than with other set-ups. However, in some contexts, it can look a little boxy and closed. And on the web, there is the problem of the text in a justified column becoming full of gaps and ugly if word wrap is not an option.

CAPTIONS

Attention grabber! Captions immediately draw the reader's eye, and it can be a good idea to formulate and design the first sentence in the caption as a title or question to grab the attention of the receiver and draw them in. The designer can also help the reader to identify a caption more easily by applying a different typeface.

It is common to use a sans serif, which contrasts with the roman typeface in the body text. Another is to set the caption flush left, with a ragged right-hand edge, in contrast to the justified body text.

Each picture should have its own caption, and if there are several pictures, the designer should not position all the captions together, far removed from the images. This would make it more difficult for the receiver, who would have to flick from one place to the other. Receivers often prefer the caption to be placed under the picture to which it refers, which is not always practicable.

SCROLLING PROBLEMS

Web design has its own specific typographic conditions. Visitors don't really like having to scroll, i.e., work their way down through an endless mass of text. To avoid this, web designers usually try to make the pages short, often using long lines to fill the screen's wide format – resulting in terrible readability, of course.

Are there any better solutions? Yes, in fact there are several.

One solution is to edit the text to within an inch of its life and so make it shorter.

Another is to create two or more columns, or split a longer text over several pages.

A third solution is to fill up the long columns that demand so much scrolling with attractive and exciting pictures, which makes the scrolling a pleasure.

Word spacing

The spacing between words on a line has to be big enough for the individual words to be clear. However, it must never be greater than the line spacing, as this encourages the reader's eye to join up words on different lines (which merge with each other) instead of reading line by line.

If the spacing is too small, the words flow into each other, which makes reading difficult.

In printed media, the *standard alignment* (the norm for letter spacing) is usually the best option. On the web, however, a slight increase in the distance improves readability.

Character spacing

The space between characters must not be so small that some characters overlap each other, or so large that the word formation dissolves. Once again, standard alignment is preferable.

Generally, reducing the distances between the letters is called *tracking*, while *kerning* involves the designer reducing the distance between certain letter combinations, while increasing this distance for other combinations.

For headings, the alignment should be reduced, but in extremely small text (6 to 7 pt) it should be increased slightly (something usually taken care of automatically by the software). It is also important that the alignment is constant throughout the entire text.

Words in upper case in body text should always be S P A C E D O U T, with the space increased equally between each letter. Lower-case words should never be spaced out, as the word formation breaks down and reading is made more difficult.

Text against background

Readability also depends on the contrast between the letters and the background.

TEXT AGAINST COLOUR

Most readers prefer black text on a white background, but dark green or blue text on a white background also gives acceptable readability. The designer should avoid combinations of complementary colours, which have a tendency to interfere with each other – red text against a green background, for example, creates a psychedelic effect.

TEXT AGAINST PICTURES

The designer should also avoid using busy pictures as the background to body text. However, if this is not possible, there can be certain solutions.

Against a (fairly) uniform background, choose a large and legible type size for a typeface that offers strong contrast.

Against a busy and complex, non-uniform background, simply insert a transparent light tint block, over which the text will be clearly legible.

Shadow the text or give it a contour to make it stand out against the different elements of the busy background.

Another solution is to opt for a really large type size that will have no difficulty standing out against the background. This may, of course, require the text to be edited to make it shorter.

Ink and paper

The choice of ink and paper also plays a role in readability. The printer has to check the ink settings throughout the printing process to avoid grey or fuzzy letters.

There are various grades of paper that the designer can choose from. On poorer paper, it can be technically difficult to reproduce the text in Bodoni, for example, since its fine strokes disappear against an uneven surface. A bold sans serif such as Futura would probably be a better choice.

A top-quality calendered (gloss) paper, however, offers no limitations in terms of typeface, but the designer should bear in mind that such paper reflects light, which can irritate the reader and compromise readability.

Language, content and the reader

Typographical factors are not the only things to affect readability.

The language itself – the choice of words and sentence construction – and the reader's motivation and ability to understand are key to the success of the message.

ABOVE / Using type against a background can be a problem for the reader. Contrast is the solution – dark or black letters require light or white backgrounds, and vice versa.

STRONG TYPOGRAPHY

The designer often chooses to intensify and highlight a word or section, using various strong typographical features.

It is important to remember that too much intensification can lead to nothing looking important. It all cancels itself out and the designer is back to square one.

Headings

As the first thing the reader usually encounters, the heading is the starting point for the message. The rules are as follows:

Use a type size that is large enough to clearly mark the difference from other text.

Make sure that the line arrangement in the heading fits in with the linguistic content and the general design.

A two-line heading should have the long line at the bottom, and a three-line heading, flush left or centred, should have the longest line in the middle.

Avoid hyphenating headings.

Preferably use fixed (equal) word spacing.

It is best not to adapt parts of a heading to a given width.

Optical letter-spacing

Designers should always apply optical letter-spacing to a heading in upper case. This means adapting the distance between each letter to achieve a harmonious word formation. By scrutinizing the heading, the designer will be able to see where letters clump together and where they are too sparsely spaced. Letter-spacing takes training, but is absolutely vital for book covers and film titles.

Bad spacing

Good spacing

Sub-headings

These have two main tasks. The first is to help the reader to develop an idea about the general content of the piece, and the second is to present the content of the section immediately below.

The typography must ensure a clear contrast between the sub-headings and the body text. While there are many ways of achieving this, the designer must choose the best solution for the particular context. However, the most common options are:

A semi-bold sub-heading against lightweight body text.
An italic sub-heading against upright body text.
A sub-heading 4 to 6 pt larger than the body text.

In a complicated text, which requires several different levels of heading, the designer should try to create as great and clear a contrast between them as possible.

When deciding on the typography of essays and of literary manuscripts, the designer should, however, tread carefully, as too dramatic a jump in size between the different levels of heading can create confusion on the page. A good starting point may be to set the lowest heading level in italics at the same size as the body text, and the next level up in a lightweight upright typeface that is around 4 pt larger that this, and so on – see the golden ratio earlier in this chapter.

The designer should also carefully consider the position of a sub-heading. In terms of content, it belongs to the text that follows it, so there should be less space below the heading than above it. Beware of headings floating indeterminately between two blocks of text.

New paragraph

The reader wants to be able to navigate their way through a column of text as easily as possible, so it is important to make it clear where a new paragraph starts.

INDENTS

These are one solution. The designer makes the first line of the new paragraph start a short way in from the margin, often using an indent the size of an *em space* (the width of a letter m in the relevant font). The em space can be found as a specific character in modern software.

An indent should not be inserted after a heading or sub-heading, as these have already signalled a new paragraph.

BLANK LINE

In complex texts, for example technical or scientific memoranda, it may be justified to mark a new paragraph with a blank line, and web designers in particular often use a blank line (or half a blank line) between paragraphs.

It may seem like madness to a book designer, but the screen is a rather different reading surface. A long column of text on screen can become too compact with just an em-space indent, whereas blank lines give it a positive lift.

However, in books and magazines, the blank line breaks up the text too much and impedes reading.

Completely omitting indents or other markings seriously compromises readability.

Individual words and characters

Sometimes the designer needs to draw attention to a character or an individual word.

This can be done in various ways:

Drop capitals
Italics
Semi-bold
Small capitals

Drop caps are an effective and elegant way of marking the start of a text. However, the designer should avoid using too many in one text, as the reader is inclined to try and identify which word they form together. In other words, a lot of energy is misdirected.

Italics are a common, simple and clear way of emphasizing a word in a text.

Semi-bold can be a little too striking in a literary context, but is ideal for textbooks.

SMALL CAPS are specially designed upper-case letters at the same height as the lower case, and can make a word stand out in an elegant and subtle way. Always use the proper small caps for the typeface in question, as they are made slightly thicker and wider to fit in with the lower-case context. The small caps so readily provided by much computer software are actually just the normal upper-case letters in miniature, making them too thin and difficult to read.

The methods of emphasis used in printed media are much less successful on a website. Both small caps and italics are difficult to read on screen – bold works better, as does changing the colour of the text.

BELOW / A drop capital – as with this O in *The New York Times Magazine* – helps the reader to find where to start, and also contributes to creating an attractive whole.

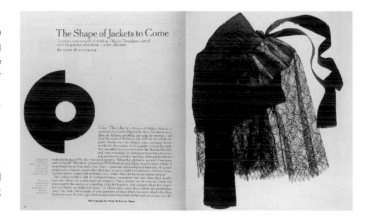

THE TYPOGRAPHIC WHOLE

The whole often says more than its parts, with the overall typographic arrangement also conveying a message. There are three design principles to consider:

The symmetrical approach
The asymmetrical approach
The contrasting approach

The symmetrical approach
This approach is a classic that appears in all typographic contexts. The designer achieves an elegant, harmonious balance by having headings and other texts oriented around a vertical axis.

The asymmetrical approach
Asymmetry introduces dynamism as the vertical axis is abandoned. Flush right or flush left headings and texts combined with diagonal shapes create a lively impression – it is best not to take this too far.

The contrasting approach
The strongest typographic arrangement, contrast appeals directly to the receiver's emotions, and can be achieved in several ways.

SIZE CONTRAST
Large against small, this is achieved by choosing a large type size to contrast with a small one, or a wide column contrasting with a narrow one.

STRENGTH CONTRAST
This is created by opposing strong, bold headline letters with lightweight letters to create an exciting effect.

SHAPE CONTRAST
Putting upright upper-case letters against italic lower-case letters, or choosing a sans serif typeface to go with a script, can result in contrasting shapes.

COLOUR CONTRAST
As you would expect, this involves reproducing part of the headline in a colour and the rest in black, or placing a logo in white against a strong background colour.

Typography can be said to be the shape of the text, its body. In the next chapter, we'll be looking into its soul: the content.

BELOW / An elegant typographic symmetry makes a good contrast to surroundings that include strong colours and form.

BELOW / Asymmetry can help give life and power to a typographic arrangement.

OPPOSITE / The designer has a palette of contrasts to use – large against small, strong against light, italic against upright, or a range of competing colours.

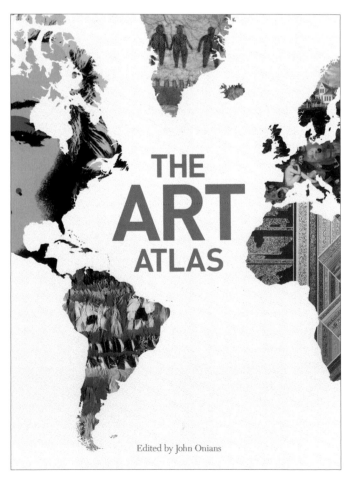

THE ART ATLAS

Edited by John Onians

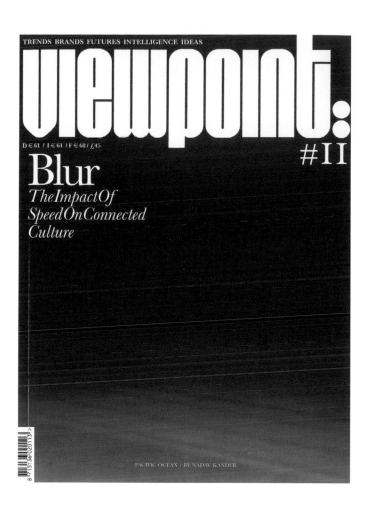

SUMMARY

'Why 9/11?'

VISIBLE AND INVISIBLE TYPOGRAPHY

Visible typography: means that the letters take on a personal design, which reinforces the message (for instance in a newspaper header or in a logotype).

Invisible typography: forms a silent link between author and reader, between sender and receiver (as in a work of literature).

THE LETTERS

Romans: characterized by the difference between thick strokes and fine hairlines and the fact that they have serifs (the letters' heels or feet).

Sans serifs: characterized by their even design and the lack of serifs.

CHOOSING A TYPEFACE

The typeface must suit the context (*congeniality*) and be *readable*.

Readability refers to how easy it is for the receiver to read a text. Factors crucial to readability include the typeface itself, type size and line length.

TYPOGRAPHICAL REINFORCEMENT

Reinforcement refers to the need to highlight more clearly various parts of a text. The most common means of reinforcement are the use of headings and sub-headings, and the marking of new paragraphs (Indents).

THE TYPOGRAPHIC WHOLE

The whole also conveys a message.

The *symmetrical* approach is experienced by the receiver as being organized, harmonious and elegant.

The *asymmetrical* approach is dynamic and attractive.

The *contrasting* approach is experienced in an intense fashion through contrasting sizes, strengths, shapes and colours.

9/
TEXT

"It was a wrong number that started it, the telephone ringing three times in the dead of night, and the voice on the other end asking for someone he was not. Much later, when he was able to think about the things that happened to him, he would conclude that nothing was real except chance. But that was much later."

ABOVE / Both captivating and mysterious, the first three sentences of Paul Auster's novel, *City of Glass* (1985), effectively draw the reader into the scenario.

'But that was much later.'

Paul Auster is a skilled writer who knows how to start a text. The set-up of the novel City of Glass, *the first book in the New York Trilogy, is evocative in its intriguing contrast between the event described and the viewpoint chosen. The novel's opening creates great expectations on the part of the reader, who wants to know who the speaker is and who is the person he is not. The reader can't wait, and has to read on.*

GOALS

These need to be formulated at every stage of communicative work, and that goes for visual as well as verbal communication.

What does the text have to achieve? Influencing and changing someone's emotions or attitudes? Teaching something?

WHO IS THE READER?

Writers have to know who they write for. A young person who has bought a piece of software and wants to know how it works?

Writers have to put themselves in their reader's shoes and think about the reader's needs, without losing sight of themselves completely. This demands intuition as well as factual knowledge, and writers have to ask themselves whether they have sufficient background information. They also have to work out in which way the reader can derive benefit from the content of the text. He or she will constantly be asking 'Why should I be reading this? What does it have to offer me? What have I got to gain?'

Much of the work of writing thus involves preparation, but this is something well worth doing. The more impressions you amass, the more you will be able to express.

CAPTURE INTEREST

Naturally, it is vital to capture the reader's interest. The most important thing has to come first and it must feel relevant. Often, however, introductions tend to be long-winded, more like a tentative attempt to get off the ground. One effective tactic is simply to cross the whole thing out.

The text should ideally be like a shark, biting at the beginning, firm flesh in the middle and a powerful tail. That's what writing courses always tell you. And you should also make links to topical events, such as an eclipse of the sun, a visit from a foreign president or a head-butting footballer in a World Cup final.

Introduce variation

Variation is important, as language that varies in rhythm and tempo excites interest and encourages forward movement.

If the text starts calmly and gently, increase the tempo towards the middle or end, otherwise there is a risk of the piece becoming monotonous. If the text starts by describing something specific, don't wait too long before shedding light on the whole. If, on the other hand, a writer starts with the big picture, he or she will soon need to look at the details.

For variation, writers should switch between long and short sentences. Something has to happen *in* the text, but it is important to remember that something also has to happen *with* the text.

Be concrete

It's important not to use descriptions of a product's design and function that are too sweeping or generalized.

Instead the writer should look at the concrete details. It is better to state that every tennis racquet is tested and the tension of each individual string is checked rather than making vague claims that everything is tested carefully. These details are meaningful.

Use metaphor

Language and imagery come together in a rhetorical device, metaphor, that allows us to describe something more convincingly by drawing comparisons. 'We launched our action plan yesterday,' says a proud manager, who would never dream of going to sea.

Some metaphors soon become overworked, but this kind of language – whether used of a tepid business presentation or of bittersweet memories – can be appealing and effective. And strong like a bear. Or sensitive – cry me a river.

Be sensitive

What is it that makes a text so interesting? What makes individual words so beautiful? Is it their sound or their meaning? Or a synthesis of the two? A carefully chosen word or phrase can really draw readers into the atmosphere you are creating.

Pitfalls

Getting the writing wrong can pose problems.

One of the most common faults is missing out steps in reasoning, making a story hard to follow. Lack of a causal connection is a common mistake. You have to remember that what is blindingly obvious to the author might leave the reader completely in the dark.

Finally

Work towards your goal. Do the words chosen help to get the message across?

WRITING FOR A NEWSPAPER

Enough of general advice, and over (very briefly) to practical journalism. First the journalist has (once more) to be very clear about the audience being written for, and, when this is known, the better the content can be adapted to expectations. The angle of the article is crucial to how the text will be read and understood.

Structure

The structure of the text is important. The headline starts the story; strong wording captures interest and creates expectations ahead of the text itself. As above, make links to something the readership knows, surprising them with an unusual statement, or provoking them with a pointed question.

The job of sub-headings is to draw readers through the text. Sub-headings are important as they often act as a kind of short cut through the article, enabling readers to make an assessment of whether the content is interesting or not. Sub-headings also make the order and structure visible, and these must be logical.

Titles vs. headlines

Choose between a title and a headline. Titles present or offer a hint about the content of the piece of text. It might be something academic and passive such as 'The behaviour of wolves'.

A headline, on the other hand, should forcibly capture interest and stimulate the reader – for example 'How to protect yourself against wolves'. This hints at something concrete and promising.

The writer must follow up the headline immediately in the text, so that the reader quickly understands the transitions and links.

Lively language

Long and complicated words have to be swapped for short and simple ones, and a personal and lively language should be used, which fires the reader's enthusiasm. It's also about winning the reader's trust through judicious use of examples from reality.

ABOVE / Dave Eggers's *Timothy McSweeney's Quarterly Concern* abandons almost all imagery to assert the primacy of text, both for its literary and journalistic potential – the journal has brought together a host of major writers – and as the source of visual interest, despite the use of only one typeface: Garamond.

'HOW TO PROTECT YOURSELF AGAINST WOLVES'

Page 19 is a disaster.

The meeting is in 15 minutes.

HP Office Jet Pro K550

Probably the fastest ink-jet printer in the world.

Product benefits:

Too fast.

Doesn't blend in.

People will talk.

Porsche

WRITING ADVERTS

Here we leave the world of newspapers and enter the ad agency, heading for the copywriter's room. The copywriter is working on a product that promises a solution to a problem (an instrumental message) and the planning work is in full swing. First, a problem experienced by the target group is identified; then, a promise of a solution; and finally, evidence – how the solution works. The conclusion challenges the reader to act (to make a phone call or buy the product).

If the product promises an enhanced emotional experience (through a relational message), there can be more freedom in the structure of the text.

Ten general pieces of advice on the art of writing advertising:

1. Have the reader in your mind's eye.
2. Start with the headline.
3. Follow up the headline in the text immediately.
4. Be concrete and not too witty.
5. Write in the active voice and remove most of the adjectives.
6. Cross out everything you can.
7. Remove your favourite bits without crying (kill your darlings!).
8. Don't be ingratiating, but do be quite personal.
9. Check the text against your strategic and creative goals.
10. Have someone read what you have written.

Short or long text

Many professionals claim that all advertising texts must be short, as people don't read long texts. However, this is a misconception. It isn't the length that determines whether a text is read or not, it's the reader's interest. Therefore an interesting, well-structured and well-worded text will be read, whatever its length.

WRITING WEBSITES

On the web, text can be read in two ways – in the traditional way on screen from a particular site or blog, or as hypertext.

Site text

Concise language is required on the web, as text on screen will be read approximately 25 per cent more slowly than on paper. Web language often means that articles and journalism that were originally written for a newspaper will require editing and abbreviating for online publication.

In addition, visitors also dislike scrolling, which means that short columns of text are required (ideally no more than the length of a screen).

SHORT WORDS

Along with short sentences and short paragraphs, short words are also very important when writing material for the web. Ideally each paragraph should deal with a single idea or message, and experienced web writers recommend *one sentence for one idea, one paragraph for one context*, and this has now become a rule of thumb.

HEADINGS

As visitors can enter a site from all possible directions, headings should be informative but not necessarily long, to make the content clear to those who have just arrived.

'Side headings' suit the screen well, as the screen format is width-oriented and there is often plenty of spare space at the edges. If the web designer creates two columns, an effective arrangement can be achieved, with side headings in one column and running text in the other.

DON'T USE LOTS OF COLUMNS

Whether a particular piece of text is long or short, the writer and the web designer generally agree that it is important to avoid the text running into several columns. If the columns are longer than one screen in length, visitors will then be forced to scroll both up and down.

BLOG TEXT

How do bloggers write? Often, though not always, they will skip the introduction and the background information, and their text is direct and concise. Visitors can work out the context from the previous entries in the blog, and this kind of writing style is ideal when there are lots of people who want to follow the entries and take part in ongoing discussions of a topic.

BELOW / Clarity and simplicity are vital for UNICEF's website, which needs to serve numerous different functions.

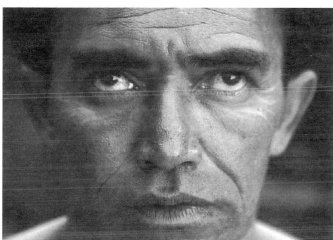

ABOVE / It takes 119.5 seconds to serve a pint of Guinness. Playing on the strapline – good things come to those who wait – this commercial creates a lyrical atmosphere; the voiceover takes us into the mind of the surfer, waiting for the great wave, making inventive use of the whalers' wait for Moby Dick in Herman Melville's epic novel.

LINKS

Traditionally, links are shown in a different colour from other text, which makes them easy to find. They should also change colour when a visitor clicks on them, partly so that he or she knows that something is happening, and partly so that he or she can also see what has already been clicked on when revisiting the site at some later date.

Links should highlight the location, not the action that is required to get there. Visit our store is preferable to visit our store.

Extremely long texts should start with a table of contents with internal links to the sub-headings in the text below.

Hypertext

This has no beginning, middle or end – instead it consists of a number of independent chunks of text from several different sites, which the visitor puts together in different combinations.

This means a blurring of the boundaries and of the distance between writer and reader, and many people think that this heralds a huge change which will see power over information move from a minority to a majority.

Control over the way our past, present and future are described has always rested with a limited number of authorities. Now these decisions are passing to the majority of writers and readers, and this might change the world at large.

WRITING TV SPOTS

The texts for a TV spot must, by necessity, be short. You can't fit all that many words into 15 or 30 seconds.

Often it's better to have sounds tell the story. Tyres screeching on asphalt are more effective than having an actor tell us that a car is coming.

Some sequences don't require a single word, as moving images, sound effects and music do the job. But when words are needed, the writer should remember that the voiceover doesn't necessarily need to describe everything that is shown in the picture. The job of the dialogue is to provide information both backwards and forwards. What situation is the person in? What is the problem? What happened earlier to create this situation? How is the person going to get out of it? What is the solution?

The dialogue should also characterize the person who is speaking (tense, anxious), the person being spoken to (calm, secure) and possibly also the person being talked about (honestly, respectfully).

It is clear that the text needs help from the image, which will be dealt with in the next chapter.

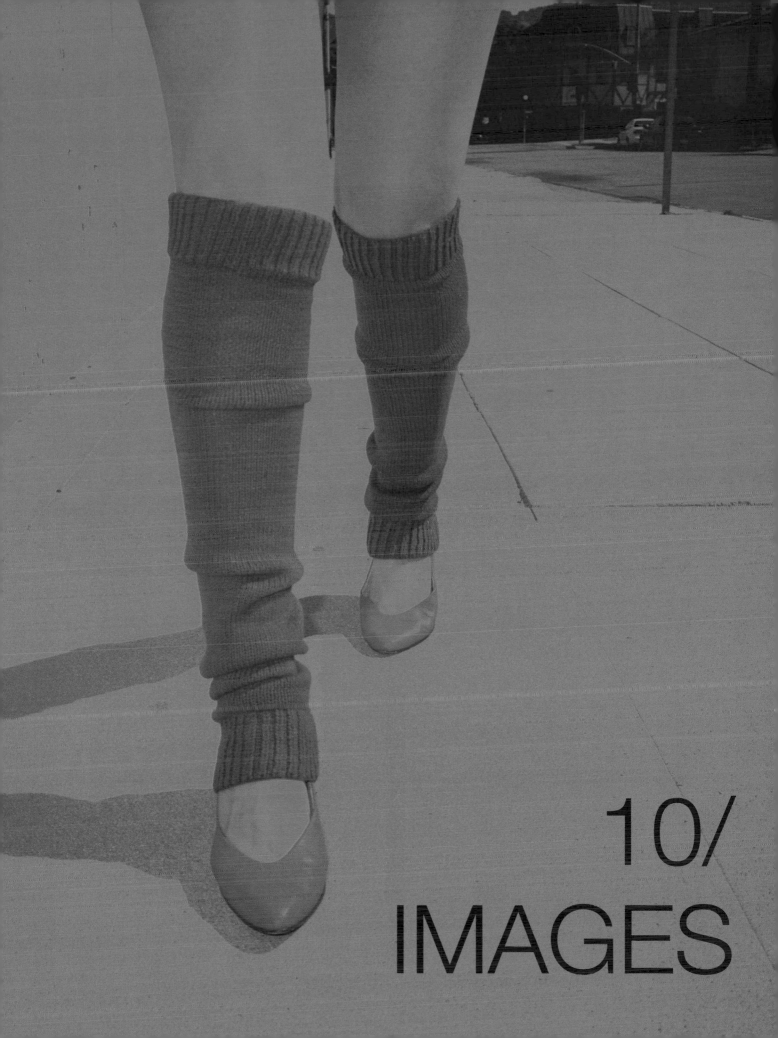

ABOVE / A strong picture does not just
describe emotions – it creates them.

'The camera was my signal for help, nothing more.'

*As the black clouds chase across the autumn sky, the huge cruise
ship slowly sinks.*

*One of the passengers, a lorry driver, is woken by the vessel
starting to capsize. Miraculously he manages to reach as far as
the huge ship's keel, which is still above the surface of the water
in the severe storm. A man is there before him. They are only 25
metres apart, but despite the short distance, each has no idea of
the other's existence. Shivering in the cold, they sit waiting for the
best moment to slither down into the dark water without risking
being dragged down into the depths by the sinking ship. The lorry
driver takes out his camera. It is small and easy to use, with a
flash. He fires off a few flashes to attract attention in the icy dark.*

Many people can still see the picture in their mind's eye. None of
those who are mourning people who died on the MS *Estonia* will
ever forget it. The picture that was never intended to be a picture.
When the flashes went off, the film was exposed. We see a man
in a red life jacket and, despite the water and light damage, we
can clearly recognize the fear in his eyes. The picture gives us no
more information than that, leaving us to face it alone. Perhaps
this is what gives it its strength. This picture doesn't *describe*
emotions. Instead its austere content *creates* emotions. We
become engaged and involved. Minimum action seems to have
created maximum emotion. It becomes our picture, and it moves
us deeply.

MILEPOSTS IN THE HISTORY OF THE IMAGE

Our search for the origin of the image starts off back in the
Paleolithic era. Here we find carved hunting scenes, a ritual
attempt at capturing the game on which survival depended.
These first examples of pictures, perhaps 30,000 years old, are
found in caves, some of which were used as homes.

Later on this whistle-stop journey through time, we find
images mainly in religious settings. In the West, churches were
filled with frescoes and mosaics. The space was filled with pictures of the powerful individuals of the day, alongside religious stories. But it wasn't long before ordinary women and men, often
depicted at work, were also able to see themselves on a painted
screen. The artists were keen to describe reality and influence it
too. Here the image became a tool for change.

Depicting reality soon became even easier and faster. The art of photography developed quickly during the nineteenth century. 1839 was the magic year when Louis Daguerre in France first published his method of producing a photographic image on a silver-plated copper sheet.

In 1895 the Lumière brothers constructed the first film camera, which was also a projector. Moving pictures were born, and spread like wildfire across the globe. Charlie Chaplin, with his jerky gait, was among the first to strut across the screen. And much of the world sat spellbound by tales of the past, present and future in the darkness of the cinema. Over 50 years later moving pictures reached the home.

Roll film is invented, colour too, and cameras get smaller and smaller, these days fitting in a breast pocket.

And now film itself is passé. Digital cameras let us experience recorded reality, still or moving, on the computer screen, on the web and on mobile phones.

Pictures fascinate us. They carry with them the memory of their subject and also its absence.

THE IMAGE REVOLUTION

We are in the middle of a revolution – an image revolution that is set to turn everything upside down. Up on to the barricades climb the digital cameras and camera phones.

We get our pictures instantly and we combine entertainment with practicality. The picture becomes our shopping list. We could even open the fridge, photograph the shelves and when we get to the supermarket click on the picture to see what it was we were out of – cheese and marmalade.

We keep diaries, but instead of writing 'dear diary' we upload the picture of the day to our computers and our lives are on display.

We share our pictures. Family, friends and colleagues see what we see and are virtually there with us, wherever we are. 'This is me at the exhibition, me with the artist, just look at those paintings!'

We get used to images. That visual sense of exclusion described in the introduction to this book has been toned down. We dare to talk about pictures, judge and analyse them. And at least some of us dare to reflect ourselves in them.

Balance

The deluge of images might therefore create a balance between the left and right sides of the brain, between sense and emotions, between text and image. The 'word people' might lose some of their social advantage. Concentration on linguistic skills in child-rearing and education may be superseded by equality between verbal and visual. We can always hope.

But many take a pessimistic view of this enormous flow of images, thinking it makes visual expression and the use of images banal. The distance is lost, and criticism and analysis with it. After all, what is there to analyse in a picture of a fridge? What is there to comment on in the flow of images of pouting mouths and naked sex which are so easily available from the internet? Nothing. The image is losing its value and we get rid of it as soon as the mobile asks whether we want to delete or save.

Screen reality

Will the flood of images become so great that we lose contact with reality? Will the image become a membrane between us and real life? Writer Susan Sontag said that we are increasingly discovering the world by depicting it and then viewing the image we have created. We will soon be living in a screen reality – a substitute for real experiences – and may become emotionally stunted, suspicious and narrow-minded. To avoid this we must constantly mark the border between image and reality.

ABOVE / Pictures – paintings, photographs or films – have always been used to influence us. Contexts have been (and still are) religion, science, news and advertising.

Three groundbreaking examples are above – Michelangelo's *Creation of Eve* (1510), an early daguerrotype (1837), and Nick Ut's photo of a napalm attack in Vietnam (1972).

AMATEURISM

At the same time as media power is becoming increasingly concentrated (with fewer and fewer people owning more and more of the media) the opportunity for individuals to access new and private media is rocketing. You can't surf the net these days without being greeted by 'Welcome to the Andersons' Website', or the equivalent. Many sites are just for relatives and friends, others for special interests from fly fishing to bootleg Dylan tracks. Some fight for environmental issues or against terrorism. Others set up news sites and blogs, challenging news.bbc.org.uk and cnn.com.

Is the power of the media under threat? Maybe. Newspapers and TV channels now even encourage their readers and viewers to send in their pictures and video clips for publication. Seen any signs of spring? Send them in. Car accidents? Let's have them. They say that only a few minutes after the tsunami disaster in Thailand, images were flooding in to newspaper editors the world over from mobile phones. These pictures first filled online editions and then paper editions with a never-ending flow of images.

A new journalism is born?

Are we witnessing the birth of a new kind of journalism? The old journalistic megaphone, loudly passing on the news from a few large news companies to each and every one of us, has had its day. Today it's the other way round. The news networks suck up text and pictures from the general public like a vacuum cleaner and send them on to increasingly niched channels. The new journalism might have lost the right to claim it gets out there and goes digging for stories. Rather it *processes* them. Editors develop and rework the incoming material to a greater and greater extent instead of initiating it and creating it themselves. Then the readers and viewers take up the attractive texts and pictures and add additional blog entries and video clips from Google. Together all this fills a small megaphone, the reach of which includes both editors and readers. The readers have been transformed into writers, viewers into TV producers and listeners into songwriters.

People no longer seem to want to see themselves solely as consumers but as participants. This shifts the centre of power from traditional media to media owned by active, involved citizens.

So what about the photographers? Will this flood of images change things for the professional photographer? After all, the purveyors of news don't have to hire expensive reporters and photographers any more when their readers and viewers do the job themselves, and the paparazzi on their Vespas are facing stiff competition. Amateurism is spreading, and the skilfully taken

BFI OW / Today's news is not only documented by professionals – amateurs on the spot also provide photography, often using camera phones.

ABOVE / A significant strength of images is their ability to show the contrasts of life. This photograph by Spencer Platt of affluent Lebanese looking at a destroyed neighbourhood of Beirut in 2006 concentrates on the differences between life and death, wealth and poverty and hope and hopelessness.

photograph is seeing itself vanquished by a grainy picture of a celebrity's lover. Taken with the help of Sony Ericsson.

New advertising production

Advertising photographers have been swimming against the tide for a long time, largely thanks to clients choosing to do the advertising job with their own digital cameras, which can produce good pictures quite easily. Photographers are too expensive, they say.

Photographers have another competitor in 3D technology, which can provide pictures and visual layouts which are far too expensive to produce using traditional methods. A person (a mountaineer) is shot against a green background (green screen) and can then be placed in any picture you like (the top of Mount Everest).

Knowledge and insight

What will it take to regain this lost ground? The answer, as is so often the case, is *knowledge*. If the photography industry is not to die out, like the composing rooms and process engraving companies before it, photographers have to become better at working in partnership with subeditors and picture editors at newspapers or TV channels and art directors at ad agencies.

Photographers have to realize that a picture never appears in a vacuum but always in a context of text and other images in a certain medium, in a certain place, at a certain time. And pictures always have a purpose. If photographers understand the underlying assumptions in terms of news evaluation, target groups, message

and potential effect, they will become modern visual media workers with bright futures. The photographer must have the whole picture clear in his or her head. It's no longer enough to be a stonemason, you have to be a temple builder too.

Nor is it easy to convince clients to go for quality when they are muttering 'this will be fine, that will do for us'. Why bother when they can earn several hundreds of pounds from their own, slightly slapdash, anodyne amateur production. It's like the waiter who, otherwise faultless, spills a few drops on the guest's table without wiping them up. Poor service becomes the norm.

GENUINE QUALITY

Those fantastic photographs and amazing film sequences which move between sender and receiver bringing the message to life and making it unforgettable – do they really exist? The lover of order might well ask this question after the pessimistic viewpoint of the preceding few pages. Yes, they definitely do. They can be found in some newspapers with an expressed and professional picture policy, which will attract skilled photographers. They exist on some TV channels, which take a serious look at everything from major, wide-ranging reportage to locally filmed interviews. And they appear in some advertising campaigns, so powerful that no one can prevent themselves watching.

They exist in reality, they exist in this book; they are important and worth encouraging and preserving. It's just that there's a risk there won't be as many of them around tomorrow.

THIS IS WHERE THE PICTURE WORK STARTS

The picture taken by the lorry driver (back at the start of the chapter) was originally not intended to be a picture at all. It was more a signal for help. But those working with news and advertising need pictures, real pictures. So what *is* a picture, an image?

According to theory, there are three types of image: the *visual image*, the *internal image* and the *technical image*. The visual image is created when part of reality hits our retina. Associations and interpretations then convert it into an internal image, of our own. The technical image is reproduced on paper, film or screen and competes for our attention with such tempting visual experiences of reality as a flower, a cat, a man, a woman.

We will return to visual and internal images later. For now, let's take a closer look at the technical image. What exactly is it?

First, there is its *construction* – the way the image is built up. It is here that we distinguish, for example, between painting, drawing, photography and film.

Then we have the *function*, which tailors the image for art, news or advertising.

Finally comes *circulation*, where receivers in different media, such as art galleries, newspapers, TV or the web, consume images.

In the media contexts examined in this book, we tend to find photographs and film used for news and advertising in the press, the web and on TV.

Working with images

Which professionals are involved in production work on photographs and film sequences? Of course there is a client, who may be an editor, picture editor or subeditor at a newspaper or TV channel. The client may also be a creative director, in charge of art directors and designers at an advertising agency or web design company.

The photographer and the cameraman carry out the commission and deliver it for reportage or advertising campaigns.

The receiver, the viewer of the image, notices the image and allows him or herself to be drawn into its world.

All three have a personal and special relationship with the image, which can be described on the basis of three different perspectives, which were introduced in Chapter 3.

The client must work according to the *perspective of intention*, as far as the image is concerned, i.e., the goals, message and context of the image.

The photographer works according to the *perspective of proximity*, which covers framing, composition and meaning.

The viewer, finally, examines the picture on the basis of perception, experience and interpretation. This is called the *perspective of reception*.

THE CLIENT'S PERSPECTIVE

We will start with the first perspective, the client's.

GOAL

WHAT DOES THE CLIENT WANT THE IMAGE TO ACCOMPLISH?
Inform, illustrate, show, explain, teach, frighten, entertain? Rock the boat, convince, persuade, sell? Change attitudes, convey powerful emotions? The answer is here somewhere. What we have to do is find it and it is vital that we make the right choice.

WHO DOES THE CLIENT WANT TO REACH?
Which target group will encounter the image? And what are the characteristics of this group – what are their insights, their needs and their dreams?

HOW DOES THE CLIENT WANT TO REACH THEM?
Where will the image be published? In which medium? In a newspaper that the target group is expected to read? In a magazine or on a television channel? Or in an advertisement, on a poster, on a website? What are the technical requirements? What are the restrictions? Will the newspaper reach the right person? Would a television channel or website be a better option? Questions, questions.

MESSAGE

Images build messages – strong ones too – and they also set the stage for them. What technical images are available and what can they achieve?

There's no doubt that categorizing images is a very risky business. The boundaries we draw can be seen as far too narrow or far too vague, but one effective categorization might be the following:

Informative, giving relevant information without value judgements
Explicative, explaining an action, a situation or course of events
Directive, indicating or encourage a certain opinion
Expressive, communicating strong feelings using powerful means

INFORMATIVE
These images record large and small real events and appear in the news as reportage and documentary items. This category also includes the simple and direct product images which fill catalogues, advertisements and e-commerce websites. Arrangement and direction on the photographer's part is restrained.

EXPLICATIVE
Explicative images include, for example, X-rays that help explain illnesses and accidents, or pictures that give instructions on how to put together a newly purchased garden chair. This category also includes images depicting the wonderful situations and the surprising events of life. Explicative images give away the fact that a certain amount of arrangement and direction has been involved on the part of the photographer, but this should not be excessive.

DIRECTIVE
In the third category of images, *directive images*, the sender and the message are more visible. Somebody wants to influence people in a certain direction and the arrangement and the direction are designed to that end.

EXPRESSIVE
Finally, expressive images demonstrate a personal approach. They may be poetic, experimental, highly associative and even non-representational. Naturally, these will involve considerable arrangement and direction.

All these types of image are used to convey messages. They dramatize the staging of news, and in advertising they reinforce instrumental, problem-solving messages. And they also envelop newspaper reportage and relational product messages in a feeling of well-being.

Informative

Directive

Explicative

Expressive

ABOVE / Categorizing images is difficult, but here is one attempt, with examples of different approaches to recording the aftermath of the New Orleans hurricane.

IMAGE RHETORIC

The images in the four categories become willing aids when a decision is made to increase the impact of the message. The sender then moves to a strong and persuasive choice of image in order to create a more intensive experience for a newspaper reader, or to stimulate a consumer reaction in the viewer sitting on a sofa in front of the TV.

This is called rhetoric, the art of speaking well and captivatingly. Transferred to a visual context, the image's persuasive function, image rhetoric, appears. But a warning is needed. Persuasion often makes the receivers less involved, making them feel that conclusions have been reached over their heads.

A *convincing* approach is preferable as it involves the receivers, who are then able to draw their own conclusions.

A master of image rhetoric (particularly in advertising) makes the following clear to the receiver:

CONSTRUCTION
How the goods or services are built or put together.

FUNCTION
How it works in practice or which sensory reaction is aroused.

STATUS
The social reaction created.

BELOW / Presentative images show a product or place with a rhetorical flourish, an exciting angle or an interesting view.

BOTTOM / The sleek design of a new Volvo is given prominence in this presentative photograph.

FOUR RHETORICAL IMAGES

So how does this work in practice? Well, senders have four types of image to assist them. These are derived from the rhetorical *figures* (tropes) that are part of the classical speaker's repertoire. Converted to the world of images they perform the following tasks:

The presentative image *shows.*
Metonymy *illuminates.*
Synecdoche *indicates* and *proves.*
Metaphors and similes *compare.*

The presentative image shows

A presentative image is used when the sender wants to *illustrate, present* or *show* what something looks like and put certain features under the spotlight. We are constantly surrounded by such images: a picture of a product or an environment, or a portrait.

The origin of the presentative image lies in the informative. Raising the image from this level up to what is a simple but nevertheless rhetorical level demands particular tactics.

A picture of a bicycle can be brought to life by ambitiously taking pains with the background and the lighting. Or why not hang a helmet on it, setting in motion an action, a hint at a course of events?

The choice of lens is also important. Wide angles can revitalize the dullest product or packaging. A hand holding out a camera, say, brings the message to life and also gives an idea of size.

A snowboard looks well designed for the steep hills of the Alps. We notice the colours and the construction, which encourages speed and inspires trust.

For his website Pierangelo Federici in Venice selects a picture, showing the remarkable sinking city, taken from the water. The sky is blue; St Mark's Campanile is visible above the roofs.

In consultation with their ad agency the stressed advertising managers at a major car manufacturer choose a studio image of one of their models for a product catalogue. The car is clearly defined against the softly lit background, skilfully highlighting the new design.

The picture shows the car directly, simply and without fuss. Details of function and status are minimal.

Metonymy illuminates

The stock market plummets, shares fall dramatically in value. How can a subeditor depict this? It isn't easy, but *metonymy* comes to the rescue. It *illuminates* a kind of closeness between two concepts or, as rhetoric has it, a change of name, or in our case a change of image. The subeditor swaps the stock market for Wall Street and, with the help of image metonymy, what was abstract and hard to capture immediately becomes concrete and easily comprehensible. The French government thus becomes the Elysée Palace and the British Prime Minister becomes 10 Downing Street. What could be easier?

BELOW / Showing a photograph of the government – a row of people in suits – can look dry. Metonymy can provide a solution – the Elysée Palace is far better.

LEFT & BELOW / A synecdoche image allows us to build the whole from a part. A seagull helps us to imagine the whole seascape and the gondolier summons up images of Venice. The lone toothbrush betrays a single life, while two suggest coupledom.

Synecdoche indicates

The rhetorical substitution, synecdoche, *indicates* something by a *part* standing for the *whole*. In the context of the news, a police badge can be used to represent a police constable, a stethoscope a doctor or the entire medical profession. And when a wide area of coast is to be depicted, a picture of a single seagull will do the job. The receivers create the rest of the sea landscape in their heads, building the waves, rocks and islands on the horizon. And the more they build themselves, the more involved they become.

In the same way, the concept of coupledom is built from the basis of a picture of a glass with two toothbrushes in it, and the concept of singledom from a similar image that shows only one toothbrush.

One recent picture that attracted a great deal of attention, and succeeds in involving us deeply, was of a woman tenderly being cared for by a paramedic after the terrorist attack in the London Underground. It will be some time before we forget the strange face mask she was given to heal her burns. The whole picture, of the terrorist bombing, the Underground and the bus, we build up ourselves in our mind's eye.

A gondolier in his black, narrow vessel, complete with its passengers, is part of the whole of Venice. Probably the most characteristic image, they think in the small office by St Mark's Square. And the site takes another step towards completion with this synecdoche image.

Synecdoche proves

When an image is used – primarily in advertising – in an attempt to *prove* that a product message is relevant and correct, synecdoche is also used.

How does this work? The art director *adds*, places the product in a certain context, in an environment, so that it becomes a natural part of the whole. In other words, the receiver sees both the part and the whole. In this way the sender attempts to prove the product's characteristics, which the receiver must immediately understand and find trustworthy.

The snowboard is filmed 'in action' in a glorious natural environment. You feel you would be able to master the most precipitous and dangerous hills aided by the functionality of the snowboard. A hint of status is added by a sign for an exclusive resort standing in the background.

For a poster campaign focusing on road holding, the car company chooses an image of their latest model on a challenging road surface in strong sunshine. The landscape creates a dramatic impression – the driver seems to be the master of the situation in this safe touring car.

Information on function is very clear, as is status, since the car is being driven in a beautiful, desirable environment.

Metaphors and similes compare

'It's a difficult job but someone's got to do it.' To make sure that others really understand this we often spice up our language. Instead of just saying that we've got a tough task to perform, we bring in a comparison from a completely different context – the world of bullfighting. We 'seize the bull by the horns', which is a *metaphor*, drawing similarities between our world and a different

BELOW / In synecdoche images for advertising, we almost always see both the part and the whole, and the message becomes clear – the functionality and exhilaration of the snowboard or the speed and style of the car – while in Absolut Vodka's famous series of ads, we are lured into the image as we search for a bottle.

ABSOLUT VENICE.

one. Shakespeare has Romeo poetically declaim, 'It is the east, and Juliet is the sun.' And when Billie Holliday sings about strange fruit, we know what she means: black men dangling from trees in Indiana.

Elsewhere we hear such expressions as 'the light at the end of the tunnel', about hope for the future, 'zipping through the rush hour' and politicians who 'lay their cards on the table' and finally 'throw in the towel'. And we all know that necessity is the mother of invention.

Closely related to the metaphor is the simile. In a pop song, we hear: 'Ain't that a shame, my tears fell like rain'. Or as another singer put it 'Why is my heart so frail? Like a ship without a sail'. Comparisons with the animal world are common. 'Sly as a fox', 'happy as a lark'.

The linguistic metaphor suggests similarities between things from different areas in order to clarify, reinforce and shed new light on a message by means of *comparison*. Image metaphors are created in the same way by producing a comparative image.

But the sender doesn't make a clear comparison between two images side by side. Instead the picture of the event (in the paper) or the product (in the ad) is replaced by another image from a linked or distant context. This forces the receiver to make what is known as an *associative leap* from one area to another in order to better understand the newspaper article or the features of the product or service.

The metaphor has two parts: the actual element (the original image) and the image element (the image of the metaphor being used for comparison). We'll use another example of advertising from the world of driving.

The *actual element* is represented by a car.
The *image element* by an arrow.

The intention is obvious. The arrow encourages the receiver to make associations with something fast and thrilling. The car borrows the connotations from the arrow, creating an exciting link.

The receiver is expected to understand that the car is very *fast* – the word *as* is important in this context. It states that the car is like an arrow and the expression 'fast as an arrow' should immediately spring to the receiver's mind. The sender has *compared* the properties of the car with those of the arrow, and has also *replaced* the car, or a picture of the car, with another image, a picture of an arrow. Construction and function thus become clear, as does status to a certain extent.

Positive and negative

A distinction can be made between negative and positive metaphors. This may seem obvious but it is worth pointing out. A negative metaphor is used when the message has to do with something dangerous which the receiver must keep away from.

BELOW / To make us understand the car's speed, the art director and photographer have replaced the image of the vehicle with the image of an arrow.

ABOVE / Amnesty's hard-hitting campaign against female circumcision encourages us to register support at their website to exert pressure on governments around the world.

A computer operator uses an image of a dying dinosaur to draw attention to the need for new, upgraded equipment (otherwise the company will die). The negative metaphor is used in dramatic storytelling and thus in instrumental messages.

A positive metaphor involves making a comparison with something safe and attractive and can be used in non-dramatic storytelling and thus in relational messages.

Advanced

It should be emphasized that in image rhetoric the metaphorical approach is the most advanced. It takes a lot to hit on that perfect metaphor which will resonate with the receiver. Boxing champion Muhammad Ali always shouted to his opponents 'I will float like a butterfly, sting like a bee.' The opponent understood and had every reason to shake in his shoes.

However, metaphors make great demands of the receiver and if he or she fails to find the key to the comparison, a flop is on the cards. The risk lies, not as so many people think, in drawing a metaphor from too distant an area. The risk instead lies in using common, tired metaphors, or bizarre ones. A flying bird is presumably far too weak as a metaphor for an airline, and the same goes for migrating birds for an estate agent.

Possibilities

Advanced abstract metaphors tend to miss their target. In image rhetoric, non-representative shapes and colours, which tend to

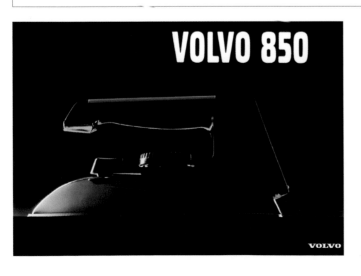

LEFT / To communicate the car's safety on the road, the art director and photographer have replaced its image with a household object: it runs as smoothly as an iron.

ABOVE / Press the 'control' button and and the ability to delete wrinkles becomes active – software becomes metaphor in a Saatchi & Saatchi campaign for Oil of Olay.

Presentative image

Synecdoche image

Synecdoche image

Metaphorical image

offer far too many possible interpretations to the receiver, act as warning signs.

So senders also have to watch out when illustrating metaphors. Choosing to illustrate the headline 'Time to sharpen your mind' that advertises a college with a picture showing a pencil sharpener isn't a good idea. The message doesn't lead anywhere. The same goes for the headline 'Swings on the stock exchange' in a TV financial programme, accompanied by a film of a children's swing. Instead they create a kind of circularity in the interplay between text and image, which doesn't benefit the message.

In Venice, the head of marketing, in consultation with his staff, chooses a green emerald as his metaphor. It is beautiful and mysterious, with great integrity. Androgynous and transcending borders. Just like the Venice Carnival. He looks pleased.

Volvo is a well-known car. This means that the car company and its ad agency can really give their advertising all they've got, including using metaphors. We have already seen that a car model is as fast as an arrow. But is it safe? A picture of an iron will do the job. The message? The car runs on the road as smoothly as an iron, of course. The metaphor made it an incisive message.

Metaphor can be over-extended sometimes, but when it really hits home, really makes the point it is aiming for, there's nothing to beat visual communication decorated with metaphors.

Case study: Rallying

Motor sports will form our final example of image rhetoric.

Rallying is a race for specially modified cars over long distances in poor terrain. The race is a tough test of speed and reliability. If you don't end up in the ditch, your gearbox is likely to pack up.

A newspaper is preparing a feature on the sport and the editorial team are focusing on the cars. The editor looks through the car archive and finds a photo of a rally car at a suggestive low angle, showing powerful tyres, bumpers, mud, dents and stickers – a *presentative* image.

In this editing work the metonymic image is left at that, but in order to further demonstrate the power of the sport, the editor brings up an image of the car in motion and trims it so that the picture is filled by just one of the wheels. Gravel and mud spray out from the tyre as it ploughs its way to the finish. It is a *synecdoche image*, showing a part, a detail, and letting us build the whole, the stress and strain, the audience along the road, the finish line, the winner's trophy, champagne being sprayed.

In a neighbouring office in the same building, a designer is working on a poster for the company behind the rally car. But this time it's a model for us ordinary, sane drivers. Reliability, safety and speed are the nuts and bolts of the message and the designer wants to demonstrate visually that the car will keep going practically anywhere. In the picture we see the car in very demanding terrain. We understand. It is a *synecdoche image* with both the part and the whole (as is always the case in advertising).

For an ad, an image of a hurdler is selected. It creates a comparison between the characteristics of the car and a fast, technically skilled athlete, flying over obstacles surely and speedily. The image of the car has been replaced by the image of the hurdler. We make an associative leap from the world of cars to the world of athletics and as soon as we have set foot on the track we understand the comparison. It is a successful *metaphorical* image.

LEFT / The range of images that can go into the depiction of a rally car – from a presentative shot of the Subaru all the way to a metaphorical shot of a hurdler.

CONTEXT

Irrespective of whether the sender uses informative, explicative, directive or expressive images, and irrespective of the image rhetoric chosen, the photograph or film now needs to be placed in a particular *context*. It is there, among other images, headlines, intros, columns, captions and logos, that the image plays its part in conveying the message.

The context may be *internal* or *external*.

Internal

The internal context of the image reveals its inner life, which can be created in different ways.

Everywhere we see dramatic images that are full of contrasts. In a fashion magazine the model displays a white silk dress in a dark and dirty factory setting. In the TV crime drama, the last and decisive battle is played out in the disused mine or at the deserted city docks.

Contradictory elements in an image, which don't seem to fit, arouse great interest in the receiver. Out of this clash, something new and exciting is born.

But a tranquil image can also radiate a calm lack of drama. The water shines like a mirror and in the misty morning light the city slowly comes to life.

External

The external context, the immediate environment in which the sender places the image, is important. The image can either harmonize with its environment or clash with it and create contradictions, conflict and contrast, like an image from nature against a glass and concrete wall in the city slums, or a picture of a caffè latte on an illuminated bus sign in the November gloom.

The context transforms the image

The secret of the image thus sometimes does not lie in the image itself but in what surrounds it, often making the image the subject of a remarkable transformation.

BELOW / Anything can happen to an image in an external context. A few short words, like yes or no, can completely change our interpretation of a photograph.

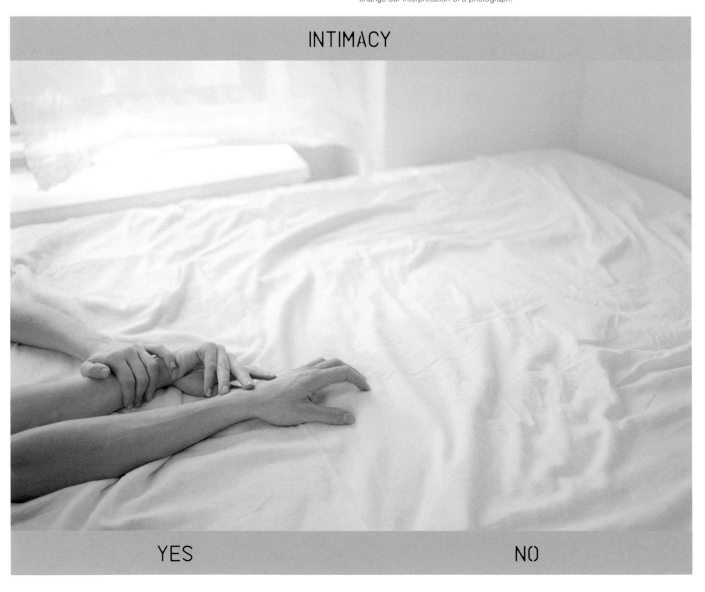

INTIMACY

YES   NO

□ flawed?

□ flawless?

Is beautiful skin only ever spotless?

campaignforrealbeauty.   Dove

ABOVE / By inviting us to chose the
heading, and thus the message, this
advert makes us participants.

Like a chameleon, the images will change according to the context in which they are viewed. The author Susan Sontag points out how different any one image can be when viewed on a contact sheet, in a gallery, on a placard at a political demonstration, in police records, in a photography magazine, in a book or on the living-room wall.

A simple, and actually quite harmless, image of a political demonstration can, in combination with a headline, text and design, be the most powerful and dramatic experience of the day for the receiver.

Headlines and other texts that appear next to the image are the most common examples of an external context that can change the content of the image from case to case.

The sensual image shown here takes on a completely different meaning depending on the text the sender chooses to place next to it. As we saw in the discussion of context earlier in the book, the external context can explain, reinforce and change the way an image is interpreted.

The heading 'intimacy' explains what we see in the image. The heading 'yes' gives an impression of a strong, shared, safe and loving encounter. An alternative heading – 'no' – gives completely different signals and associations. Here we see oppression and submission, changing the image and the message.

It is also the case that the various parts of an image are interpreted in different ways in different contexts. In one context a body might be experienced as soft and appealing, while in another it is experienced as hard and threatening.

HOW DO THE CLIENTS GET THE PICTURE THEY WANT?
The strategy is now agreed, as are the goal, the target group and the medium. The message looks strong in its draft form, but pictures, photographs or drawings need to be added. There are two distinct ways of working, each of which has its own advantages and disadvantages:

Hire a photographer
Approach a picture library

Photographer
There are many advantages to hiring a photographer. The company gets exactly the picture it needs. The partnership benefits the image and the message, as the photographer's expertize takes the client's ideas further and the finished result is often a pleasant surprise. The image is also tailored for a particular report or advertising campaign, and the client has exclusive use of it.

Picture library
The alternative is to search through a picture library (if we're talking about stills). This can be done by visiting the library, or searching on CD-ROM or via the web. This is considerably cheaper than the first option but, on the other hand, the client has to be content with the images that are available.

The picture editor in a picture library provides both *rights-managed* and *royalty-free pictures*. In the former case, the client pays for the picture depending on how and when it is to be used. In the latter case the client pays a one-off fee and is then free to use the image as he or she sees fit.

Some companies commission picture libraries to create an *image bank*. The aim is to profile the company in a certain way and in a coherent style. However, often the templates for the images are too narrow, having the opposite effect and making the company look uniform and rigid. It should be obvious to everyone that it is the specific message in the context of a specific activity that should determine which pictures are used. Nothing else.

THE PHOTOGRAPHER'S PERSPECTIVE

Despite the growth of amateurism, it is only in exceptional cases that a client takes their own photographs. Instead they order pictures from the photographer and therefore have to be aware of the opportunities offered by photography and film.

CATEGORIZING IMAGES

Let's start with the photographer's attempts to categorize pictures by looking at an example from an acclaimed exhibition in New York in 1978, entitled 'Windows and Mirrors'.

Windows

The first group, windows, covers photographs which depict reality in a direct and natural way. Photographers open the lens like a window on the world around them and record events without adding very much of themselves. They photograph what they see and what they have been commissioned to immortalize, such as a product under studio lighting or a person at work.

Newspapers, magazines and television are examples of media where these window images are shown and, of course, they also turn up in advertising.

Four motifs are particularly common. These are: *subjects* – people and animals; *objects* – things, and the relationships between subjects and objects; *situations* – events and actions; and *environments*.

This *objective* camera-as-window approach is used in an amusement park. A roller coaster is photographed at a distance, and it is easy for the observer to judge the height, length and the number of death-defying hills.

Mirrors

The second group, mirrors, covers personal photographs that reflect the creator of the image behind the camera and hint at a directing and organizing approach to the world (reminiscent of visible typography).

'I don't photograph what I see, I photograph what I feel,' a photographer explains. Strong emotions, such as hate and love, are projected on to the motif, and the finished photographic image sends back these same strong emotions, and looks the receiver (and the photographer) straight in the eye.

Window

Mirror

Mirror images tend to be found in photo galleries, but are also seen in newspapers, on television and in adverts.

This *subjective* camera-as-mirror approach is used to photograph the roller coaster from below to reinforce the sense of dizzy height. It's plain to see that the photographer is wary of heights.

First person

The subjective camera can also act as the eye of a person (also called *point of view shot*, or *POV),* which means that the receiver sees with someone else's eyes, the lens of the camera.

Back to that roller coaster. The camera is now right at the front of one of the cars, which quickly hurls itself down one of the steepest parts of the track, and the fear of heights is even clearer.

All-seeing eye

This means that the subjective camera can act as a free and all-seeing camera eye, as in a film or a computer game, and moves in the image space without being directly linked to a particular person or role.

The camera now seems to have wings and it flies above the roller coaster, sometimes nose-diving down towards the shrieking passengers.

Personality, time and responsibility

Let us leave the windows, the mirrors, the points of view and the all-seeing eye and instead try to work out what it is that makes a good photographer.

Maybe the required elements for a good photographer are personality, time and responsibility.

A skilled photographer allows his or her own personality to interact with the personality of the subject. After all, each subject contains something exciting, melancholy or frightening, and by opening up to these associations, to memories or to pain, the photographer can bring all these emotions together in an impressive photograph.

The photographer must be well-prepared, and must be ready to wait for the events to be depicted. He or she allows them to happen and attractive pictures will then be the result. Hurried and exaggerated arrangements should only be made in cases of extreme emergency.

The photographer takes responsibility by taking the camera close, but not *too* close, for example, to a person whose portrait is to be taken. There will always be a limit that must not be overstepped, and if it is, the subject will then lose their integrity and their dignity.

First person

All-seeing eye

ABOVE & LEFT / The wide, horizontal format invites a strong response, while a vertical format will feel tighter, but is useful for portraits. The square format can feel rather static, unless it is filled with an attractive composition.

THREE STRONG TOOLS

We now move on to the innermost secrets of the photographer's perspective of proximity, where we find the following three tools: *cut*, *composition* and *meaning*.

CUT

The motif (a beach) must be chosen and the viewpoint decided. The cut (a child with a beach ball) is the part of the motif captured by the limits of the lens in terms of height and width. The cut determines the format.

A photograph is happiest in the right shape and the photographer discovers, somewhat reluctantly, that the motif tends to find its own format, like a soap bubble, which determines its own size and characteristics.

The rectangular format

All formats have their own intrinsic energy, created by the tension between height and width. The greater the difference, the stronger the energy and dynamism, and the rectangular format is therefore the format which best attracts the eye of the receiver.

The *horizontal* rectangular format opens itself invitingly to the receiver. Like the broad white screen in the cinema or a window with panoramic sea views. Appropriately enough, *landscape* is the popular term for this format.

The *vertical* rectangular format is also common. Unlike the calm, horizontal landscape format, this creates dynamic movement vertically. Portraits, for example, are actively scrutinized by zigzagging from the top downwards and this format is known as *portrait*.

The vertical format can sometimes be experienced as being tight and ungenerous, like the narrow door that leads to the tempting beach outside.

The square format

This is less common in visual communication. Photographers even feel a certain amount of resistance to it. Nothing happens, many of them complain. This is probably because it is seen as static and lacking in excitement, and the square is a universal symbol for a lack of change.

Format is partly dictated by historical context, and is part of the atmosphere of the period. Churchill and Hitler look best in a square format, as that was the technique at the time. But news items and documentaries are now shown in widescreen, making these historical figures look strangely cut down.

The divine proportion

Humanity has always tried to determine mathematically the most beautiful and harmonious relationship between length and width. The answer was to be found in *the golden ratio*.

The Greek mathematician Euclid, who lived in the third and fourth centuries BC, outlined the golden ratio in his book *Elements*. It can be described as a line cut such that the smaller part (a) has the same ratio to the larger part (b) as the larger part has to the whole line:

$a:b = b:(a+b)$
$b:a = \phi = [\sqrt{5}+1]/2 = 1.618 \ldots$

The golden ratio can more simply be described (and is possibly easier to understand) by using the classic number series worked out by the Italian mathematician *Fibonacci* in the thirteenth century. This is based on the series 1, 2, 3, 5, 8, 13, 21, etc., in which each number in the series is the sum of the two preceding numbers, and where the last numbers calculated come increasingly closer to the exact relationship. This proportional relationship is used in architecture, in sculpture, in designing furniture and other everyday objects, in typography for books and magazines and, of course, in determining picture formats (for instance, 8 cm high, 13 cm wide).

BELOW / By using the golden ratio (also known as the divine proportion), attractive proportions of height and width can be created – here, 8 cm high by 13 cm wide.

COMPOSITION

Whatever the cut and the format, the picture must also have a clear design and composition.

The composition must be compatible with the meaning of the picture. A photograph that is to convey drama is, consequently, built up from strong contrasts and dynamic diagonals, while a poetic image is composed with a considerably lighter touch. This applies to stills as well as film.

There are countless principles for composing pictures. The task the photographer faces will demand many and sometimes tricky decisions, but also offers a wealth of opportunities, which are explored in what follows.

We'll start with the basics.

A&O

This stands for 'attracting and orienting', the fundamental requirements for an image.

Without the attention of the receiver, the photographer won't get far. The photograph must therefore first and foremost *attract,* which the picture as a whole often can. But a selected, dominant element might be more successful in attracting the receiver's eyes as a kind of starting point.

Orienting is just as important. The photographer has to create a clear way into the landscape of the image and there show how and in which order the various elements are to be read.

Images that are too overcrowded will be rejected by the receiver. Simple and pared down images are preferable. Take a leaf from the gardener's book, who knows that removing a few leaves and pruning a plant doesn't mean extinguishing life but granting it.

THE STRUCTURE OF THE IMAGE
The structure of the image refers to a consistent internal form.

Symmetry and asymmetry
The first question the photographer often asks is 'Where shall I place the subject I am going to photograph?'

Photographers often decide on a *symmetrical composition,* which means that the person, the tree or the car is centrally placed in the picture. The human eye is predisposed towards symmetry, which creates a pleasing order. This form of composition is called axial (as in typography) as it starts from a central axis. The picture radiates harmony and power, which in some circumstances can be precisely what the photographer is aiming for.

But some may find the symmetry monotonous and so try to give the image some movement.

BELOW / A successful composition demands a dominant element, which immediately attracts the eye, then guides viewers into the different parts of the image.

TOP / In this photo by Lee Friedlander, *Hill Crest, NY* (1970), the rule of thirds is used in a free and personal way. © Lee Friedlander, courtesy Fraenkel Gallery, San Francisco.

ABOVE / The asymmetrical picture becomes symmetrical if a gentle finger is placed over the girl (left); important elements are placed according to the rule of the thirds (right).

Asymmetrical composition, where the person, the tree, the car, is placed slightly to the left or the right in the composition, can create dynamism. This is not only about where exactly in the picture the photographer places the subject, but also about how much empty space is freed up. In a good asymmetrical photograph, a tension immediately arises between contrasting large and small areas.

Images in thirds

The rule of thirds can be a handy guide when you are trying to achieve a suitable asymmetrical composition. The photographer draws two lines dividing the format into thirds, or four lines dividing it into nine. This is a simple way of creating a dynamic grid of squares. Then these areas have to be filled so as to create contrasts between the larger and smaller areas. The most important

ABOVE / This is a picture full of
contrasts – light against dark, horizontal
against diagonal, warm against cold.

part of the picture (perhaps a face or an eagle) is ideally placed on
one of the crosses and the photographer immediately then gains
a strong composition, as all these intersections have something
magical about them.

Contrasts

The dynamism of images that are full of contrasts attracts the
human eye, which is drawn to the lightest part of an otherwise
dark picture or is greatly attracted to a conflict between two elements in the image, one large and one small.

Size, shape, strength and *colour contrasts* are the most common (as in typography). A powerful and dominant element tells us
that this is the starting point of the picture. The contrasts can then
orient the viewer further through the image.

Composition is all about directing these forces in order to
create strong pairs of opposites. As we all know, opposites
attract, and it is often extremely important to manage the tension
between order and chaos by emphasizing, by under-emphasizing
and by exaggerating.

The pairs of opposites can be:

Large / small
Straight / curved
Near / far
Black / white
Dark / light
Heavy / light
Inside / outside
Horizontal / vertical
Positive / negative

A balancing act

The perspective of a photographer on achieving balance is illumi-
nating: 'Fascinated, I gaze into the viewfinder. I move the camera
so that the cyclist is in the left-hand side of the picture against a
light background. I compensate for his presence on the left with a
larger area gleaming attractively on the right. The two shapes, the
cyclist and the light window, balance each other.'

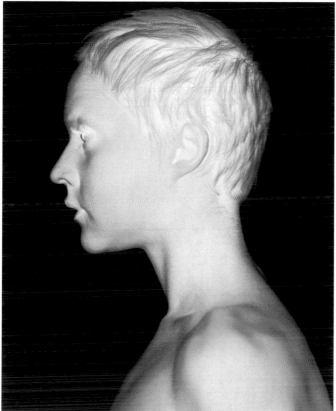

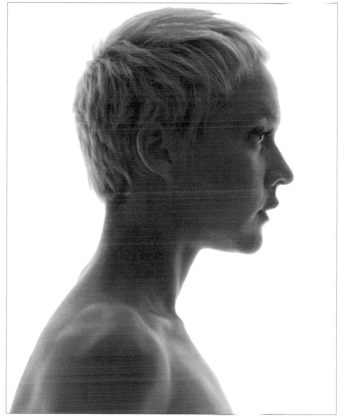

TOP / Besides balance, contrast can be the soul of an image – here distance and proximity, coldness and warmth, and movement and stillness all meet.

ABOVE / More powerful contrasts – this time negative against positive.

BUILDING UP IMAGES

The composition of the image, and the interplay between its various parts, are both part of building up an image.

Areas of the image space

The space in photographic images is made up of:

Foreground
Middle ground
Background

In the large courtyard by the glazed entrance to the Louvre in Paris the water stands out in the *foreground* of the picture, while in its *middle ground* we see part of the entrance itself with its characteristic glass pyramid. In the *background* the receiver sees the main building of the Louvre, in one of whose galleries the Mona Lisa smiles her intriguing smile behind bullet-proof glass.

IMAGE DEPTH

Some images lack any depth and the receiver's gaze cannot wander particularly far. Such images are often perceived as both flat and unwelcoming.

In other images the gaze can range across forests, mountains and seas. And in sequences of images a sense of life and rhythm can be created by switching between different depths.

Overlapping elements

One basic approach is to allow one detail to partly cover or hide another. The receiver immediately perceives one as being close (in the foreground) and the other as further away (in the background). This is known as *graduating* the image space.

Large elements

Equally fundamental is the method of allowing one large element to dominate at the front of the image. When this technique is used, everything else in the image is seen in a kind of depth relationship to this.

Dark elements

Proper depth is created when the photographer allows part of the cut which forms the foreground to be very dark. The human eye then registers the depth of the image, and if the middle ground and the background are light, the experience of depth is reinforced even further.

BELOW / An image full of depth, with water in the foreground, the glass pyramid in the middle ground and silhouettes of the Louvre in the background.

ABOVE / The dark element in the foreground – the back of a man – helps to convey a feeling of depth, as does the blurred background, in this famous image by Robert Doisneau, *Kiss by the Hôtel de Ville* (1950).

Blurred elements

The receiver also perceives an image as being deep when the photographer allows the middle ground and especially the background of the picture to be blurred. The same thing happens in real life where the eye suffers from a limited depth of field.

Some photographers fall in love with *selective blurring* and have the main motif, a person, blurred and the background in sharp focus. Images like this tend to bemuse the receiver, but can be justified when maintaining the anonymity of the subject is a consideration.

LIGHT IN IMAGES

We cannot see without light, and images cannot be created without light. Light is thus a prerequisite for the image, but also part of the composition.

Composition using light

Using lines, shapes and fields alone, it can be difficult to achieve either a real sense of depth or an exciting composition, but great things can be created with the help of light. Shadows appear and the surface gains in volume, the circle swells into a sphere and the square into a cube.

Light is also a major source of information, enabling the receiver to understand whether in the world of the image it is day or night, indoors or outdoors. Light also conveys more sophisticated information about danger and security. Dark images are naturally seen as more dramatic than light, which instead convey feelings of freedom and innocence.

Natural light creates a special atmosphere, and artificial light a completely different one. Sometimes a combination of these different kinds of light can be the most effective.

Direct light — Indirect light

Front light — Back light

Side light — Shadows

ABOVE / Natural light helps to give a documentary feel to a picture, as in this photograph by Jens Lucking.

RIGHT / A variety of lighting directions are employed in fashion shoots – such effects, and the shadows they create, can be particularly striking in black and white.

Lighting

Different use of lighting allows the photographer to create hard or soft light:

DIRECT LIGHT

This hits the subject directly and often creates hard shadows.

INDIRECT LIGHT

This is bounced off a studio screen or a wall before reaching the subject. This reflected light softly models a face, for example.

FILTERED LIGHT

Light passes through a colour filter to introduce a particular colour. Using this technique, the photographer can also contrast several colours, e.g., a cold bluish tone and a warm red.

Direction of light

The direction of the light source in relation to the camera can considerably change the subject, as anyone who has ever played with a torch in front of a mirror knows. If the torch is placed under the face, a frightening expression is created, while light from the side gives a considerably kinder-looking face.

Possible directions are:

FRONT LIGHTING

The photographer has the light behind him or her and it falls directly on the subject, flattening the subject so that the person looks like a cardboard cut-out.

BACK LIGHTING

The light source is behind the subject and shines directly towards the camera, creating a dark silhouette effect, and the photographer adjusts the exposure in relation to the background. If he or she judges the exposure in relation to a person's face, the background will be very over-exposed.

SIDE LIGHTING

When the light comes from the side, it softly and naturally models the subject and its volume, much as daylight through a window does in a room.

Shadows

Light and shadow in an image are crucial for the receiver's perception and interpretation. Images which completely or partly lack shadows often give a hard, eroded impression, and without a shadow, the location of a foot, a bucket or a lantern in the image space will lack definition. Shadow anchors the subject and provides information on the characteristics of the floor, for example – sanded or unsanded, wet or dry.

A basic rule is that light should come from the top left-hand corner and the shadow will then be formed in the bottom right-hand corner.

ORIENTATION

Most pictures have inherent motion, and the elements of the image grab the receiver and take him or her with them. The elements can be oriented in countless different ways, but the five most common are:

Horizontal
Vertical
Diagonal
Circular
Triangular

Horizontal

A horizontally oriented image is experienced by the receiver as calm and harmonious, as the motion energy will not be particularly strong. Horizontal motion dominates, of course, and this will be reinforced by a horizontal format, but it would be countered by a vertical format.

Vertical

The receiver perceives a vertically oriented image as somewhat more dynamic. Vertical motion dominates, reinforced by a vertical format, though it is countered by a horizontal format.

Diagonal

Real speed and dynamism do not really appear until the image is oriented diagonally. A line or space becomes most active if it is oriented from corner to corner.

The human eye is used to an organized interplay between the horizontal and vertical, and the diagonal puts this interplay out of true. The diagonal also creates a strong sense of depth, which effectively draws, and almost throws, the receiver into the image.

ABOVE / Orientation and format reinforce one another, though sometimes a clash between a tall building and a horizontal format can create tension.

This orientation often focuses on a single point a long way into the picture. Lines and spaces are then *converging*, i.e., moving *towards* this point. They can also be *diverging*, i.e., radiating *from* a certain point.

The diagonal orientation can also be built up from several diagonals in different directions. The photographer knows that sometimes you have to balance too powerful a diagonal with a lesser one in the opposite direction.

Circular

Compositions that are circular give the impression of both harmony and unbroken movement, and the circle is quite rightly a universal symbol of wholeness and completion. The composition might consist of a group of friends standing chatting. The oval, a cousin to the circle, is also common.

Triangular

The triangle is a symbol of the tripartite nature of the universe – sky, earth and humanity – and it can be used either upright or inverted.

The upright version (in which one of the sides forms the base) gives a light and harmonious impression, as in a group portrait of three people. A picture similar to an inverted, precarious triangle creates considerably more dynamism.

MOTION IN IMAGES

A still image stands still, obviously, but an effective way of creating a sense of movement is to use the *motion blur* that has occurred naturally, or to simply plan for it when taking the photograph. In a picture of a hand, for example, not much blurring is needed for the still image to come to life. It is the contrast between

BELOW / Converging lines can help give a sense of perspective, drawing the viewer into the image and giving it life.

BOTTOM / The circle and the triangle are two arrangements that can add interest to photographs of groups of people.

The 180-degrees rule

ABOVE / A person shown in continuous movement should be filmed from one side only. To ensure a stable sequence, a Steadicam can be used.

the sharp and the blurred, the still (the beach) and the moving (the waves), that creates the sense of movement.

Appealing direction

The photographer can also use the *direction of movement* of the image to carry the receiver away. An image will always have a direction, and thus seems to be heading a certain way, like a face in profile or a galloping horse. The photographer can use the direction to keep the receiver in the picture by having the directions run towards the centre of the image. Of course he or she can also open up the image and let them head outwards towards other images or other material.

Photographers often talk about a picture's 'home side' and 'away side'. This means that a direction from left to right is seen as moving away, while a direction from right to left will be seen as moving home.

It's important to always allow space for direction and movement in the image. If the express train is heading in a particular direction in a picture, the train needs room to move, otherwise the edges of the picture will swiftly bring the train's movement to a shuddering halt.

Agreed direction

There is thus a kind of unspoken but still clear agreement between the photographer and the viewer of the image when it comes to image direction.

It is important to remember that this tacit agreement applies only in the West. The story is told of an international pharmaceutical company which learned a rather expensive lesson in an Arab country. People who saw the advertisement could not understand why an apparently well and happy person would take medicine in order to become really ill (and one can only agree with them). It was only later that the marketing department realized that Arabs don't just read text from right to left, but also pictures.

The 180-degrees rule

If a film cameraman shows a person in continuous movement, in several sequences of film, their appearance, the direction of movement, the speed, lighting, sound and colour must match from picture to picture. Otherwise there is a risk that the receiver will not be able to follow the story.

The cameraman should not film the subject from different directions, but only from *one* direction within a sector of 180 degrees. In this way the audience feels that the person really is going in a particular direction. If sequences are filmed outside these 180 degrees, it will often look as though the person has turned round and is now on the way back again, which can confuse the audience.

In televized football matches, viewers can avoid this confusion through signs ('reverse angle'), which indicate that a certain sequence is filmed from a different point and that the player isn't scoring an own goal.

What is good film camera work?

A good film sequence should be built up simply. The main event must be clear, and ideally the image should not have more than one subject at a time, and everything unnecessary and disruptive should be removed.

It's important not to use flat lighting. Instead light the scene so that different objects become separated from each other and thus create depth. The cameraman can also use a short depth of field so that objects both in front of and behind the main subject are blurred.

Camera movements

The film camera often stands still but of course it can move too.

PANNING

This is when the camera is moved horizontally during recording, for example across the windows on the wall of a house.

TRACKING

This describes the camera travelling next to something that is moving (some trotting horses or a speeding car).

TILT

This vertical camera movement enables the camera to follow parachutists from the second they leave the plane until they land on a church tower.

ZOOM

This means two things: firstly zooming in, using the lens to come closer to the subject (a person talking) and secondly zooming out, backing away from a close-up and instead showing more and more of the surroundings (the person is talking to an audience).

FILMING INTERVIEWS

When a reporter carries out an interview, it can be filmed using a method called *shot/reverse shot*, which means that the television viewers see the reporter asking the questions and the interviewee when responding.

However, often the person interviewed is long-winded and the visual narrative suffers, so the reporter is cut in reacting to what the interviewee says. This shot is called a *cross-cut*, which adds variety and life to the interview.

Another common feature is a *two-shot*, where the audience sees the person being interviewed slightly to the left of the picture and the shoulders of the reporter to the right. A *reversed two-shot* is when the audience sees the reporter slightly to the right from the front, and the shoulder of the interviewee in the foreground on the left.

The pictures of the interview must match its content, otherwise there will be a double message. If, in a report about a street robbery, an elderly lady expresses her deep fear of leaving her flat, she must be filmed in her flat. Another person also interviewed, who doesn't think it is dangerous to go out, can be filmed in the street (or maybe even in a park after dark). The context thus reinforces the news item.

DISTANCE AND ANGLE

The photographer chooses the distance from and angle to the subject at the moment the photograph is taken. Depending on the subject and the context, the photographer can choose between:

Close-up
Mid-shot
Long shot

Close-up

Every day we see stereotypical close-ups in newspapers and magazines, and for ceremonial occasions such as weddings and major birthdays. But in fact close-ups are fascinating because they create intimacy. The smallest object can be loaded with meaning and we see it with new eyes.

Close-ups of a person can be arranged in different ways. The most common and probably the most conventional method is to place the face precisely in the middle of the format.

LEFT / In a news report about street violence, a frightened elderly lady is filmed inside her safe home, thus implying that she is too scared to go out ...

ABOVE / A girl's legs in close-up, her cropped body in a mid-shot, and the whole person in the long shot.

RIGHT / The worm's eye view (above) immediately creates a sense of superiority, while the bird's eye view (below) creates the opposite, inferiority.

It is considerably worse to have too much space above the face. The result often creates a sense that the person in question is slowly sinking down and out of the picture.

Instead, a more exciting approach is to place the person higher up and actually cut slightly into their hair or even forehead. This gives a sense of closeness, roughly like getting together over a small table in a café.

Mid-shot
These are ideal for clarifying personal and social relationships, focusing on the person as the subject.

Long shot
Long and extreme long shots allow space for the setting and the atmosphere. The person can be depicted at work and at play, in the city and in the countryside.

These three types of picture can be used in a single context to work together effectively, e.g., in a magazine article.

ANGLE TO THE SUBJECT
The camera angle is not unimportant in image composition – two common and very useful angles take their names from the animal kingdom:

Worm's eye view
Bird's eye view

Worm's eye view
The photographer creates this effect by placing the camera low down, which can make a person in a picture look very important, even superior.

Bird's eye view
Here, the photographer places the camera high up, which has the opposite effect, making a person in a picture look less important, even interior.

Both views can be used in dramatic storytelling, where the status of the characters is fundamental.

ABOVE / Disruptive elements in a photo can be removed. Focusing on one part of the picture or dramatizing it can enliven an image.

IMAGE PROCESSING

It is very rare that an image can be placed directly in a visual arrangement in its original form. As a rule images need to be processed in some way.

Cropping

This is one of the most common actions carried out by the photographer, but often it is the designer who finally decides on the relationship between height and width.

An image should ideally be cropped to improve or reinforce its form and content. Cropping gives the image a new format, which in turn should influence the design of the magazine page on which it will appear.

Doing it the other way round, fixing on a certain design and letting the cropping be determined by the amount of space left on the page, is a much worse approach. And the crop that results will usually be poor.

In practice the cropping process usually involves:

Reducing
Focusing
Dramatizing

REDUCING

This refers to the removal of disruptive elements in an image. These may be an eye-catching detail in the background or half of a person on their way into or out of the picture.

FOCUSING

This emphasizes part of the picture. A person who plays an important role can thus easily be brought forward or a frightening detail can be served up to the receiver in a surprising way.

DRAMATIZING

A picture can have life shaken into it. Maybe there is an extreme contrast to exploit, a reflection in a window or a blinding reflection of light. The photographer can also tilt the picture and thus gain a different and dramatic perspective. The sea leans and the road goes straight up into the sky.

REMOVING THE BACKGROUND

In many images the central subject is drowning in a busy background. The solution to the problem is often simply removing the background altogether to liberate the main player in the image (a technique used in *vignettes)*.

Even with a calm and neutral background, there can be reason to remove it, in order to create a clear focus, for example on a face.

RHYTHM

Photographers sometimes try to create a kind of filmic effect despite having only still pictures at their disposal. Here they put the photographs together in sequences which are all linked together and form a suggestive whole.

It is important to create an exciting rhythm with pauses and changes in tempo, as in music. Pictures which are similar in colour and cut, frame for frame, won't create good films, articles, advertisements or websites. Instead the photographer should go for rhythmical contrasts which create visual collisions (as with Eisenstein in Chapter 2) so that long shots are placed against close-ups and light against dark.

COLLAGE

Plenty of good images to choose from, a generous newspaper format and a staging which will only gain from being portrayed in a multifaceted manner – these are the ingredients not only for a designer's perfect day, but also for a collage that, correctly executed, can be exciting and appealing.

It's important for the subeditor and designer not to make all the pictures the same size. Otherwise the collage runs the risk of being an impenetrable mass, like a chess board. A better approach is to give one image the starring role and allow it to dominate. This creates a stronger dynamic whole and gives receivers a clear way into the material. They quickly understand where they should start looking.

It is also important that the images are allowed to convey different kinds of information. A close-up creates a portrait of a person and a full shot gives a sense of the setting, which is important to the context.

The *before and after* message requires access to two images which together show what something used to be like and what it was like after a specific action was taken. A factory building was renovated (in a newspaper article), the coastal idyll was smashed to pieces by a storm (in a television newscast) and wrinkles disappeared (in a TV advertising spot).

The style might be a little hackneyed, but the receiver appreciates the clear lesson, even if (in the example of advertising) it is done with an ironic glint in the eye.

BELOW / Using plenty of strong images can create an exciting collage – it is important to use contrasting sizes, crops and colours, as in these spreads from

Italian magazine *Colors*, designed by Fernando Gutiérrez.

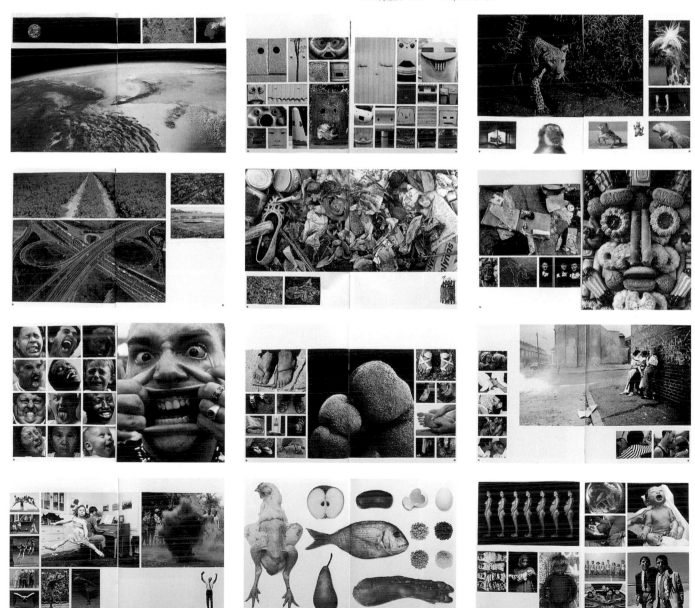

ABOVE / Soft cuts create suggestive sequences, which gently weave the whole film together.

EDITING

This is possibly the most important phase in making the story in a film attractive. The tempo and rhythm are crucial to the audience, as a fast tempo creates exciting tension, while a calm tempo turns the film into a poetic or epic tale. Double exposures and frozen images add new dimensions to the storytelling.

Editing can make things move fast, as in a film when the journey from New York was shown in two cuts. Passport checked at JFK, a dry Martini knocked back on the plane, passport checked again on arrival at Charles de Gaulle.

Cuts can be *hard* or *soft*. Hard cuts create a dramatic break in the film, as in the classic *The Deer Hunter* in which the audience was brusquely moved from a small town in the US to fighting in 1970s Vietnam.

Soft cuts aren't as easily recognizable, especially when sequences merge into each other.

What are known as *cutaway shots* can often be used in film. They can be photographed from a completely different angle and are a kind of transitional image that is useful in countering contrasting or jerky cuts, e.g., in news reports.

They can also be used to consciously create surprising and exciting breaks in the chain of images.

MEANING

Many things contribute to the meaning of an image. The intention of the client sets off the photographer, who, with cuts and composition, takes the image towards a meaning, which in turn meets the eyes of the receiver. Maybe the receiver sees what the client and the photographer see, maybe not. However, one thing is certain, which is that the receiver doesn't merely consume the image passively. Instead the receiver becomes a co-producer, creating his or her own meaning for it.

This is not to say that the work of the client and the photographer is meaningless, but that dedicated effort increases the chances of influencing the receiver as intended. It doesn't mean you should hand over an unfinished image, as some artists do, to the receiver (who will do their own thing with it anyway). That's just a poor excuse for not finishing your work properly.

Next we'll find out a little more about this co-producing receiver, but let us first attempt to summarize the difficult art of adding pictures to a message, or staging.

ADDING THE PICTURES

Four points for the subeditor, art director and designer to consider:

Personal attitude

You have to look to yourself and come to terms with your feelings ahead of the job. Is it relevant? Exciting? A waste of time? What can be improved and what opportunities are there?

Message

Should the picture support an instrumental message, which promises to solve a problem, or a relational message, which promises well-being? Should the page of the newspaper be filled with a current event dramatically staged or is a non-dramatic image required, describing something which has already happened?

Angle

Will a direct window image work, as an attempt at objective reporting, or a subjective image reflecting the client and the photographer?

Does the subject demand an informative image, an explicative or directive one, or possibly an expressive image that will inspire certain emotions in the receiver?

Reinforcement

Is stronger language required to convince the audience? Can metonymy, synecdoche or metaphor be brought into play?

THE RECEIVER'S PERSPECTIVE

The receiver, the viewer, takes visual impressions from the image with the help of *perception*, *experience* and *interpretation*.

PERCEPTION

Let's begin with perception, our visual impression, with which we fill our consciousness.

The components of the image
The image is filled with large and small components and they are more interesting than one might think:

Dots
Lines
Spaces

These can appear in different sizes, shapes, colours, structures, shadows and lightnesses. Together these small components in various guises form what we, in everyday language, call pictures.

The smallest components are *basic elements*, which have a kind of non-meaning. If dots, lines and spaces are put together into an interpretable combination, they are *part meanings*.

Eye-movement cameras show that our eyes move jerkily over an image before we read it as a whole. The pattern of movement and our reading of the image are naturally affected by our interest, knowledge and familiarity with images. Law students may prefer pictures constructed simply; picture editors may be attracted by more demanding ones.

Small dots together form changes in colour, which in turn form a grain in something that looks like wood. Viewers possibly see a planed board or two in front of them, and these form something that looks like a ladder.

If the viewer then combines a number of part meanings into a larger unit, the result will be a *full meaning*. The picture before the viewer might consist of a ladder and 13 planks. The receiver has built a jetty and is soon gazing out over the water of the small bay.

The image thus consists of:

Basic elements
Part meanings
Full meanings

FIGURE AND BACKGROUND
If the viewer is to be able to make any sense of the picture at all, something must take on the role of a figure, a central eye-catching element, which clearly stands out against a background.

EASY TO IDENTIFY
The simpler the figure, the more likely it is that the viewer will perceive it correctly. Circles, squares and especially triangles are all easily identified shapes which the eye is eagerly drawn to. If the figure consists of several parts and these appear next to each other, there is a greater chance of the viewer seeing them as a coherent whole.

BELOW / Seeing an image, the viewer will start to build it up into a whole. Basic elements create part meanings, which in turn create full meanings.

DIFFICULT TO IDENTIFY

The main figure is clearly sought after and is eager to appear, but may also elude the viewer, who is forced to shift their way of looking at the image. Now the viewer sees a fine glass goblet, now two profiles. Pictures like this can be fascinating, but can also be perceived as elusive and hard to interpret.

THE MONITOR OF THE BRAIN

According to gestalt psychology the brain has been blessed with a sense of order, helping us to organize the chaotic world we live in.

We try to put together all the signals from the world around us into manageable and comprehensible wholes, or gestalts, on the basis of our ability to see shapes and patterns. Almost by reflex our eyes and brain turn slight differences in colour in the moss into a path which will take us out of the forest.

To survive, animals and people alike have to quickly identify risks wherever they appear: movements, contrasts, a glimpse of a detail that, with other impressions, means danger, creating life-saving tenths of a second. The hen wasn't a fox's prey, at least not today.

GOOD AND BAD GESTALTS

Visual communication isn't always that dramatic. Gestalt psychologists tend to talk more about good and bad gestalts. Bad gestalts are rejected by the viewer as it is hard to bring any sense of order to them. The eye flits aimlessly around.

Good gestalts are characterized by simplicity, contrast, regularity and continuity, and thus capture us immediately. They are derived from the *gestalt laws*, which are based on the knowledge that the human eye and brain find it easier to read pictures in which different elements or figures form wholes that can be interpreted.

In the early twentieth century several gestalt laws were formulated – three are particularly applicable to visual communication:

The law of proximity
The law of similarity
The law of closedness

The law of proximity

Figures that belong together should be close to each other. If some people in an image are standing close together, they are naturally seen as a delimited group with something in common.

The law of similarity

The viewer also easily reads an image in which different figures are similar to each other. This identification is made easier by a group wearing similar clothes, for example, like football players wearing identical colours and sponsors' logos.

The law of closedness

If some figures close off a composition from the outside, it is easy for viewers to identify and interpret elements delimited in this way.

The image can be composed so that a window, tree branches or a group of people frame or close off part of the picture from the rest of it. A person who is in this closed space in the image is experienced by the viewer as being part of the group or, conversely (and more excitingly), as having been captured by it.

Proximity

Similarity

Closedness

EXPERIENCE

So much for perception, now on to experience.

We reflect ourselves in pictures, but we see someone else who is living another life in another reality with completely different experiences. The picture shifts angle and approach and suddenly we have another sex, another skin colour, we are at our most beautiful or our most ugly. We are participating in a war, committing murder, making peace.

But how do we make these experiences our own? What is it in the image that constantly creates the attraction, the fear and the mystery, on an emotional level? To answer this question we will borrow some theories from the world of the theatre, where dramatists and dramaturges often make three demands of a play.

Space
Focal point
Point of pain

Space

All storytelling must take place in a space of some kind. The drama has its stage, backdrop and wings and the image has its cut and format. This is where everything happens and it is towards this space that the receiver's eye is expectantly directed.

Focal point

But the space isn't quite enough. The viewer needs an eye-catching focal point, which must step forward and detach itself from the background. Like the main role on a stage, a figure, a gestalt, a person, an event, maybe more, will create attraction and excitement. Like the child and parent in Maria Miesenberger's picture.

Point of pain

But the viewer is still not completely satisfied. A point of pain is needed. This can be completely visible and clear, and speak directly to the viewer, but can of course also be invisible and perhaps touch the viewer disturbingly.

This point of pain is the image's communicative engine, constantly working to reach its audience, and it must tug at the

BELOW / To reach out to the viewer, a photograph needs a space, a focal point, and a 'point of pain'. They can all be found in this work by artist Maria Miesenberger (left), while the shocking photograph of an Iraqi prisoner (right) also contains a point of pain, like all pictures of abuse and torture.

ABOVE / Something is wrong – according to Roland Barthes, the little boy's cap in this image is too big, and therefore not his own. This query creates heightened interest and raises questions for the viewer.

viewer's heartstrings. A memory, a weak position, a conflict, a lack, a loss must emerge, as with Miesenberger's picture.

There is also a point of pain in the image of the lone Iraqi prisoner on his flimsy pedestal. He is draped in black, with a hood, connected to electricity and the floor seems stained with blood.

Does this picture also contain a secret? Maybe. There is something beyond the shocking image which reveals torture and war crimes. It must be the scaled-down composition and simplicity, which becomes a kind of archetypal image of human pain and a symbol of vicarious suffering. The outstretched arms in the shape of a cross reinforce this experience and possibly this is the image's secret, which we take to our hearts and never forget. Maybe pictures like these can change attitudes to war and the other horrors of our world.

We will leave this hook for another point, which shares some of the same features.

SOMETHING IS WRONG!

A point, a remarkable point, will take us further on this journey through the land of secrets and experiences. The French image rhetorician Roland Barthes claimed that there are two categories of image. One he called *studium*, the other *punctum*. The first group of photographs can be analysed verbally, while the second cannot be captured in words.

Studium

This refers to a general observation of the world around us. The motif is there but does not arouse particularly great interest and Barthes believed that pictures like this belong more to the photographer than the viewer. They are not 'experienced'.

Punctum

In an image there is often something the viewer perceives as being wrong without really being able to put a finger on it – the punctum. It is as though one piece of a jigsaw was missing and this forces one to look for an explanation, which is not always obtained.

Barthes gave a name to a kind of wordless point, an emotional thrust, an arrow that is shot out from the image and hits and wounds the viewer, who realizes that some experiences cannot be turned into words, but instead create layer upon layer of meaning. Quite a few words to describe something which can't be described using words!

ABOVE / In this photograph by Robert Capa taken in Barcelona in 1937, there is not only a punctum (it looks like the girl has done up her coat with the wrong button), but there is also a creeping presence of something dangerous – it can't be seen in the image, but is only hinted at outside the frame.

THE ADJOINING ROOM

Some images offer an exciting interplay between what viewers see, and what they don't see but suspect exists outside the picture's frame. Here, people (in the image) are frightened by the air raid warning (outside the picture) and head for the shelters during the Spanish Civil War. This is called the relationship between the *positive* and *negative* room of the image and can also be described as the relationship between the room and the adjoining room (with other voices and events).

It is as if the very edge of the image attracts the eye and the viewer asks what is going on outside it. There is of course something above, below, to the left and to the right of what we see and also behind what we see (as well as behind the camera itself). Outside the cut the photographer has chosen or outside the cropping carried out by the subeditor or designer, there is an invisible, attractive, external context.

The negative space has a strong and unique charge. No image draws as much life from what is shown as it does from what is not shown.

The viewer constantly fills in what is outside the image, completing the negative space.

INTERPRETATION

It's not always easy to read, express and agree on what an image contains and means, and the interpretations of any group of viewers will often diverge wildly. The image sneaks away from its purpose and fertilizes the viewer's imagination. From this point the viewer 'owns' the image, and it is here that the greatest difficulty in visual communication lies.

Some behavioural researchers also claim that most viewers have the developmental level of a ten-year-old when it comes to photographs and illustrations. If this is true, it means that few people understand the language of images or the messages where the image plays an important role. It also means that just as few people appreciate the art and finesse of the photographer.

Unambiguous

The image on the next page will serve as an example. Most people will agree that it shows a house reflected in water, so establishing the image's *denotative content*. This is called the image's *core meaning* or *basic meaning*, and refers to the meaning of the image

ABOVE / There are three levels of image experience and interpretation. The denotative content gives us a basic meaning, the connotative content adds additional meaning, and there are also private associations, which we as viewers make on a very personal level.

that most people will interpret in roughly the same way. The image becomes unambiguous and the visual communication has every chance of being successful. Denotation is a process carried out by the left hemisphere of the brain.

Ambiguous

But now it gets more difficult. If the group of viewers continue to interpret the image, going into greater depth and trying to agree on what is going on, they soon notice that the debate becomes intense and extended.

The images become ambiguous and the chance of communication can be made more difficult, or even lost completely. If the house is reflected in the water, shouldn't it be upside down? Is the picture of something else? A terrorist attack? An earthquake? Mental illness? We are approaching the image's *connotative content,* a kind of *additional meaning* or *connotation*, which is strongly influenced by the viewer's experiences and associations. The ability to associate is one of the typical characteristics of the right hemisphere of the brain.

The connotations are culturally dependent and therefore shared by different groups with the same shared values and interests.

Private

A third level is *private associations*, where the viewer is completely alone. The viewer might have a very personal relationship to the picture because when it was taken – in Venice last year, during the carnival, there was a bad smell, the viewer felt dizzy and some people in masks appeared threatening.

Personal and universal

The strictly personal interpretation need not result in a communication disaster. The photographer knows that an image that deeply moves one receiver in the right way will in all likelihood do the same to others. The most personal is also often the most universal, as we see for the second time in this book.

ARCHETYPE

This is the term for an unconscious symbol that originates from our genetic inheritance. The psychoanalyst Carl Jung originally coined the term after the Greek *archetypos*, which means 'first of its kind'.

According to the theory, through archetypes we perceive a kind of contact with our ancestors, even with the very first humans. Our unconscious uses archetypes to tell us something that we would be wise to listen to.

There are archetypal *gestalts*, such as the mother, the father and the village elder, and there are also archetypal *events* such as birth, marriage and death. Sun and fire are examples of archetypal *objects*.

There are many people who doubt the existence of archetypes, while others strongly feel the presence of the existential in the face of images which have eternal motifs such as clouds and the horizon. This is why images with seductive views of the sea, of wind and water, as their background, are so common in car advertisements, for example. Human companionship around the burning campfire on the beach is also, as we know, common the world over.

IMAGE ANALYSIS

There is a widespread disinclination to analyse images. This may be because analysis says so much about the person doing the analysing.

There is also a paradox here. In analysing a photograph, we have to use words, and these belong to a completely different language from visual language. This translation work, which must then be done, can completely mislead, as the photograph is filled with wordless secrets.

Parts and the whole

Nevertheless, we start the analysis. It breaks an object into pieces, with the aim of understanding and describing the constituent parts, their relationship to each other and to the whole.

Many people are sceptical about taking an image to pieces, as they want to experience it as it is, as a whole, and are perhaps happy merely to say whether it moves them or not. But in professional visual communication work, more is required. A subeditor, an art director and a designer have to go further than merely saying that an image is good or bad. They must be able to determine whether the photograph has communicative force or not.

A METHOD FOR IMAGE ANALYSIS

Image analysis therefore becomes necessary in all visual communication. One method of analysis is based on asking the following questions:

What is the picture of?
How is it built up?
In what context is it shown?
Who is it aimed at?
Who is the sender?
What is its purpose?

Let's take another look at the advert from Chapter 2 with the baby in the dark cellar.

Of?

The picture is of a baby who is preparing to inject the content of a syringe. With the help of his mouth, the baby tightens a cord around the upper arm in order to find a usable vein.

With only a nappy on, the baby is sitting on a tiled floor, in a dirty corner of a cellar. On the floor there are remains from earlier injections. Beside the baby's face a name is reproduced almost like a heading: John Donaldson, age 23.

BELOW / Archetypes can move us profoundly, resonating with a collective unconscious.

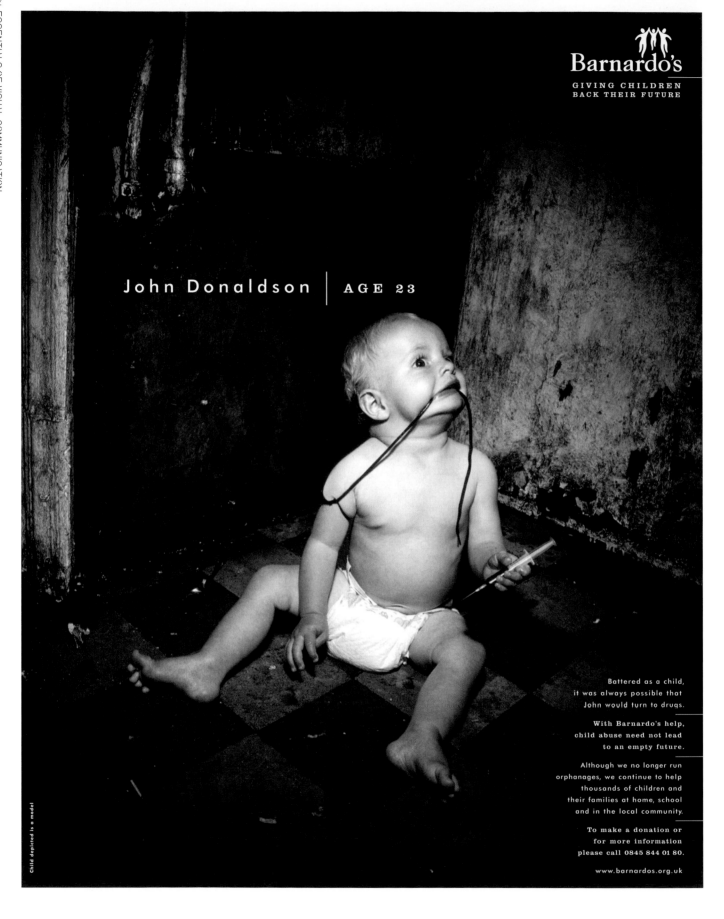

Built up?

The baby is placed in the middle of the image space, almost completely centred. The photograph is taken from a bird's eye view. A ceiling lamp lightens him up and makes him the central figure, in strong contrast to the dark cellar. His strongly twisted head as well as his arms and legs all point in different directions, creating an effective focal point.

Context?

The picture is shown in an advert, which forms the image's inner context, supplemented with the name, age, a text column and a logotype.

The advert is part of a campaign, and is reproduced in its external context in several daily papers in Britain, where it is competing with the news, with its distribution of text and images.

The external context of the image includes this book, in which it is being analysed.

Aimed at?

Who is the target group? In this case it is the readers of the papers, who represent a rather broad cross-section of the general public.

Sender?

The sender is the children's charity Barnardo's, whose vision is that the lives of all children and young people should be free from poverty.

Purpose?

The image is the most important part in this instrumental message, which clearly and dramatically points out the problem: poverty leads to child abuse, leading children to grow up to be addicted to alcohol and drugs.

In the same picture, with the help of a name and age, childhood and manhood, presence and future, are woven together creating a message, which doesn't only attract our attention but also arouses strong feelings. The image wraps up 23 years to one dramatic point. The name charges the message with a personal focus without losing its universality.

It is a synecdoche image, with the intention of affecting viewers by showing the part (the baby, doomed from birth) so they understand the whole (poverty, and what it leads to).

Barnardo's feel they can stop this dangerous development by means of support and help for the children and their families, at home, at school and in the local community. But this demands economical support and Barnardo's urges us to donate.

As donors we all become troubleshooters. If politicians and authorities are influenced by the campaign and the debate that it creates, they can also be participants. Reinforced or changed attitudes can lead to financial backing from these politicians, allowing Barnardo's to provide support and better surroundings for the children to get their future back – as the tag line reads.

Dramatic pictures, like the one we have just analysed, are used in what we will be looking at in the next chapter: design.

SUMMARY

'The camera was my signal for help, nothing more.'

THE IMAGE REVOLUTION
The image is in the middle of a revolution. Amateurism means that the general public are increasingly providing the news media with pictures, and companies are producing their own advertising images.

THE PERSPECTIVE OF INTENTION
This covers the work of the client under three categories:
Goal: the ambitions for the image, for the target group and for the choice of medium.
Message: instrumental, relational, dramatic or non-dramatic staging.
Context: the surroundings in which the image is reproduced.

Categories of image
Informative: giving the relevant information without value judgements.
Explicative: explaining an action or course of events.
Directive: indicating or encourage a certain opinion.
Expressive: communicating strong feelings using powerful means.

Image rhetoric
The convincing function of the image:
The presentative image *shows*.
Metonymy *illuminates*.
Synecdoche *indicates* and *proves*.
Metaphor *compares*.

THE PERSPECTIVE OF PROXIMITY
This covers the work of the photographer under three categories:
Cut, where the subject is captured and cut.
Composition, in which the image's line, volume, space, light and colour are composed to form an attractive and orienting whole.
Meaning, the meaning and content that the photographer and the client want to get across using the image.

THE PERSPECTIVE OF RECEPTION
Covers the receiver's/viewer's encounter with the image:
Perception: the eye receives visual stimuli, which are sent on to the brain by the optic nerve.
Experience: consists of a personal feeling, an assessment of stimuli and processing the impression.
Interpretation: in which the viewer expresses the meaning of the image (in *image analysis*).

11/
DESIGN

ABOVE / You have to sketch, turn and twist to find the optimal form that is both personal and reaches out to the receiver in the intended way.

'You only get one chance.'

Visual communication is like a market, with traders at their stalls trying to attract the attention of passers-by, show off their wares and convince people that they need the products. The traders reinforce their attacks with inviting, appealing body language.

Of course, successful design relates to the way visual elements are put together – whether the receiver first sees a heading or a picture, and whether the composition is simple or over-complicated. When it comes down to it, well-organized design is easy to read, and muddled design difficult. The former signals gravitas and relevance, the latter the opposite. First impressions are crucial, with the sender often getting only one chance.

It turns out that an awful lot of things have to be just right for a few tomatoes to change hands.

FORM AND CONTENT

The term 'form' relates to *how* the visible shapes or configurations have been created, and to how the various different parts have been arranged.

The term 'content' covers *what* these different elements are filled with and also what thoughts and types of information are being conveyed.

Form and content are considered to be mutually interdependent. The form cannot exist until it has some content to present, and the content does not truly exist until it has taken shape in the design process.

At the same time, it is important to remember that the content should lead the form, and not vice versa. The insightful designer also knows that the combining of text and image cannot save or hide a bad idea or poor content (or at least not more than once). You can't make a silk purse out of a sow's ear, and ignoring that fact will only make any lack of content even more marked.

Graphic design will draw the receiver's eye to the right place, and the content gets the receiver to understand. The interplay between the design and the content is what creates that all-important first impression, paving the way for *the message*. Design + content = message.

However, something is needed to spice things up, which is why the designer will add an exciting idea, be it simplicity, drama, surprise, refinement, human warmth and finally a pinch of humour.

TEXT AND PICTURES – THEN AND NOW

Design is one of our most important cultural expressions, taking in everything from architecture, fashion and interior design to industrial design, crafts and visual communication.

Way back in time, designers painted pictures or characters on cave walls, pressed carved pieces of wood against soft clay tablets, chiselled letters in stone or painstakingly produced thick manuscripts.

The graphic designer and book printer were once one and the same person. But as the art of printing developed and became mechanized as demand for printed information increased, two separate professions were created.

Books, plays, pamphlets, posters, flyers and signs were designed, illustrated, printed, bound and read in an ever-increasing flood, but mass production did little for quality.

In the nineteenth century, *William Morris*, the British author, painter and designer, took up the cudgels against this decline. Morris, who set up the Kelmscott Press, came to have a huge influence when it came to demand for high-quality craftsmanship and choice of genuine materials.

The poster art of *Henri de Toulouse-Lautrec* played a crucial role in the development of communication using text and pictures. With his alluring images of scantily clad artistes in the cafés of Paris, the *fin de siècle* artist became history's first art director (or is that perhaps a slur on his artistry?).

In the 1920s and 1930s, deeply inspired by Morris's Arts and Crafts movement, an architect by the name of *Walter Gropius* founded one of the world's most influential design schools, the *Bauhaus*. This German school of architecture, arts and crafts, photography, dance and much more besides sought to create a bridge between art and industry, in the spirit of Functionalism. Form and function became buzzwords and visual communication formed an important part of the teaching.

Jan Tschichold, the author of *Die neue Typografie* (1928), came to personify the strictly functionalist and asymmetrical style of graphic design prominent during the period that followed.

In the 1950s, interest shifted to the other side of the Atlantic. *Saul Bass* created revolutionary film posters, minimizing the use of predictable film images and instead using strong graphic elements. He also applied the same approach to epoch-making title sequences and end-credits for films.

Alexey Brodovitch was born in Russia and worked in Paris before leaving Europe for America in 1930. He came to have a major impact on American graphic design (including that at *Harper's Bazaar*) with effective use of white space and contrasts between photographic images and eye-catching layouts.

The 1960s were shaken by the creative revolution on Madison Avenue in New York, with the advertising creatives seizing power from the go-betweens and accountants. Copywriters and art directors established a deeper partnership, resulting in a stronger and more effective interplay between text and pictures. Leading lights included *Bill Bernbach* of the advertising agency Doyle, Dane, Bernbach, *Herb Lubalin*, graphic designer, and *George Lois*, art director, with *Andy Warhol*, artist, filmmaker and media man, overseeing the whole movement.

Towards the end of the last century, the American *David Carson* challenged good taste with his deconstructionist approach, integrating text and pictures to such an extent that the pages of the magazine *Ray Gun* were more like lithographic works than journalism.

Neville Brody, British newspaper and magazine designer and one of the shining design stars of the past few decades, put everything back on an even keel, with white space and clear organization for text and pictures. His best work could (and can) be seen in the publications *The Face* and *i-D* magazine.

Founded by a number of designers (including Alan Fletcher and Colin Forbes) in 1972, the studio *Pentagram* has worked successfully with visual profiling, but also with adjacent branches of design such as products, interiors and architecture.

BELOW / Three milestones in the development of graphic design: Henri de Toulouse-Lautrec's first poster, *La Goulue* (1891), created for the Moulin Rouge dance hall, a poster (1955) by Saul Bass for the film *The Man with the Golden Arm* and a cover (1939) for *Harper's Bazaar* by Alexey Brodovitch.

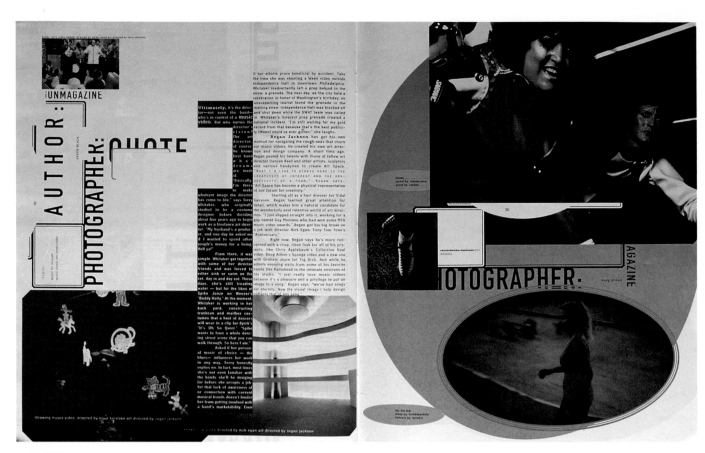

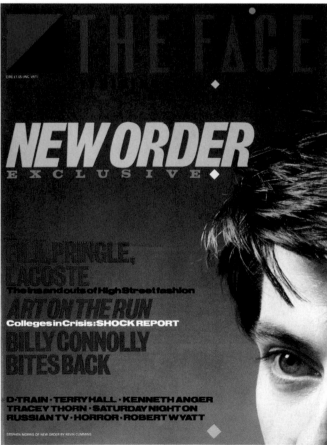

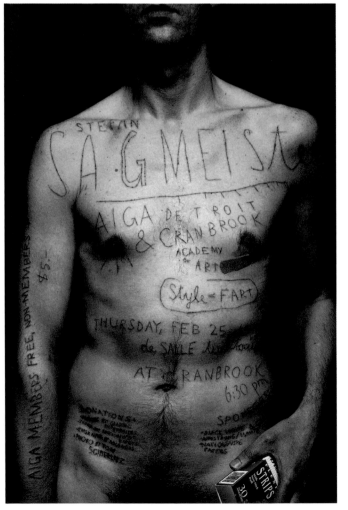

ABOVE / A deconstructivist spread for *Ray Gun* (1995) by David Carson, a striking cover for *The Face* (1983) by Neville Brody, and a highly personal lecture poster (1999) by Stefan Sagmeister (which even makes use of his own person).

ABOVE / This commercial for Sony Bravia
by Fallon really grabs the attention –
streets are filled with colour, as is the
television screen.

The British designer *Peter Saville* is famous for his record sleeves and posters for a number of artists, but he also finds clients among the fashion and advertising industry.

Jonathan Barnbrook, the British graphic designer and typographer, adds a social conscience into his work, which becomes a weapon for social change.

The Austrian *Stefan Sagmeister*'s extremely personal approach and his self-exposure inspire many designers, among them *Jan Wilker* of Germany and *Hjalti Karlsson* of Iceland, a design duo with clients in the film and music industries.

Innovative graphic design and advertising are also found in Amsterdam at the advertising agency *KesselsKramer*. Other advertising agencies are taking up the design banner, for instance *Fallon*, which is based in London, Minneapolis, São Paulo, Singapore and Tokyo.

Graphic design is now a thriving, international industry, with emerging stars constantly adding new elements to the design mix.

TRIANGULAR DRAMA, AGAIN

It is time again for the triangular drama between the client (with the perspective of intention), the receiver (with the perspective of reception) and the main figure in this chapter, the designer, whose perspective of proximity means being completely immersed in the letters, the images, the colours and, of course, the whole entity, the design.

However, it is important for designers to look *inside* themselves and ask how they as messengers are reacting to the messages they are working on. They must also look *outwards* in order to take on board the views of clients and colleagues.

But there's more to it than that. It is also necessary to look *backwards*, in order to remain anchored in the essential early parts of the communication chain – the goals and strategy – and then to look *forwards* in order to properly study just how the messages affect and influence the target groups, the business world and society.

HOW DOES THE DESIGNER CHOOSE?

The independent artist starts working with brushes in hand, in front of a taut blank canvas. The canvas is like a stage, where anything can happen and where the work can seem like controlled randomness.

In visual communication designers also start with a blank space – the search is on for the best arrangement of text and pictures.

STOP!

Before the brain, eye and hand rush into any communicative design, it is vital to stop for a moment. What is the aim and what is the message all about? These are two key questions and it's often worth writing the answers to them down on paper. 'Pleasant, warm atmosphere' (before designing menus for a café) or 'the dialogue energizes the play and thus vitalizes the auditorium' (before designing a poster for a theatrical first night).

A design commission comprises different parts (strategy, text, image, format …), which can be compared to shards of pottery. You have to look for something within yourself which corresponds to each of these shards and try to put them together. And once you've got it right, and the pottery vase is complete and the creative context justified, it's time for the following important points:

Planning

This involves evaluating the assignment and looking ahead, based on goals, time, budget and design constraints. What could take longer than anticipated? Where is the weak link? And what help is available?

Sorting

Look over all the available material such as text and pictures. What has the highest priority? What is the order of importance?

Weeding

Anything which fails to make the grade, in terms of its design, content and technical aspects, should be taken out, or its deficiencies addressed.

Organizing

This is the stage before the start of the project. Is this work best suited to one particular individual or a team? Who is best suited to do what on this assignment? How will this affect the schedule?

Costing

Building up an idea of the financial side is vital. What will it cost? What will the most expensive item be? Is there a cheaper alternative? Is there a contingency? When will the costs be reviewed?

Designing

The brain, eye and hand are finally given free rein, so the design work can focus fully on the message. At last!

SKETCHES

At the initial creative stage, the designer has to transfer thoughts into concept sketches to test them out. This is usually done on a computer screen, but a felt-tipped pen and paper, or even a biro on the back of a beer mat, will do the job.

The concept sketches are then developed into sketches for presentation to the client, and then into sketches for the supplier, giving instructions for technical production.

EXCITING SPACES

The sketches indicate various spaces which the designer can use to further strengthen the message.

Landscape

A horizontal rectangular space creates strong tension between width and height, attractively stretching out to the sides. The receiver's eye seems to move easily and naturally across it, and the designer can strengthen the first impression of width by cropping the image and allowing it to completely fill a double-page spread in a magazine, for example.

Placing several pictures in a kind of film sequence as a border from left to right also attracts the receiver. Colour can be used to link things together and give a pleasing perception of width – blue grapes on the left send signals to a blue vase on the right. It is important to make use of the natural way of reading from left to right to capture the attention of the receiver.

Portrait

If the designer turns the space about a central axis, it then becomes a vertical rectangle, which behaves in a very different way. The tension between the height and the width creates an energy that pushes upwards and downwards. This space is, of course, perceived as considerably narrower than the landscape rectangle, so the receiver's eye can thus quickly zigzag through the content.

This is probably the most common shape, as it works in most contexts. Think of all the A4 sheets and other standard formats that pass through our hands over the course of our lives.

Square

According to many photographers and designers, a square is a space where nothing happens. With the equal length of its sides, it is seen as almost devoid of tension. But if they look carefully, they can see that it has a strong inner power. The square can be filled with an active arrangement of content which competes energetically with static uniformity, such as a design which radiates out towards the corners.

Other spaces

The circle and the triangle, which along with the square make up three basic options in the world of design, are exciting and unfortunately uncommon. Why aren't books about football round and why isn't a movie poster for François Truffaut's triangular drama *Jules et Jim* also triangular?

CHOOSING THE FORMAT

The energy or tension in a space is created by its frame. Once the designer has decided on the height and width of a space, its format is also determined.

But first it is necessary to think about the following:

Function
Message
Cost
Distribution

Function

This often determines the choice of format. A poster requires a large format, a cinema ticket a small one, while a phrase book has to fit in your pocket.

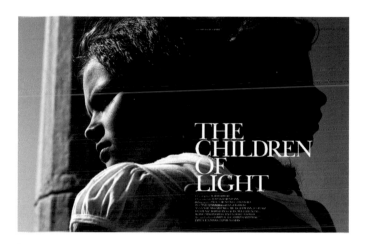

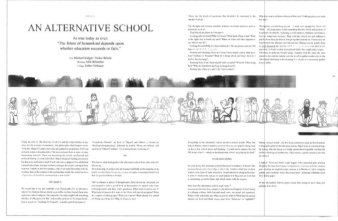

ABOVE / The German magazine *kid's wear* creates appealing forms with the help of exciting contrasts between colour and black and white, photography and illustration and portrait and landscape shapes.

ABOVE / CD sleeves make considerable demands of the designer, but design studio Intro have brought life to a square cover for Razorlight (left) while Circuit73's design for the beeps exploits the potential of the CD's circular format.

Billboards in town centres are often considered extremely large, but at the same time many people fail to see them. One effective way of checking whether a message is capable of reaching its audience is to photograph the arrangement of text and images using a mobile phone and then hold it at arm's length. If you can make sense of it like that, it ought to work out on the streets too.

The message

A book about marathons might logically have a landscape format, and a brochure about the Eiffel Tower a portrait format.

However, a different, unusual format is often needed to match the message. A full page in an evening newspaper is a conventional choice, while two half pages, one on either side of a double-page spread, is a more creative option (Romeo on the left and Juliet on the right).

The cost

Money also helps determine the choice of format. A 24-page brochure costs more than an eight-page one, of course, as the editorial work, picture and illustration costs and paper requirements are proportionally greater.

Distribution

Often a brochure has to be dispatched to prospective customers, so weight and format become key factors for distribution costs, such as postage. A website is probably the cheapest solution for reaching a wide audience.

STANDARD OR SPECIAL

In advertising, it is fairly easy to choose the format, as the advertisement price list states which formats are available.

For books and printed material, there are two options to choose between:

Standard format
Special format

Standard format

By far the most common standard format is the A-series, used for a great deal of printed material in many countries, particularly in Europe. If an A4 sheet is folded in half, it becomes A5 format, which in turn is folded once to produce A6 format.

The proportions of the A-series deviate from the golden ratio and are therefore considered unsuitable for books with one column of text per page, for example. The column width is far too broad if the format is used to the full. However, the A-series is excellent for magazines, brochures and product sheets, and allows the designer to arrange the text in several columns, and leave plenty of space for pictures.

Special format

There is no need to feel constrained by the standard formats when an exciting, incisive message may require a special format.

The publishing industry uses several special formats that have almost become standard in their own right. Paperback books are often printed at 190 x 110 mm (7.48 x 4.33 in), an attractive and functional format that is also good for readability and allows a reasonable length of text line. Many other books are printed at 210 x 130 mm (8.27 x 5.12 in) format, which fits well with the proportions of the golden ratio and gives a reader-friendly impression.

TYPE AREA

The type area is the space on the page taken up by the body text (and pictures), described as a measurement of height and width. If the designer divides the type area into smaller sections, these are called columns.

A whole range of factors affects where the designer places the type area. How much text is there, and how many pictures? Is the

LEFT / An example of the standard dimensions for margins in fiction, helping to ensure a comfortable read.

ABOVE / A boundless image with a strong message – a Nike trainer bursts through the billboards in a subway in Singapore.

designer looking for a light and airy impression, or the reverse, a compact and dense one? In this context, *margins* have an important role to play, as without these receivers would not be able to perceive any order. It is margins that group text and pictures into units. These should have a clearly defined size and above all be larger than other white space on the page.

In books and in printed material aiming for high quality, the margins should be given harmonious dimensions, and should increase from smallest to largest in the following order:

Gutter (inner margin)
Header (top)
Outer margin
Footer (bottom)

HELP IN DESIGN WORK

Tables are very common in printed and digital contexts, creating a *grid* of invisible lines dividing the page, often into three columns. The first column may then be used for headings, the middle one for text and the third for pictures and illustrations.

The tables are a kind of well-organized car park, providing consistency and uniformity.

MORE HELP

The web designer often has problems with visitors whose web browser and personal settings completely destroy even the most careful and beautiful design.

Style sheets are often a good solution (as are PDF files), as they lock the design the way the designer intended it to be seen.

However, there are some pros and cons with both locked and free, flexible design.

Advantages of locked design

The web designer's pages are almost identical to those that are seen by the visitor to the website. Any printouts of the page always work properly.

Disadvantages of locked design

If the visitors' screens are narrower than the width stated by the web designer, visitors will have to scroll horizontally, which may get on their nerves.

Advantages of flexible design

The design adapts to the visitor's environment, screen size and web browser.

Disadvantages of flexible design

The text lines can become too long on large screens, causing readability to suffer. A large amount of irritating empty space may also be created.

BASIC DESIGNS

Whatever the space, the format or the type area involved, and irrespective of whether the designer is working in a printed, a moving or an interactive medium, the basic design must be decided upon, and the character of this design should fit the goal and the message.

A&O IN DESIGN

A skilled designer is clear that design is not the end in itself, existing only for its own sake. Its main task is to pave the way for the message by:

Attracting
Orienting

Attracting

An effective design is one that attracts the receiver through its distinctiveness and its power. The receiver may be captivated by *one element* of the whole production, for example a large and exciting image or a dominant heading, or by the interplay that exists between them.

The receiver may also be attracted by the *whole*, with each individual element combining to create an overall experience. It hardly needs pointing out that a well-structured and consistent design gives a professional and credible impression.

Horror vaccui is Latin, meaning a fear of empty spaces in an artistic context. This fear is expressed in cluttered design, completely filled with letters, images and colour accents.

The solution is to make sure that there are white, airy spaces. An image will attract extra attention if it is surrounded by generous expanses of white space. A heading makes more of an impact if it is set in black in a suitable size, with plenty of space to breathe.

BELOW / Dominant elements attract the reader, as with this front and back cover from *Eye* magazine.

TOP / Generous white space helps to emphasize dominant and attractive elements, as in this animated website for the Leo Burnett advertising agency.

ABOVE / A newspaper attracts through having an inviting whole that also orients the reader among text and images, as in the innovative *Folha de S. Paulo* in Brazil.

Symmetry

Asymmetry

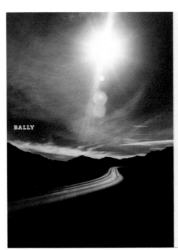

Open design

Closed design

ABOVE / Efficient attraction and orientation can be created with symmetry or asymmetry, and open and closed design, as seen in covers by David Pearson for Penguin, the profile of the Young Vic theatre by Intro, an ad campaign by Boris Bencic for fashion brand Bally, and spreads for *Rolling Stone* magazine art directed by Fred Woodward.

Orienting

The receiver also has to be guided through the material. It must be clear in which order visual elements should be read – like an attractive tourist map with a clearly marked historical walk around Venice, from St Mark's Square in the west to the beautiful square of San Stefano, and then on to ...

In newspapers, orientation can be made easier by using vignettes which guide the readers through the pages, helping them to find their way. Several possible ways in should all bring them to interesting material.

SYMMETRY AND ASYMMETRY

As in typography and picture composition, a *symmetrical composition* means that headings, images and logos are placed along a central axis. The composition is perceived to be calm and harmonious, almost grand, and the receiver finds it easy to read and understand the message.

Symmetry works well for content with a little grandeur, like a government. However, in another context, the composition can seem far too static, particularly if the subject is a dynamic one, such as bullfighting in Seville or a police chase in Berlin. The twentieth-century Austrian artist Friedensreich Hundertwasser detested symmetry so much that he always wore odd socks, and was also a great supporter of a different kind of composition.

An *asymmetrical composition* creates dynamism and tension. The axis has been thrown out, to be replaced by an interplay of contrasting designs, colours and spaces.

OPEN AND CLOSED DESIGN

Another basic in the design world is open and closed design, each of which generates a very different reaction in the receiver.

The open design is generous, welcoming, often non-dramatic, inviting and free. Closed design is exciting, dramatic, but perhaps a little mean and claustrophobic.

TAKETE AND MALUMA

In the theatre, the director chooses between two ways of building up a scene. With their unusual, almost onomatopoeic names, they can easily be transferred to the design world.

Takete represents the heated, dazzling and dynamic design, which has a strong, perhaps even disturbing, effect on the receiver.

Maluma stands for warmth and humanity, a design that has a gentle and positive impact on the receiver.

THE OPTICAL CENTRE

Let's now have a look at a few lithographs on the wall at home. They are usually framed within a mount so that the motif is not quite in the centre, but slightly above the centre point. Why?

Because the motif is placed at the optical centre, just above the exact centre. If text and pictures are arranged around this point, the designer can be certain that material will not appear to drop out of the frame, as it might if placed it at the exact midpoint.

The reason for this is that the eye first reads (scans) the upper section of a space and then the lower part. The cut-off point is at the exact centre (or along the centre line), so any design elements

ABOVE / If the title of a book is placed on the cover at the optical centre, it will create a harmonious whole.

placed there will be saved until scan number two, and will be perceived by the eye and brain to be a long way down the space.

You can use a compass and ruler to calculate exactly where the optical centre is, but it is better to develop a feel for design and let the eye find the best place for a heading or an image.

In general, the upper part of a format is felt by the receiver to be more positive and attractive than the lower part.

OBVIOUS DESIGN

The receiver is not able to process an infinite number of design elements, and becomes uncertain when faced with too busy a design, and stressed about not finding a way in.

A design which makes the receiver feel stupid, for example when trying to navigate through a website that is far too complicated, can generate a lifelong hatred of the product or company.

Good design has to signal a degree of obviousness, supporting and justifying the inclusion of the various elements. If its purpose isn't clear, it shouldn't be there.

PSYCHOLOGICAL DESIGN

Psychology and design – what can these two disciplines offer each other? Gestalt psychology, which we have already come across in the previous chapter, doesn't just help the photographer

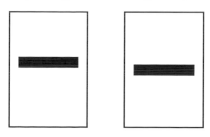

working on an image. For the designer too, the three gestalt laws are useful tools:

The law of proximity
The law of similarity
The law of closedness

The law of proximity
Designs that appear close to each other are perceived as belonging together. They form a unified whole, a gestalt in fact.

Here, too, the most important tool is white space, which delimits and links up, as the illustrations below show.

The law of similarity
Designs which are similar to each other belong together. This law comes into play when the designer of a catalogue or site wants to make receivers aware of recurrent technical facts, for example. These may be highlighted using a uniform typography, vignettes and colours to help receivers find what they are looking for.

The law of closedness
This applies when the designer wants to separate off (enclose) certain information, such as product descriptions or prices, with the help of a frame or background colour. The result is a good, clear structure.

FOUR DESIGN PRINCIPLES

Attraction, orientation, spaces, format, basic designs and the odd dash of psychology combine to form the pillars of the following four classic design principles:

Contrast
Balance
Alignment
Rhythm

CONTRAST
The helicopter takes off, giving the tourists a bird's eye view of Manhattan. They can soon see the rectangular grid system formed by the avenues and streets. But look, over there is the curve of Broadway, winding its way in stark contrast to the right angles! And suddenly there is an enormous green area, Central Park! The island comes alive, with the contrasts keeping at bay the monotonous uniformity that you might otherwise see from the air.

It is the same in visual communication, where contrasts in size, strength, shape and colour can make for dynamic and exciting design.

A contrast in size is particularly useful, as it can make for a way into the visual arrangement, a fact welcomed by the receiver. In the same way that a door to a building indicates that the visitor should knock and enter there, the contrast in size signals that the receiver should start looking and reading.

A good way in might well be a dominant image, a bold headline, an initial letter or an arrangement of text and pictures in strong colours.

ABOVE & RIGHT / To entice the eyes, a contrasting element is necessary, whether it is a dominant text arrangement or an attractive colour palette.

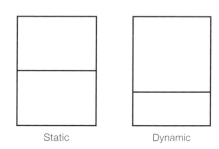

Static   Dynamic

The illustration above shows two different relationships between spaces. In the left-hand layout, they are both exactly the same size, which gives a static and uninteresting impression. However, in the right-hand one, one space has been made dominant, which immediately creates a contrast, giving a much more lively design and a clear way in.

The photographer applies the *rule of thirds* when composing a photo, but it is equally applicable here. The designer draws two or four lines to divide the format into thirds or ninths, making it easy to create a design that is both full of contrast and attractive.

LEFT / The gridded streets of Manhattan can be seen clearly from a helicopter, but Broadway cuts through in contrast.

BELOW / Posters for the Norwegian music festival Trollofon by Grandpeople, known for mixing typography and illustration to create lyrical designs with attractive contrasts.

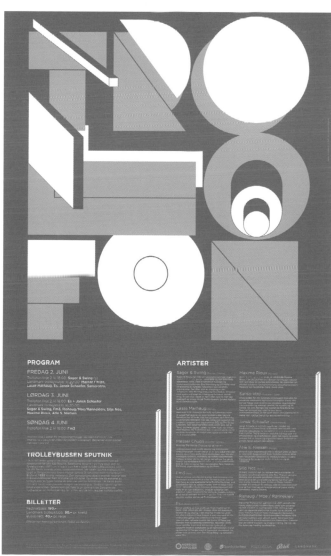

MATADOR

35
MILÍMETROS

*Gabriel Figueroa fue el mejor director de fotografía de México.
Trabajó con todos los grandes y en su archivo personal guardó a lo largo de los años
cientos de tirillas que utilizaba para hacer pruebas de luz. Con la paciencia
y la minuciosidad de un monje amanuense, su hijo, Gabriel Figueroa Flores,
ha restaurado los mejores fotogramas de películas hoy míticas de Luis Buñuel
fotografiadas por su padre. El sueño de todo cinéfilo.*

ABOVE / Fernando Gutiérrez from
Pentagram achieves a good balance
through the careful placement of simple
elements in the magazine *Matador*.

In summary, contrasts create:

A dynamic and exciting design.
A way into the visual arrangement.

And just as in typography and image work, the four contrasts work their magic everywhere in the media:

Size contrast
The most common form of contrast, with the designer simply placing a large image in contrast to a small one.

Strength contrast
This may involve striking arrangements of large black headings and dark pictures contrasting with airy typography and light illustrations.

Shape contrast
The designer may choose a frameless image to contrast with a traditional rectangular photo or a round one with a square one.

Colour contrast
The use of contrasting colours offers endless possibilities. The designer can have a colour picture that contrasts with a black and white image, a heading in a colour along with a black sub-heading, or a background colour on one of the facing pages in a double-page spread.

BALANCE
The designer does need to ensure that all of the various elements are brought into balance, so that the layout does not tip towards one side or the other. The whole magazine spread could capsize if the designer places a very powerful image in one of the bottom corners, or unthinkingly makes use of too strong a colour for a tint block.

The most common and the easiest way to achieve a balance is, as we have already said, to establish an axis to create symmetry. Images and text are laid out in the middle of the format, producing a harmonious but also elegant impression.

The opposite is asymmetry, where shapes and spaces are placed in strong contrast to each other. Even here, the skilled designer will be able to create balance.

ALIGNMENT
The designer needs to ensure that headlines in a newspaper or magazine are always placed at the same height from the first to last page, that pictures are inserted according to a set pattern, that the margins are the same size all the way through, and that the navigation tools are positioned consistently on every page of a website.

To help in this process, the designer uses grid lines, which generate a template for the design. But don't overdo it. Some magazines, e.g., French *Vogue*, only use templates for parts of the magazine and allow freedom of expression in others.

ART
INTO
ARCHITECTURE

by Joseph Giovannini

Nixon was President, the design material of choice for corporate America was chrome, and Frank Gehry was running a conventional architectural practice. Trained in the conservative architecture school at the University of Southern California and in the detail-oriented Los Angeles firm Gruen Associates, where he worked from 1954 to 1955 and again from 1957 to 1960. Gehry seemed destined to run an upper-middle-quality office, but for his inspired flaw. As a USC student, he switched from art to architecture, and the lateral slide would typify his entire career: while he maintained a practice consonant with the expectations of his time and place, he led a double life, spending time with the Iconoclastic artists of Venice Beach who were devising new ways of interpreting space, light, and materiality. At his 1969 show in the Riko Mizuno Gallery, painter Ed Moses took a buzz saw to the roof and opened an oculus to the sky, exposing the ends of the rafters. To materialize light and to paint the air, the artist—working with assistant James Turrell—stood on a ladder and threw rice dust high into the space.

Frank Gehry's raw, expressive buildings disturbed the prevailing architectural ethos in the early 1970s by introducing the irrational into a profession dominated by the rational. Subsequent projects confirm the artist's sculptural approach to architectural design, and reveal the influence of the many years he has spent in the company of artists.

Santa Monica Place
1980

above and facing
page: Gehry house
Santa Monica
1978 renovation

Artists like Larry Bell, Billy Al Bengston, Tony Berlant, Robert Irwin, Moses, and Doug Wheeler invented the conversation Gehry was really listening to, and what he heard differed from what he had learned at USC and Gruen. The Venice artists, most associated with the Ferus Gallery, were pursuing two artistic initiatives. They brought art off the pedestal, out of the frame, and off the wall, utilizing space and light as its subject matter; and they were performing half-serious, half-madcap, quasi-architectural interventions in their own studios, building impromptu moments. Moses, for example, sandwiched wood studs between panes of glass in his bathroom, and Bell created a parallelogrammatic room with all walls leaning toward the beach, Bengston continuously rebuilt his studio, testing out recycled aircraft materials. The efforts that would later emerge as formal installations in museums and at specially chosen sites had a relationship to the raw, ongoing, never-finished, at-home construction performances that were undertaken by artists simply because they wanted to; it was a way to talk both to each other and to their art.

It is hard to remember how strictly codified the practice of architecture then was. Its design by many highly regarded firms was academically formulaic. The plans by The Architects Collaborative (Walter Gropius's successor firm in Cambridge, Massachusetts) for the national headquarters of the American Institute of Architects

in Washington, D.C., built in 1970, generally embodied the prevailing ethos and rules: exposed structure, defined circulation, the materiality of materials, all in the name of simplicity. From the point of view of architectural professionalism, Gehry indulged in deviant behavior when he brought the artists' experiments into his designs. In this new lexicon, materials need not be pure, they could be broken and even chaotic. Collage common. Forms need not be pure, they could be broken and even chaotic. Collage constituted fair compositional technique. Just as Robert Rauschenberg made artworks out of discarded objects he found in his forays into the trash heaps of

Vitra International Furniture Museum, Weil am Rhein, Germany 1989

American Center, Paris 1994

Nationale-Nederlanden building, Prague 1996

Catia rendering of the Guggenheim Museum Bilbao exterior

International Furniture Museum (1989), across the border from Basel, where compound curves form a constantly evolving shape that motivates visitors to walk around the building; the forms are in ever-changing relationships to themselves, curves playing off curves. From the point of view of Gehry's [...], the building signaled that he had at last achieved an independence from insights borrowed from his artist mentors. He understood the spirit behind their observations and ten years after the house, made his own independent breakthrough. Architects are said to mature late; Gehry was 60 years old. For inspiration, he now was looking at the sails of magnificent galleons, and at the folds in the drapes of medieval marble sculpture. Anything was fair game.

In their independence from the academy and from the usual rationalities of architecture—the most expensive and therefore most rationalized of the arts—Gehry's buildings embody an especially American attitude that perhaps represents the first significant original architectural idea to land on European shores since Frank Lloyd Wright's Wasmuth portfolio, a German publication of his Oak Park work, which had a great impact on European architecture. The spirit that Gehry's work in Europe incarnates—first Vitra, then the American Center in Paris (1994), the Nationale-Nederlanden building (nicknamed the Fred and Ginger tower) in Prague (1996), and the Guggenheim in Bilbao—is American in its wildness. Gehry was exporting raw, generous, Western vitality to the old world.

Consider his design for the Guggenheim Museum Bilbao. The tough industrial cityscape of this Baroque capital requires a building that can stand up to the context, and the mandate of the museum itself stipulated an architecture able to broadcast its presence and establish a wide sphere of influence. The cultural ecology of Europe required no less than a Sydney Opera House for Bilbao: in a unified

The cultural ecology of Europe required for Bilbao: in a unified Europe where nations advance, stellar buildings will help no less than a Sydney Opera House **are receding in importance as cities define the cultural pecking order.**

Europe where nations are receding in importance as cities advance, stellar buildings will help define the cultural pecking order. Bilbao leaders want their city to be no less than the capital of the Atlantic seaboard in Europe's newly reconfigured geocultural map, and the Gehry building, combined with the Guggenheim collection, will help promote that claim. Of all museums, the Guggenheim knows the power of a building to define an institution. Gehry has delivered a building that at least matches the brilliance of Wright's New York Guggenheim vortex, and the inexplicability of its forms will draw thousands of visitors to its mysteries.

The inspiration for Bilbao occurs at a mature point in his use of the new language of curves. Sited along Bilbao's industrial riverfront, next to a bridge, in the bowl of the city's valley, the building turns and scrolls along the river, bracketing the bridge and its highway and absorbing them into its force field, then coming to a head in a dense, imploding entry where the curved walls turn and surge up into a spray of white water: the movement of the forms gives the building an energy and life just at the edge of tumult. The central organizing space for the vast museum recalls Wright's rotunda and is meant to provoke site-specific artistic responses. As the request of the Guggenheim, Gehry has not sought a neutralized atrium, but one that stands on its own as an architectural work.

The irony of the design is that without looking technological, its artistic imperative required advanced computer technology. Gehry

designed the building with sheets of paper that he rolled and taped by hand, much like a sculptor working clay or a first grader cutting-and-pasting. Baroque craftsmen might be able to carve by hand focal moments on a building, but the sum total of long curves Gehry proposed far exceeded the capabilities of conventional construction practice. Gehry had turned to the computer to execute the Fishdance restaurant, and with his design for the Walt Disney Concert Hall in Los Angeles (still unbuilt) and then the Guggenheim, his reliance was complete. Associates in the office located Catia software, used by the French aeronautical firm Dassault to model jets such as the Mirage, to "build" the necessary drawings.

Catia enabled Gehry to digitize points on the edges, intersections, and surfaces of his hand-built models he was therefore able to use the computer not for representational purposes but as part of the construction process. For Disney Hall, this meant that a disk sent to a computer driving cutting tools in a

quarry in the south of France could automatically carve out stone without the usual shop drawings. One computer could speak to another. The same program allowed the Italian construction firm Permasteelisa to build with great accuracy and little waste the monumental webbed fish overlooking the Villa Olimpica complex in Barcelona (1992). The computer has enabled Gehry—and the profession—to realize architectural complexities that would have been impractical only a few years ago. It also challenges the assumption of simplicity necessitated by industrial repetition, which has long formed the conceptual basis of architectural Modernism. The computer can handle uniqueness rather than repetition without punishing costs, and in the long run it has the potential of shifting practice to a post-industrial paradigm based on electronics rather than mechanics.

The creativity of artists who do not finally exceed their inspiration eventually tires and expires, but Gehry clearly has sustained a body of work that has emerged with a logic and life of its own. Whatever derivations may have sparked his first break-out designs no longer direct his imagination. In a practice characterized by grasping beyond what he has already reached, Gehry has achieved an originality that not only influences architects but also the artists who were his first inspiration and example.

GUGGENHEIM MAGAZINE FALL 1997

ABOVE / A bold design for the magazine of the Guggenheim Museum by the art director J. Abbott Miller, which does not follow a strict grid but lets text and images reflect one another to create an organic and balanced whole.

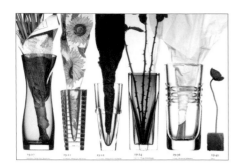

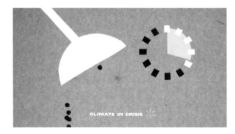

ABOVE / Varied, surprising reinforcement schedules can help take the receiver through material, as here in (from top to bottom) a brochure for glass manufacturer Orrefors, an article on profiles for design magazine *Creative Review*, a piece on choreography in arts magazine *Esopus* and a public information film for Live Earth.

RHYTHM

A well-thought-out design is based on rhythm, which takes the receiver on a journey with the help of variety – exciting switches between close-ups and long shots, between different sizes and directions, soft and hard shapes, cold and warm colours. The receiver should not be able to predict everything that is to come. Humans seem to be the only members of the animal kingdom who get bored, so it is important to stimulate them.

Visual forward momentum

Let's take a closer look at rhythm. In the pop world, an intro sets the tone of the song. The verses contrast with the chorus, creating forward momentum, and break into a short interlude to keep monotony at bay.

The dramatist creates a similar forward impetus in theatre and film. As we have seen, visual communication requires the same kind of forward momentum. It is needed in the design of advertisements and posters, but also in media made up of a series of pages and sequences that follow each other. The sender wants the receiver to read on in a newspaper or brochure, and wants the surfer to click through the website from the start page.

To the expertize of dramatists and music producers, we should therefore add a little psychology of learning.

The psychology of learning

This talks about *reinforcement*, which, transferred to visual communication, means that alluring texts and images make the receiver feel stimulated, entertained, full of new knowledge and,

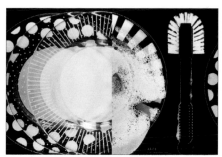

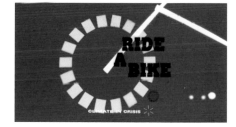

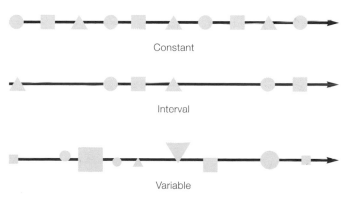

in turn, 'rewarded' for paying attention, reinforcing the receiver's willingness to move forward in the search of more experiences. Without this, the sender ends up allowing the receiver's concentration to waver and their interest to wane.

Reinforcement schedules

The pattern by which the reinforcements recur is called a reinforcement schedule, which can be designed in various ways, although the overall requirement is that it must always drive the receiver forward.

Reinforcement can come *constantly*, which means that the receiver is taken forward by texts and pictures in a fixed and repetitive way. In the end, the schedule becomes far too monotonous and predictable in its logical progression.

Constant

Interval

Variable

Reinforcement schedules

ABOVE / Closeness, distance, light, darkness and rotated images, together with strong typographical elements, combine to create a captivating design.

Fixed-interval reinforcement means that the reinforcement comes at regular intervals, but in between this reinforcement there may be less attractive sections, which can cause the receiver to lose interest.

The preferred choice is a *variable-interval reinforcement* schedule, as the reinforcement is irregular and surprising in terms of time and intensity. Text and pictures create a stimulating and attractive entity, which takes the receiver forward with the help of exciting change and variation.

It is important to have a common thread that runs through the whole production. This thread may be as wide as a motorway, but could also be as thin as a hair or as complex and interwoven as a bird's nest.

Just like on stage in a play, the pauses are crucial. They have a vital role in the whole piece, but can also be used to highlight and focus on something important, as a pregnant pause creates drama.

Impact on memory

A varied and surprising reinforcement schedule not only creates captivating forward momentum but also a positive impact on the memory. It is easier for viewers to find their way back to a particular place in a course prospectus or on a site if they can fix a specific detail in their memory – a standout shape, colour or size. Like when you're trying to find that great place for picking blackberries: 'I remember now, it was just past that hollow tree trunk.'

Quality naturally

The quality of the reinforcement is also significant, as it must be perceived to be important.

The designer knows deep down that a varied and surprising schedule cannot save poor content. Yet again, you can't make a silk purse out of a sow's ear (for the second time in this chapter). The key is to help the receiver take on board the material in the best possible way, rather than trick them into paying attention.

NEWSPAPER DESIGN

Let's now look at how the four design principles are applied to newspapers, TV, the web and advertising. We'll start with the one on the kitchen table.

There are three approaches to newspaper design.

The first is *technology-based design,* which means that text and pictures are positioned where they fit in and not according to order of importance.

In *surface-based design*, it is the design that leads the way rather than the content.

Content-based design means that the subeditor allows the news to determine the layout. Items considered important are given pride of place and less crucial items have to make do with what space is left. This helps the reader to choose articles without having to check every little detail on a page. Reader surveys show that readers spend half their time scanning pages – good design could cut this scanning time down, thus increasing the time spent actually reading.

Genres

A newspaper or magazine is full of different genres, all of which make up the whole and feature a particular kind of content.

These include news and reportage, leaders, commentaries, domestic and international stories, financial news, culture, columns, reviews, notices, entertainment pages, cartoons and advertisements.

The various genres are placed according to a particular pattern in a newspaper, which the reader gets to know. A news article looks different to an editorial piece. *Vignettes* are small items combining text and picture that are used to signal the nature of the genre on a page, again helping the reader to find their way.

The all-important top left corner

In many papers the most important part of the front page is the top left corner, where subeditors will put the day's main news. It does not need the most space or the most dramatic photo. Often, all it needs is a headline and a few columns – the news itself is enough.

In order to balance the picture-free left-hand corner of the page, there is often a large, dominating photo that is linked to a different news item. This creates an equilibrium between verbal and visual elements, and often between complicated and simple ideas – between the housing crisis and football.

Headlines

These have to work as optical magnets, drawing the readers' eyes so they don't miss any interesting news. They also have to convey the main content of the article and generate a desire to read it.

So what is it that makes a good headline? The old news hound at the corner desk knows: a simple, straightforward idea that is positive and specific – expressed with a vivid verb in an active form, using short, simple words. That's all there is to it!

Images

Even a simple and straightforward idea often needs a picture. A headline plus photo captures the attention of the reader (some

subeditors call this combination a headline image) but it is important to make sure that the headline and the photo don't say exactly the same thing. If snow is falling in a photograph, the subeditor doesn't need the headline or the caption to say that snow is falling – the reader can already see it. It is better to use a turn of phrase that works with the image. 'Warning of icy temperatures' or 'Spring a long way off'.

An image of three politicians going in different directions outside parliament, accompanied by the headline 'Of course we can govern together' will make the reader suspect that the coalition may be unravelling and the article will reveal more. The fact that the headline and the image are saying different things creates curiosity and encourages careful reading.

Captions

These catch the eye and are tasked with describing what is happening in the photo. The caption should ideally tell its own little story.

Accompanying a photograph of an individual playing golf behind a high fence is the caption: 'Golfing prisoners – inmates held captive by their new golf course.'

Pages

The subeditor and the designer use the grid lines to lay the page out in different horizontal blocks to avoid the reader having to read all the way from the top of the page right down to the bottom and then up again (which would be like having to scroll up and down on a website). Instead, the articles are grouped together within the blocks, so that the reader can easily take in the individual article and also the page as a whole. If parts of the headline, an image or

LEFT / Most newspapers will put the main news of the day in the all-important top left corner of their front page (or of their homepage online).

ABOVE / Readers appreciate articles with elements grouped together in blocks, with headlines, pull quotes and intros, making a page appear tidy and improving readability.

parts of the body text in an *article box* stick out beyond this box, this can produce a very straggly look – designers call these designs 'doglegs'.

A good article box will have the headline and the intro, along with the start of the text, on the left, and an image on the right, creating what is known as the L-design. This layout allows the reader to move easily from the headline to the intro and then on to the body text.

The columns should not be broken up by images or other insertions, or the reader will lose the thread. The best approach is to keep text and pictures slightly separate.

It is important to allow plenty of air or white space to create contrast, rather than filling all the available space with shapes and colours. In newspaper jargon, this is called *active air*, and it is this attracting and orienting air that the reader 'breathes'.

With their straight columns, the pages of a newspaper are rectangular in shape (like the blocks of Manhattan), so contrasts, in the form of borderless images and unexpected round shapes, can add vitality.

According to the old school of newspaper design, the editor should ignore any advertisements and design the pages based only on the news. However, the new generation of designers makes sure that editorial and commercial material do not drown each other out.

TV DESIGN

When the designers at a film company or TV station aren't involved in producing the programmes, they design texts, tableaux and vignettes.

Credits
Design of the *opening* and *closing credits*, which start and round off a programme, has long been a much neglected communicative art. However, with new technical advances, these texts have not only started being appreciated (and even given awards), they have also given some status to the designers, who have been allowed out of the shadows.

The battle for viewers also requires moving vignettes and graphics filled with text, images, sound and colour for TV channels. As the channels grow in number, so do design companies specializing in this kind of dynamic design.

The TV studio
Studios also need to have a design that works. They may be *cubic*, with talking heads in close-up and video sequences in the background, along with rolling news along the bottom edge of the screen. Most TV viewers feel this to be cluttered and static.

ABOVE & RIGHT / It is crucial that television idents create a distinctive profile for a channel and ensure this is communicated effectively to the viewer, as with these examples for Channel 4, UK, by 4 Creative.

ABOVE / Strong idents for individual series, such as these by Universal Everything for MTV's History of Dance, help draw viewers back for the next episode.

ABOVE & RIGHT/ A spherical studio can open up, close in and change to suit different elements of the programme. The cubic studio has a more confined feeling.

The TV studio can also be *spherical* and dynamic when it is shaped according to the parts of the programme, following and growing with a moving presenter, inviting us into a new area, opening up rooms outside the studio, for example for a reporter with additional interviews.

The studio should create confidence in the professionalism of the production and must be functional, so that the positioning of the presenters, weather maps, picture sequences and other technology works well. The studio is a rhetorical room, created for convincing (often persuasive) slants and influence, and it has to convey and create emotions to ensure that the TV viewers are interested and involved.

There should be no doubt about who is leading the broadcast. The news anchor must come across as the undisputed central figure (a good gestalt) around whom everything revolves, and he or she must make sure the broadcast has a beginning, a middle and an end.

The studio background is important. Some are like an open-plan newsroom at a newspaper, where journalists and technicians move around in the background between screens and editing apparatus. Others place the anchor in front of a bank of active TV screens. Both cases provide a kind of promise that all the latest news will immediately be passed on to the TV viewers, as the technology is ready and waiting.

News is reported using text, stills, video, moving graphics and, of course, the spoken words of the news anchor. The message is strengthened with the help of body language, attitude, gestures, tempo, facial expressions and clothing, all of which create a certain atmosphere in the studio and in the viewer's living room ('Look at that tie!').

WEB DESIGN

Now let's switch off the TV and instead see what basic designs surfers encounter on screen. The two most common models are:

The set square

The web designer would be well advised to start design work in the top left corner (like the front of a newspaper), and then be sure that the most important features will be visible on every visitor's screen. This creates a clear, welcoming structure for the visitor, who can easily understand the layout and quickly sort out the best bits. A search function or drop-down list from A to Z would be appreciated, and should be placed in the corner of the set square.

Magazine

This approach presents large volumes of attractive content in a similar way to a newspaper, with the visitor able to browse the pages looking for items that catch their interest. Well-formulated headings, well-composed images and a host of internal links increase curiosity.

However, this generous and popular model can cause problems. There is a lot to be fitted into a newspaper's online edition, and the screen area isn't really spacious enough. This results in text often being squeezed into columns that are too narrow (with too little white space between them), compromising readability and navigability. In order to save space vertically, images are often cropped to letterbox format, which is unlikely to please the photographers. An airy design is, of course, preferable.

LEFT & BELOW / The set square model is extremely popular – Reuters keeps it to the left, while BBC Arabic puts it on the right. CNN opts for the magazine model, while the website by fortsetzungswerk for Italian video production company Studio Ennezerotre uses a free model that catches the eye and the interest of the visitor.

AD DESIGN

And now to the world of advertising, where we will examine the various design elements of an advertisement.

Images

The designer knows from experience that it is the image that attracts the receiver. The choice of this image is therefore absolutely vital.

Does size matter? Yes, a larger image will usually capture more attention, but on the other hand the advertisement will have more credibility if it is smaller and the proportion of text in it is greater. It would seem that the receiver often has more faith in text than in images.

Headings?

The greatest impact comes from headings which promise solutions to problems or increased well-being.

The combination of text and pictures is also crucial. Advertising space that is totally dominated by one image with no heading makes a major impact, but the result will often be poor. The same is true of those advertisements in which the image is accompanied by a trite headline, for instance 'Lovely!', 'Look!', or 'Act now!'

Logotypes

Right at the bottom of the page, you will often find the logotype. This must make clear who the sender is, using suitable typography, shapes and colours. If this logotype is too large, it will take away attention from other important things, while if it is too small, it will simply disappear.

Basic ad designs

It is quite tricky to describe fixed patterns and templates in an industry which is said to be so driven by the demand for innovation. But there are patterns to be found, five of them.

These basic ad layouts are on the right, and they can work as the basis of design work, or be adapted with more freedom when more expressive means are required (as is the case in many of the examples in this book).

ABOVE / A simple, fresh and distinctive advert for Lego, which has an immediate appeal and a subtle but vital interplay between image and logotype.

1.
Large square-shaped picture with heading, text and logotype. This is a classic. The large image covers two-thirds of the page, the heading, often centred, is placed underneath with the text, which is in two or three columns. The logotype is usually placed in the bottom right corner. The image may be expanded to bleed off the edges of the page. The design communicates order and tidiness, but can give a stiff impression. It makes great demands of the picture, which has to give life to the entire page. In addition, the page may end up as cluttered and confused as its context, and not stand out properly.

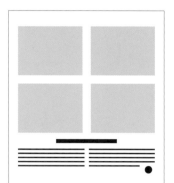

2.
Several square-shaped pictures with heading, text and logotype. This basic design is characterized by multiple images, which together cover about the same space as the large image in the previous category. The design can be varied, particularly the number of images used. The ad can be very attractive if the pictures are chosen to contrast in their shape, colours, proximity (closeness and distance), textures and depth.

3.
Small picture with large heading, text and logotype. Space is important in the world of design, and in this layout there is a lot of air to breathe. The picture does not play the same central role as in the previous basic designs, but stands back both in the form and the content of the ad. The text has the leading role, which helps to provide an air of credibility.

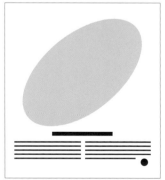

4.
Big vignette picture with heading, text and logotype. This basic design also makes attractive use of space, as a picture without a background can be appealing to the receiver. The designer can choose to let the picture dominate so there is no conflict between a heading and a picture of equal size. The spacious design will also make the ad stand out against a cluttered editorial context.

5.
Several vignette pictures with heading, text and logotype. This last basic design includes several pictures – these could be a collage in a catalogue for a furniture superstore, showing summer furniture and barbecue accessories in a soft and generous design. It is important to create a way in for the viewer – something has to dominate, otherwise the ad runs the risk of becoming an impenetrable mass. A colourful lounger can be given a starring role, while the tongs and grill stand back.

FOTOGRAFISK TIDSKRIFT
2/2004 [årgång 116]

GALLERI Poser och rörelser i dansen
INTERVJU Björn Larsson Ask
TEKNIK Överlåt arbetet till datorn

ABOVE / Simplicity can equal clarity,
and is appreciated by the readers of this
magazine, with the text and image echoing
each other on the cover.

SIMPLE DESIGN

Pure, simple design is a virtue. It is important for designers always to ask themselves, 'Is this element necessary or superfluous?' In the vast majority of cases, one can take out an image or part of a text without disturbing a message. It is in fact possible to pare down a design to a much greater degree than you might think.

Architect Mies van der Rohe expressed this approach in the classic statement 'Less is more', which means taking away everything that is surplus to requirements. The sentiment is particularly applicable to visual communication.

However, not everyone has the same opinion or taste, and too minimalist a design is seen by many as cold and lifeless – 'less is a bore'.

Sometimes design work is particularly difficult. The obvious, clear design refuses to reveal itself, and the text and pictures just don't flow properly. The reason might be that the designer has become too attached to a particular element and fails to see that this is what is blocking production of a good design.

The solution to this problem is to force yourself ruthlessly to take out whatever doesn't fit. The brutal term for this is 'Kill your darlings'!

Which brings the chapter to a similarly brutal end, making way for the much gentler subject of paper.

SUMMARY

'You only get one chance.'

A&O
The main task of the design is to pave the way for the message by *attracting* and *orienting*.

FORMAT
The choice of format for articles, adverts and banners depends on function, message, cost and distribution.

BASIC FORMS
The most common are *symmetrical* (axial) and *asymmetrical* (dynamic).

GESTALT PSYCHOLOGY
The gestalt laws are three useful tools for good design.
The law of proximity says that texts and images placed close to each other are perceived as belonging together.
The law of similarity says that visual arrangements that demonstrate similarity are perceived as belonging together.
The law of closedness says texts and images enclosed together within a frame, for example, belong together.

FOUR DESIGN PRINCIPLES
The most important is *contrast*, which creates a dynamic and exciting form and a way into visual arrangements.
Balance prevents the design capsizing.
Alignment and *grids* place columns and images according to a uniform template (in a newspaper, on a website).
Rhythm takes the receiver forwards by switching between stronger and weaker elements.

VISUAL FORWARD MOMENTUM
Telling an appealing story demands forward momentum, which draws the receiver further into the article, the advert or the website. The *reinforcement schedules*, derived from the psychology of learning, are important instruments and should be varied and surprising.

ABOVE / The whirl of confetti, with all
the hopes and dreams that each piece
of paper carries.

'Happy New Year!'

Without paper, most messages would never reach their receivers. Without paper, we wouldn't be able to read the morning newspaper over breakfast, and we would never receive a handwritten letter from a friend.

Paper is important from another point of view too. It is part of the message. The young couple are planning a fantastic New Year's party. In good time, friends receive an invitation on a unique paper made from recycled fibres with small discreet paper flags in matching shades randomly spread across the sheet. The recipients get an advance impression of confetti, champagne, fireworks and New Year's resolutions.

PAPER THROUGH HISTORY

Paper was first invented in Egypt in around 3000 BC. The Egyptians pressed together the pith from reeds to produce a smooth surface to write on. The material – *papyrus* – was stored in rolls and resulted in a revolution in the art of communication. Around 200 BC (a giant stride historically), writing material was refined when the Europeans began to produce *parchment* – tanned goat's or sheep's skin. The skin was rinsed, dried, rubbed and polished with a pumice stone to make it as soft as velvet. Parchment, which was not rolled but used as sheets, became the most important writing material up to the end of the Middle Ages.

In around AD 100 the Chinese had invented the method of suspending plant fibres in water and adding glue. This was then left to dry on a silk cloth, turning it into large sheets. In the eighth century, via the Silk Road and Samarkand, the method became known in Europe.

In the fourteenth century, this writing material was developed even further by wetting textiles (rags) that were then stamped to break them down into fibres, which finally became *paper*.

The development of printing brought with it an ever-increasing need for paper, which in the nineteenth century resulted in new manufacturing processes. The raw material became wood pulp, from which mechanical pulp (containing wood) and chemical pulp could be extracted. Mechanical pulp produces a paper which yellows over time, and therefore came to be used for newspapers, for example. Chemical pulp produces white paper, which is considerably better able to stand the test of time.

DIFFERENT TYPES OF PAPER

There are many different kinds of paper and the list below is restricted to the most common. These are:

Wood-containing paper
Wood-free paper
Coated paper
Uncoated paper
Glossy paper
Matt paper
Coloured paper
Specialist paper
Environmentally friendly paper

Wood-containing paper

As it yellows relatively quickly, this is used for simpler printed materials with a relatively short lifetime, such as newspapers, folders and flyers.

Wood-free paper

This does not yellow, which is why designers choose it for printed materials that need to last a long time and contain photographs.

Coated paper

With its extra fine surface, coated paper is suitable for the quality printing of colour pictures. The paper may be wood-containing or wood-free.

Uncoated paper

With its untreated surface, this is ideal for copying, for example, as the ink powder sticks to it easily.

Glossy paper

The shiny surface of glossy paper is good for advanced printing, with its high demands in terms of colour image reproduction. This surface, which creates reflections, may be distracting though.

Matt paper

This is common in books and magazines. The matt surface improves readability, as the reader avoids irritating reflections.

Coloured paper

As this becomes increasingly common, designers can choose practically whatever colour they like. However, it has a tendency to fade rather quickly.

Specialist paper

Produced in small quantities, these papers can produce different and exciting effects. They could be paper with an extremely porous surface, or transparent butter paper.

Environmentally friendly paper

The chemical pulp in most white high-quality papers has to undergo a bleaching process, which is anything but environmentally friendly as it uses hazardous chlorines.

RIGHT / Rob Ryan's unusual and fascinating paper silhouettes are cut out using a scalpel, and are much in demand in the fashion and music industries.

Today's environmental requirements have, however, led to the paper industry starting to manufacture chlorine-free paper, which, if it meets certain standards, is granted an environmental label such as the Nordic Swan ecolabel.

IMPORTANT CHARACTERISTICS OF PAPER

Three common paper terms deserve a closer look:

Grammage
Opacity
Fibre direction

Grammage

A paper's weight is given in grams and refers to the weight of a square metre of a particular paper. A thick paper naturally has a higher grammage than a thin one of the same type, and papers with grammages over 170 gsm are called board.

Opacity

This is a measurement of a paper's transparency. Low opacity means there is a risk of text and images showing through from the other side and disrupting reading. High opacity, of course, means the opposite.

Fibre direction

During paper production, the fibres in the pulp tend to become oriented lengthwise – to avoid them all lying in the same direction, the wire on which the pulp flows is shaken. This is particularly important for thin papers, as this process makes them stronger. Folding the paper after printing is best done along the direction of the fibres.

CHOICE OF PAPER

When choosing paper, the designer should take the following four factors into account:

Message
Text and images
Lifetime
Cost and print run

Message

The paper is part of the message, so it is important to choose a paper which harmonizes with it or reinforces it. An imposing offer from a broker might demand glossy paper. A DIY store will choose a brownish, wood-containing packaging paper for information on a weekend decking sale.

BELOW / From time immemorial we have been used to paper being flat, whether it is a single sheet or bound in a book. Su Blackwell upsets our calculations, building three-dimensional paper worlds from old books, which we approach with fascination.

LEFT & BELOW / Adventurous use of materials – holographic card on the cover of Swiss magazine *soDA*, and cheap corrugated cardboard for a series of fashion show invites by Paul Boudens for Belgian fashion designer Walter Van Beirendonck.

ABOVE / Bold contrasts between different paper stocks and varnishes can create a powerful impact, whether used for text or images – this is a collection of the work of photographer Rankin designed by the studio BB/Saunders.

Text and images

Uncoated paper is the best choice for printing text. It is pleasing to the eye and to the touch, as is a paper with a hint of colour (ivory or grey). But for a publication in which detailed illustrations and demanding photographs are to be reproduced, a completely different kind of paper is required, and a paper consultant would definitely recommend a double-coated paper.

Lifetime

A simple folder to be delivered to local households through the letterbox can be printed on cheap wood-containing paper. An encyclopaedia, which will be consulted for many years to come, demands paper of a much higher quality.

Cost and print run

The financial aspects of paper choice are important. Designers should think carefully before choosing paper for large print runs to keep down costs. For small print runs, the choice of paper has less effect on the total cost, which means that the designer can choose a higher quality paper. In general it can be said that coated paper is one of the most expensive types.

The next chapter looks at what decorates the paper, colour.

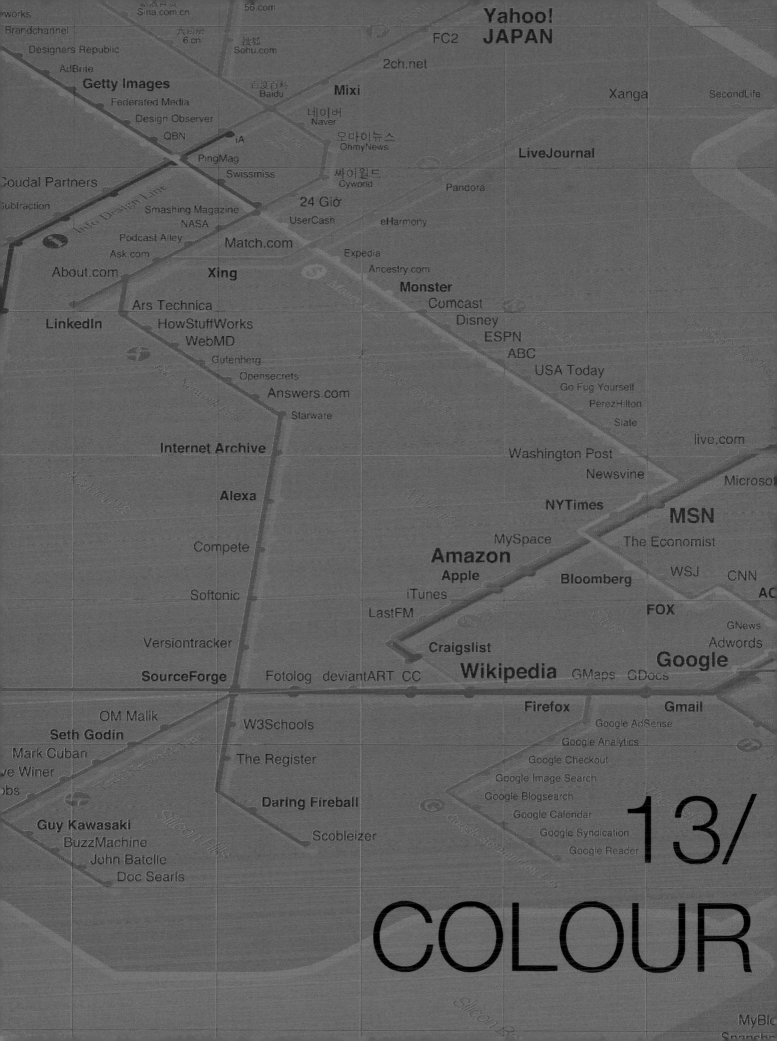

ABOVE / An image in full colour can create a powerful experience, but so can a black and white picture. This image forces us to add what is not there – the chromatic colours – and thus makes us participants.

'In full colour.'

For most people, black, achromatic colour has a special temptation. Black with white can give a documentary feel that makes us believe in something in the image. Just as often, a black and white picture invites us into a suggestive world, making us participants in a filmic sequence.

EXPERIENCES OF COLOUR

Colour perception has been important ever since the first cave paintings, which were created using nature's own colour palette of yellow, brown and red clays, iron oxide, soot, chalk, crushed berries and animal blood.

Colour is an important feature in our interior decor today, too. The right choice can create space, for example, and that narrow hall or dark stairwell will instantly become large, open and inviting with the help of light colours.

FUNCTIONAL AND NON-FUNCTIONAL

The terms functional and non-functional colours are used in many contexts, especially in architecture and industrial design.

Functional colours support and improve the product's physical and communicative functions, as a designer would put it.

Non-functional colours, on the other hand, are only a cosmetic addition. The receiver will often be confused by irrelevant and conflicting colour signals.

FUNCTIONAL COLOURS

In effective visual communication there is only room for functional colours, which are an important communicative force and should mainly be used to:

Attract
Create atmosphere
Inform
Structure
Teach

ATTRACT

A colour image in a paper attracts and grabs the receiver, just as graphical elements in strong, contrasting colours catch the eye on a website.

Many people share the belief of the Russian-born artist Wassily Kandinsky that the colours are active: 'If two circles are drawn and painted respectively yellow and blue, brief concentration will reveal in the yellow a spreading movement out from the centre, and a noticeable approach to the spectator. The blue, on the other hand, moves in upon itself, like a snail retreating into its shell, and draws away from the spectator ... Green is the most restful colour that exists. On exhausted men this restfulness has a beneficial effect, but after a time it becomes wearisome ... The unbounded warmth of red has not the irresponsible appeal of yellow, but rings inwardly with a determined and powerful intensity. It glows in itself, maturely, and does not distribute its vigour aimlessly.'

CREATE ATMOSPHERE

Colour can effectively create and reinforce atmosphere in the media. Seductive pictures with a blue sky and glistening white snow in travel brochures make us long for the Alps. Light, happy colours in red and yellow immediately create an exhilarated atmosphere in a shop, while dark, blue-green colours on a book cover give completely different signals.

In his classic film trilogy *Three Colours: Blue*, *Three Colours: White* and *Three Colours: Red*, the Polish film director Krzysztof Kieslowski has the colours play a very prominent role to accent and reinforce crucial moments. They are not imposed on the top, but are woven naturally into the imagery.

Colour can have symbolic meaning. Many (like Kieslowski) definitely associate red with love and passion. Blue is often seen as respectful, full of longing, melancholy or 'blues-like', while yellow symbolizes joy. Black stands for sorrow; white for purity or innocence. Light colours with femininity and dark ones with masculinity.

BELOW / Colour creates atmosphere both in the posters for the *Three Colours* triology (1993–4) by Krzysztof Kieslowski and also in the films themselves.

BOTTOM / Architecture can also use colour to create space and aid navigation, as at Madrid Barajas Airport, designed by the Richard Rogers Partnership.

But we should be careful. What colours stand for changes between cultures. In one part of the world, yellow can symbolize falseness, while in another it is holy. It's important to check so that your message doesn't convey the wrong impression entirely.

INFORM

Colour also communicates information in lots of different contexts. When lobsters have turned red in boiling water, it's time for the dinner party to begin. In hospitals, yellow means infection and disease, red that something is dirty, blue indicates clean materials and green means sterile.

STRUCTURE

Colours can lend structure by the colour-coding of the sections of an annual report with background colours, and giving visual elements (such as dots and lines) uniform colours. In a magazine, colours help readers navigate sections. Red signals columns, blue reportage, yellow lifestyle and pink culture. The colours recur effectively and tastefully in ornaments and headings in their respective sections.

TEACH

Effective teaching is aided by colour. Bright images or decorative tints encourage reading; colour blocks accentuate diverse parts of content.

BELOW / Colour affects us in many ways. It can be used to reinforce a commerical message, as in Fallon's 'Paint' campaign for Sony; for signage, warning us of radiation; as an aid to navigating sections of a newspaper; or, through witty adaptation of underground maps by Information Architects Japan, give an overview of web trends.

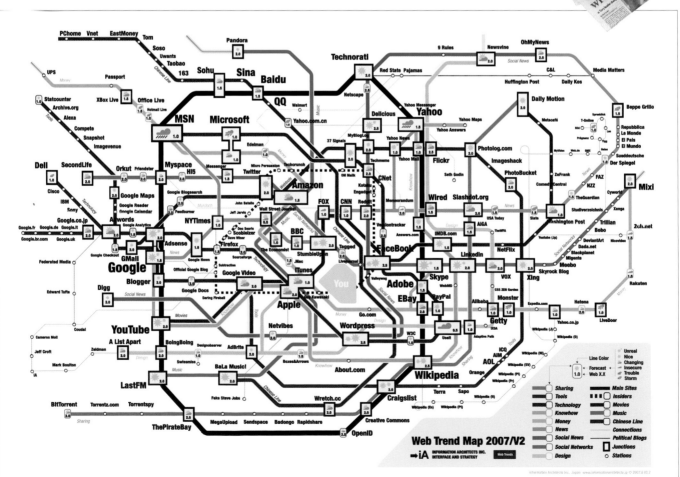

HOW DO WE SEE COLOURS?

All cats are grey in the dark, or so they say. In order to see colour, we need light, and without enough light all the objects around us look dark and depressing.

But if an object is lit by sunlight or artificial light, some rays of light are absorbed and others are reflected. The reflecting rays reach our eyes, which lead the visual impressions on to the brain, where they are converted into what we call colour. It is the ability of our nervous system to react to different wavelengths of electromagnetic radiation that forms the basis of our colour vision.

That is why we see the car as blue not red.

NATURAL COLOUR THEORY

Colours are important elements for many different professional groups. Working with colour unites the designer, the interior designer, the fashion designer and the textile artist.

One of the most common systems of describing colours used by these design professionals is the *Natural Color System* (NCS). This is based on use of colour in the environment and how humans perceive colour, and is the work of the Scandinavian Colour Institute.

The elementary colours of our vision are yellow (Y), red (R), blue (B), green (G), white (W) and black (S). The first four of these are called chromatic colours, while black and white are called achromatic, with no hue. The NCS colour notations are based on how much a certain colour seems to resemble these six elementary colours.

THE COLOUR SPACE

The NCS Colour Space is a three-dimensional model with an axis of white to black and the fully chromatic elementary colours at the compass points on the circumference. All imaginable colours can be plotted and thus given an exact NCS notation. In order to more easily understand the parts included in the NCS notation, the space is divided into two two-dimensional models, the NCS Colour Circle and the NCS Colour Triangle.

THE COLOUR CIRCLE

By taking a horizontal section through the centre of the model, we see the NCS Colour Circle, where four spaces (called quadrants) between the chromatic elementary colours are divided into 100 equal steps. The ten per cent steps represent 40 steps in the colour circle. The hue G30Y describes the degree of resemblance to green (70%) and yellow (30%).

Between yellow and red is orange, between red and blue are the purple colours, between blue and green many bluey-green colours and finally between green and yellow, greeny-yellow colours. The colours in the left half of the circle are experienced as being cold, while those in the right half are warm.

THE COLOUR TRIANGLE

The NCS Colour Triangle is a vertical section through the NCS model at one of the ten per cent steps. The section shows a particular hue, in which the designer can determine the colour's relationship to white, black and the full chromatic colour. The higher up in the triangle that the colour is, the more whitish it is, and the further down the colour is, the more blackish it is. Colours further to the side are more chromatic. The notation S1050 describes the resemblance we see to black (S, here 10%) and to the maximum chromaticity.

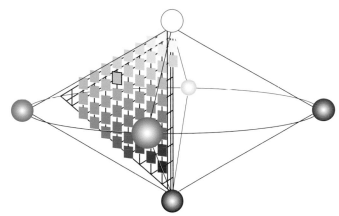

NCS Colour Space

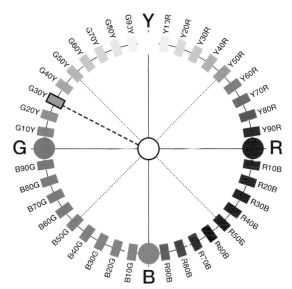

NCS Colour Circle

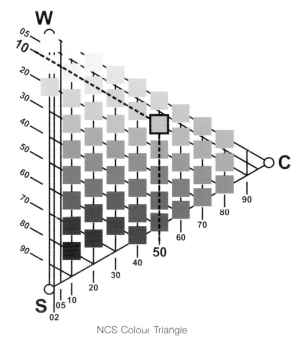

NCS Colour Triangle

ABOVE / The Colour Space, the Colour Circle and the Colour Triangle are instruments to help decide quickly and easily which colour to employ.

CHOOSING COLOURS

With the help of the Colour Circle, the PMS colours (described below) or the computer's colour palette, the designer can choose the exact colour needed for a given purpose, whether it's a colour for packaging or to symbolize a whole company.

It's important to try to imagine the receiver's experience. Is a chilly blue the optimum choice for the label on a bottle of spring water, or is this the conventional and predictable option?

Should the tea packaging be mainly green? Or would red-brown be more appropriate? Traditional and boring? How will the receiver react and what does the designer really think?

COLOUR CONTEXT

Colours are sometimes like chameleons, and change according to their surroundings.

If the designer reproduces a particular chromatic colour against different values of the grey scale, we can see how different the luminous intensity of different colours can be, as in the illustration below. The context always plays a crucial role, and that goes for colours too, which is important to bear in mind.

COLOUR COMBINATIONS

To simplify slightly, the designer can combine colours in three ways. Here we need the Colour Circle again.

Whispering colours

If the designer chooses to combine two colours in the top right quadrant, for example, they will form a harmonious whole and *whisper* to each other.

Speaking colours

On the other hand, if the designer chooses to combine together two or more colours from quadrants that are close to each other, he or she will then obtain colours that are in vital contrast to each other. Such a contrast might be the combination of a blue with a red, which will give a lively impression. These colours *speak* to each other.

Shouting colours

If the designer finally combines colours from quadrants which are opposite each other, a very strong colour contrast will be created. These colours *shout* at each other – the strongest contrast of all is between red and green.

Grey scale

Whispering colours

Speaking colours   Shouting colours

ABOVE & LEFT / A daring poster using 'whispering colours' by Intro for the British Council (left), and multicoloured ads for Apple's iPod, in which the strong colours used provide a thread between the posters in the campaign.

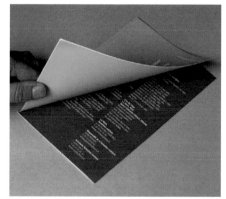
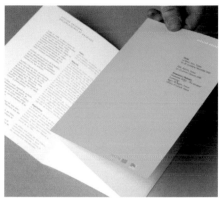

ABOVE / French designer Philippe Apeloig has developed a typography-led approach for the Paris-based film school La fémis, using overlapping type in subtle colour variations in place of images to imbue its literature with a serious pedagogical feel.

Daring colour contrasts can add a great deal to the visual message, just as badly combined colours give shrieking, unprofessional impressions.

Complementary colours

It is said that in 1799 Johann Wolfgang Goethe came to stare at a red blanket on a clothes line during a break from writing. When he then shifted his gaze to the whitewashed gable wall of a house, he saw a green blanket in his mind's eye. He called these colours complementary colours. These colours stand in a remarkable relationship to each other and have provoked lively debate over the centuries.

Besides red and green, these colours are the pairs blue and orange, and purple and yellow. Some colour theorists claim that putting these colours together creates harmony, while others claim the opposite.

COLOURS IN PRINTED MATERIALS

When the designer does not need to print four-colour images but merely wants to reproduce a logo in a certain colour, for example, there are around 1000 different colours in the *Pantone Matching System* (PMS) to choose between. These are available as printed, numbered samples and are ready mixed by printers. They are also used by computer programs, which have no limitations when it comes to colour.

The colour palettes are never-ending and will be discussed in the next chapter, which looks at visual profile.

SUMMARY

'In full colour.'

FUNCTIONAL COLOURS

Colours must have a communicative function, and should:
Attract through colour strength.
Create atmosphere with the help of cold or warm colours for example.
Inform, as in a hospital where yellow indicates infection.
Structure, as in a newspaper where different sections are colour coded.
Teach, for instance through tint blocks which emphasize and clarify certain parts of the material.

NATURAL COLOUR THEORY

The most common system of describing colours is the *Natural Colour System* (NCS), which is based on research into how humans perceive colour. This system is described in the *Colour Space*, the *Colour Circle* and the *Colour Triangle*.

COLOUR COMBINATIONS

The four quadrants (quarters) of the Colour Circle provide a general template for combining colours.
Combinations of colours in the same quadrant produce *whispering colours*.
Colours from adjoining quadrants give *speaking colours*.
Shouting colours are obtained by putting together colours from two quadrants which are opposite each other in the Colour Circle.

14/
PROFILES

ABOVE / Intentionally or not, companies are always sending signals to the outside world. Some strengthen their profile, persuading consumers to buy a product during a major campaign; others make consumers decide never to have anything to do with the company again, after encountering a drunken employee.

'Never ever.'

He's drunk and having great difficulty getting his shopping on to the conveyor at the supermarket till. He drops a six-pack of beer on the floor and it takes him forever to pick it up again.

In the long queue behind him stand some very irritated customers who want nothing more than to buy their goods for the weekend and get home. All of them have seen the company name in big white letters on his dark blue jacket. It says 'Fast Transport Ltd'. All of them form a tacit alliance. Never, ever, will we use that company to transport anything.

CORPORATE PROFILE

Producing isn't only about production, it's also about communication. If a company uses child labour in a poor country and this emerges, that's a form of communication. All decisions have a communicative aspect, as the consequences of the decision can be observed. The 'Butterfly Effect' theory comes into play – according to this the beating of a butterfly's wing on one side of the globe can cause a storm on the other. The theory is based on the view that all parts of a system are interrelated and affect the world around them.

Therefore, in all its dealings with the outside world, a company must always be clear and consistent and inspire confidence. The signals must be unanimous and this coordination, called *visual corporate profile*, is one of the most important elements of brand building. This is so important that it must have a proper and relevant name. The descriptions below make it clear that the term 'profile' is preferable to the often-used term 'identity'.

The profile not only promotes the sales of goods and services in the short term, but also secures the company's long-term survival. This is why it is important for issues concerning this corporate profile to be deeply rooted throughout the company.

The goals of this work can be summarized as follows:

Clarify the company's mission statement and corporate culture.
Contribute to a consistent and positive image of the company.
Contribute to a feeling of solidarity internally and externally.

The work on the corporate profile involves considering and deciding on a number of policy issues. The company's management must agree on three concepts and the way they relate to each other, now and in the future:

Identity – what the company is.
Vision – where you want to be in the future.
Profile – what you want to be seen as.

Identity

The company's innermost being is its identity, its soul, which is based on a history and culture that are often part of the company's very foundations.

The culture can often stem from common values such as the company's rituals (the annual football match or outing), the symbols it uses (striped ties), the language employed (which is always civilized), the music (the managing director loves Julio Iglesias) and the colours (yellow T-shirts).

The management must notice if the identity changes and try to understand why. New management and consequent changes in staff attitudes can be one of the reasons.

Vision

This involves trying to make clear to the staff and the outside world where the company wants to be in the future and which products are to be produced.

The vision statement often has a tendency to be too pompous (describing a shining utopian goal, which not only patronizes the staff but also increases the gap that exists between these words and the actions on the ground). The vision must be concrete, as the future isn't just lying there waiting to happen – it needs to be created here and now.

Profile

The profile the company chooses to convey to the outside world should be derived from its identity and its vision. But it's important to be selective about what is to be put on display. Product characteristics and quality ambitions are obvious, but internal conflicts and a lack of gender equality are things the company should keep to itself (and tackle).

THREE PROFILES

Of course the simplest way to create a profile for a company is to buy advertising space in the mass media and thus gain an opportunity to convey the messages that they want. But the signals from the company can come from so many different places, and the secret is getting them to run in tandem with each other and in the right direction.

The corporate profile is often broken down into the following three components:

Individual profile
Environmental profile
Visual profile

Individual profile

Each company has a great many ambassadors, who represent their workplace all the time. They answer the phone, meet customers, sell goods in a store, explain a service over a desk and reveal things over the dinner table.

To ensure that all these people convey the right profile of the company, the management should explain the company's goals and opportunities through internal marketing, staff welfare and training. This motivates staff and makes them realize the importance of their own contribution, which, in the long run, affects the result. People who are not properly informed cannot take responsibility, but those who are informed cannot avoid it.

Managing directors, who not only have to cope with their job but also have to radiate social expertize, are possibly the most important ambassadors. They have to be role models and mentors, as well as inspiring enthusiasm by expressing the company's goal and visions, often in the mass media. They are in the public eye even when not at work, and know that a person's clothes and even their ringtone reflect their values.

SPONSORSHIP

This gives the managing director the opportunity to be seen at public events and raise the profile of the company.

But sponsorship can also involve a more visible partnership in a *marketing activity* in which the goal is a win-win situation for both parties.

BELOW / Managing directors and founders are usually good ambassadors for a company – they will often participate in sponsorship activities for the company.

It is important to choose the right areas of sponsorship that will match the profile of the company.

A telecommunications company carefully considers which type of sponsorship they should choose. They look for something which reflects energy, perseverance, technology and overcoming hardships. They choose sailing, and resources are made available for a boat and crew in front of the media's reporters and photographers. The logo is clearly visible on the sail and 'quality time' – relaxed socializing with existing and future customers – is provided at the harbour stops at the end of each leg. Everyone can follow the crew's battle with raging seas and icebergs on their mobile phones.

Many sponsor combinations may seem dubious. Volkswagen, the German car manufacturer whose range includes popular, family cars, was chosen as the main sponsor of the Venice Carnival. Everywhere carnival-goers were able to read *'Volkswagen e il Carnevale di Venezia. Arte di strada'*. The art of the street, in other words. The car manufacturer is invading the carnival and making it possible.

We ask Pierangelo Federici how Volkswagen could have been chosen as the main sponsor:

'The German car firm is a very serious and generous sponsor. Without them we would not be able to run the carnival, at least not at its current level. You can ask yourself what a car manufacturer has to do with a carnival. But the Germans have invested long term in sponsoring experiences. A few years ago they were

behind The Rolling Stones' world tour. A great success, if you ignore the fact that Keith Richards refused to drive the Passat they had given him and instead carried on driving his Mercedes.

Venice gains help with information activities, the enormous stage in St Mark's Square and a great deal more besides. Volkswagen gain exposure for their cars and their logo all over the city. And we also help them with special events for very important customers and contacts. But I'm afraid I can't reveal any more.'

Environmental profile

The environment in which the company operates can also be exploited to highlight its profile. The exterior – the architecture – offers great potential. Sydney in Australia shows how a building can represent a whole city. Who doesn't see the fantastic Opera House before their eyes whenever the city's name is mentioned?

The environment also covers the interior premises where staff spend their time and customers are received. The first impression is crucial for a visitor entering a company. The foyer can be experienced as being formal and deserted, or warm and welcoming. A reception can be an impenetrable fortress or a smiling person.

The environmental profile also includes retail premises, and it is becoming increasingly common for architects and designers to work together to increase stores' attractiveness. They must inspire customers. Customers must be assisted by sales staff, but

BELOW & RIGHT / An environmental profile strengthens a brand – the upper-class suites for Virgin Atlantic aim to achieve this, while their in-flight magazine, *Carlos*, is printed in two colours, is illustrated with line drawings, and uses a brown paper stock for its cover to stand out from other luxury magazines.

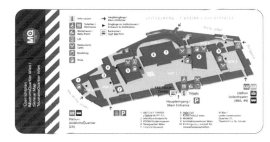

ABOVE / Vienna's MuseumsQuartier houses a range of historic and contemporary museums and art spaces, and therefore needs a uniform visual profile. In contrast to many other museums, they have chosen a playful approach by design team Buro X, rather than an over-prescriptive one.

also have the opportunity to freely wander around and discover the range for themselves. The signals from print and TV advertising must harmonize with the impression given by the store – *good retailing* in other words.

Environmental profile can also include a company's environmental awareness, which is becoming an increasingly important part of how a company is perceived.

Visual profile

The company's identity, vision and core values need to be translated into a visual language – a visual profile. The designer has to carry out in-depth research and analysis which he or she then supplements with large doses of craftsmanship and creativity to create this visual profile.

The designer must ensure that this visual profile is firmly embedded in the company, and find bridges between different departments. Danger threatens when a strategic process starts in one part of the building and a visual process in another.

It is also important to remember that a visual project can never solve problems such as deficient management, a woolly strategy or low product quality. Nevertheless it's often the case that redesigning an old, outdated visual profile can up profits by 15 per cent and lower the average customer age by as many years.

THE VISUAL PROFILE IN PRACTICE

The visual profile often replaces a face-to-face meeting and does so with the help of business cards, letter paper, envelopes, folders, brochures, catalogues, staff magazines, T-shirts, uniforms, cars, signs, flags, advertisements, packaging, commercials, websites and much more besides.

The threats to a clear visual profile are many, as it seems (exaggerating slightly) these days anyone in a company is allowed to design logos and packaging, making a consistent and professional profile difficult to achieve. The solution is a tight grip on the reins, and staff training.

CORPORATE DESIGN PROGRAMME

These tightly held reins for a company's visual profile are called a corporate design programme, and are usually collected in a *graphical* or *visual manual*, which serves as a kind of reference book, consulted as soon as doubts arise on visual production. The manual exists to be followed and therefore it is important to train the people involved in corporate profile issues.

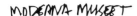

Logotype	Ideograms	Pictograms	Characters	Letter marks

ABOVE / Oxigeno, Norway (Mission Design); eBay (CKS Group); Moderna Museet, Stockholm (Stockholm Design Lab with Greger Ulf Nilsson and Henrik Nygren);

Fashion Center, New York (Pentagram); Tate, UK (Wolff Olins); Public Radio International, USA (Pentagram); Amnesty International (Diana Redhouse); Rowing, Tokyo Olympics

(Masaru Katzumie/Yoshiro Yamashita); Nederlandse Spoorwegen, The Netherlands (Tel Design); *Expressen*, Sweden; Penguin (Edward Young/Jan Tschichold/Pentagram);

WWF (Peter Scott/Landor Associates); Canadian National Railway (Allan Fleming); National Theatre, London (FHK Henrion); RAC, UK (North Design).

A corporate design programme usually includes the following:

Logotype
Symbol
Colours
Templates and rules

LOGOTYPE

A good logotype, which is the core of a company's visual profile, must first and foremost harmonize with the company's mission statement and culture. The logotype is also a visual mirror image of the company, the goods or the service. It must create confidence and trust and definitely not give rise to associations that conflict with the corporate profile. It must also meet the following criteria:

Be easy to recognize.
Be easy to read.
Work in large as well as small typefaces.
Work in a particular colour and also in black only.
Be timeless.

The logotype is the company's or the product's name, or part of it, reproduced in a specially selected typeface. It is sometimes called a *wordmark*.

The most important attribute of the logo is to stand out from the crowd, like the shields on ancient battlefields, which protected their wearer from injury, but also clearly showed who was who amid the smoke and dust, close up and from a distance.

Readability must be high, and this means that it is important to look amongst the romans and sans serifs, and not among the free typefaces.

A distinctive logotype should work just as well in a 3D animation on a huge screen in a sporting arena as it does in black and white on a consignment note or a receipt.

The timeless criterion means that it should not be trendy and tied to a particular period, as it will quickly become outdated. A logo which is in tune with the company and its operations will be long-lived, but will demand regular fine-tuning.

Another criterion for a good logotype is thought to be that it is clear and coherent enough to be used to form a pattern (such as on an exclusive carrier bag or on wrapping paper).

Name

The company's name can be *generic* (descriptive – PianoMove) or *arbitrary* (capricious and with no clear link to the business – Apple).

Internet name

Names for the web are a different matter altogether. They must be short and easy to spell, and it is also a good idea to register the most likely misspellings, which will then direct web users to the right address. The name must also be scalable so that it does not later derail the company's growth and its expansion into new areas. If the company is called 'pears.com' and wants to move into selling apples, the marketing manager is going to have problems – it would have been a better idea to go for 'fruit.com' from the start.

SYMBOL

Many companies choose to supplement the logotype with a symbol, often a simplified image. This is sometimes called a *device mark*. Looking far back into history, we can trace similarities with the mark or sign carved into the wooden handle of a stone axe. The mark became the brand of the early man, and everyone could see that the axe was his and no one else's.

A really well-known and familiar symbol can be used separately from the logotype, on corporate clothing, in a pattern or in the context of sponsorship, for example. A symbol also bridges such barriers as language and culture and thus it can be used worldwide.

Symbols can be divided into the following categories:

Ideograms
Pictograms
Characters
Letter marks

Ideograms

The actual idea behind a company's operations is show by an ideogram. The umbrella of an insurance company refers to the protection and security the company offers.

Pictograms

These are greatly simplified and stylized images. They are common in a corporate context, but are also important elements in the design programme for the Olympic Games, for example.

Characters

A company's operations will often be embodied by a character. A wasp is a cheeky symbol for a newspaper that prides itself on its investigative and revealing journalism.

Letter marks

Acting in almost the same way as a logotype, letter marks tend to consist of initials or abbreviations only.

Several criteria

In brief a symbol must be:

Simple and graphically clear.
Distinctive.
Able to be used in all contexts, irrespective of material and background.
Clear whether large or small in size, and in colour as well as black and white.

There's a story that a toilet-paper manufacturer had trouble selling their product when the packaging was decorated with a pointy and prickly design.

Sales took off, however, when a more 'comfortable' and appropriate design was created.

COLOURS

As they speak directly to our emotions, colours are an important element of visual profile. In consultation with the company's management, the designer selects a special corporate colour that will be used throughout the corporate visual profile, from the logo on the business cards to the sign high up on the roof.

Many people say that blue is the most common corporate colour. This colour is usually associated with dignity and distinction. Others say that red is the colour that will attract attention fastest and is therefore the most common (Canon, Coca-Cola, Kellogg's and others).

TV news broadcasters tend to be dressed in blue, while entertainment programmes signal excitement and fun using orange. Red colours were once used only rarely as they were considered to bleed (not stay in one place). But with today's digital technology offering perfect colour separation, this strong colour is making a comeback.

TEMPLATES AND RULES

Right at the back of the graphical manual are the templates and rules for what letterheads should look like, how the product catalogue is to be designed and how the company's logo and symbol should be used on a stand at a trade fair.

It is important that the person behind the manual does not make the rules too narrow and strict. There needs to be a certain amount of scope for adaptation and creativity.

Nor should they forget the importance of sound in delivering the company's message, and this is dealt with in the next chapter.

BELOW / Red is a desirable colour – it has a powerful signal effect, and there is stiff competition between Canon, Coca-Cola and others for its use in logos.

SUMMARY

'Never ever.'

CORPORATE PROFILE

In all its dealings with the outside world, a company must always be clear and consistent and inspire confidence.
Key concepts:
Identity – what the company is.
Vision – where you want to be in the future.
Profile – what you want to be seen as.

THREE PROFILES

Individual profile is about the image conveyed by the management and the staff.
Environmental profile concerns exteriors and interiors of office space and sales outlets.
Visual profile means translating the company's goals, visions and core values into a visual language.

The design of the visual profile is outlined in a *design programme*, and the rules for applying it in a *graphical* or *visual manual*.

The design programme includes:
Logotype (or wordmark): the name of the company or the product in a particular typeface.
Symbol (or device mark): a simplified image which attempts to encapsulate the company's business.
Colours of the logo and symbol.
Templates and rules for everything from folders to the colours of the cars.

15/
SOUND

ABOVE / 'Our editor wants us to capture the sound of death.' Cynical? Do media organizations have a duty to try and help the people whose suffering they record?

Can such unbearable images change our opinions as well as affecting our emotions?

'The sound of death.'

Somalia, autumn 1992: an emaciated child has crept out to the edge of an aid station. A Western TV crew follows, filming the hopeless fight for life. The camera glides slowly over the little body, zooming in on the flies around the eyes, counting the clearly visible ribs, recording the swollen stomach and tracking across the naked genitals. A reporter is holding a microphone to the dying child's mouth. When an aid worker asks what's going on, the reporter answers, 'Our editor wants us to capture the sound of death.' Cynical journalism?

Sound affects people, perhaps more than we realize. The soundscape is taken in and processed in the inner parts of the human brain, where feelings, memory and instincts share space.

Sound plucks at different emotional strings. Piano music creates one experience, and an annoying doorbell another. Sometimes a sound can be clear, and even insistent, but can often occur as a hidden message, and we certainly notice when it's not there. Silence can be very revealing, as when a politician is struck dumb, caught unawares by a journalist's probing question.

THE JOB OF SOUND

In visual communication, the job of sound is primarily to strengthen, unite and structure.

Strengthen

In a news item on TV or a website, sound creates atmosphere and strengthens experiences, as the receiver uses several senses at the same time, making an immediate impact. In a film scene, a huge whale dives down into the depths to ethereal trumpeting calls.

Sound can bring closeness and depth to otherwise more or less content-free images, often making the experience more vivid. Images in a travel report from the bazaar in Marrakech are brought to life by rhythmic folk music.

Unite

Sound can create a bridge between the film sequences on TV and between stills on a website, providing a sense of unbroken continuity. Music can glue together disparate scenes and disjointed clips, creating a sense of coherence.

In the classic film *Point Blank*, the hero walks with quick, echoing steps along a corridor. As he leaves the building and gets in a car, the steps still sound, continuing throughout the drive, only ceasing when he stops the car and enters a house: high drama.

Sound can also pave the way for an event by coming in early and signposting what is to come, linking everything together and speeding up the narrative. The unmanned level crossing in a picturesque rural setting at first looks idyllic in a film sequence, but not when accompanied by the crashing sound of metal on metal.

Structure

The sound technician can also employ sound to divide up or organize parts of the content, using toe-tapping jazz for one section and a calmer track for another.

SOUND CATEGORIES

The four most common categories of sound are:

Spoken word
Voiceover
Effects
Music

Spoken word

This is provided by talking heads on the TV news, including news anchors, programme and weather presenters, interviewers and correspondents. They all provide the viewer with the latest news, with their words strengthened and supplemented by the studio interior, vignettes, sound effects, lighting, colour, moving pictures and an appropriate personal manner.

Voiceover

Usually an invisible speaker, but occasionally a visible one, the voiceover is a kind of extension of the text in a news or advertising context. Instead of providing a typographical message, the voiceover presents the text in spoken form instead.

However, a voiceover runs the risk of being over-explicit, i.e., saying more or less the same thing in sound as is being said in text and pictures. It is therefore important to make the expressive elements work together, complementing each other instead of repeating each other parrot-fashion.

A dialogue (or an interview) between two people in a TV spot can also provide clear and even entertaining information about a product or service.

Effects

Sound effects can be realistic or they can be designed to create an experience.

Realistic effects may be the sound of a printing press in a large and clattering printworks, fans on the terraces cheering on their football team or a barking dog tied up outside a newsagent's.

The sounds designed to *create an experience* comprise sound effects that, to varying degrees, have been made specially for the purpose in question. A dramatically screeching car tyre or

aggressive footsteps on the pavement at night, disquieting strings or the freedom of the harp.

The sound experience can, of course, be interactive. The visitor to a website can choose the music, move the volume up or down and, in essence, can make the screen into their very own mixing desk.

It is important to be restrained with sound effects, as they can sometimes drown each other out. The solution is *interleaving*, which means 'alternating' so that dialogue does not have to compete for attention with a background sound. Speech – car door closes – speech – car starts.

Many retailers use sound to increase business in their stores. In front of a shop window, a movement sensor sets off a recording that showers the window shopper with offers. And on the way into the store, the shopper steps on a mat with another sensor, which in turn launches another soundtrack aimed at encouraging the right frame of mind to shop.

Music

Composed rhythms, harmonies and melodies make music, and you don't have to be a composer to understand that music is probably the most effective creator of atmosphere. What would a Soderbergh film be without a dramatic soundtrack and what would David Lynch's oeuvre be without suggestive mood music?

The emotional power lies in the fact that the audience often has an extremely personal relationship with certain music, and associations are quickly recalled on their 'internal screen'. This is why it is important not to split the filmed sequences in news broadcasts and advertising too much, taking in a bit of Vivaldi here, a bit of Ryan Adams there. It's better to plant fragments of a musical theme at an early stage, and then gradually develop it into a coherent whole.

A piece of music can also give quick information about time and geography. Renaissance music over footage of Rome and the Sex Pistols over punk-era London take the receiver on a journey through time and space.

SOUND DESIGN

When the door to a Mercedes shuts, you can hear a dull, mechanical sound, like you would hear from a magnificent old safe. This patented sound is meant to signal quality and safety, and is considered as important to our perception of the German luxury car as the logo, chassis and colour.

Called sound design, this indicates an attempt to weave sound into the design and the communication – all to strengthen the brand.

What about the vacuum cleaner? Shouldn't it be a bit quieter? No, if it doesn't make a noise, we consumers think it's not sucking properly. This is called *confirmation sound* – something has to be heard to happen when we press a button (on a computer, say).

Sound also crops up in the next chapter, but only as one part of a greater whole.

16/
INTERPLAY

ABOVE / 'Being too explicit is terrible.'

'You have to leave something for the audience to fill in.'

'You can decorate a Christmas tree with all the glitter, tinsel, flags, baubles and lights that you can get your hands on, making it sparkle and shine.

But you can also decorate it with just three flags, two baubles and one piece of tinsel, and it will sparkle just as much.

Being too explicit is terrible. You have to leave something for the audience to fill in.'

The speaker is an actor, giving an insight on communication.

PARTICIPATION

Without participation, there's no communication, that's obvious. The two words are actually both derived from the Latin *communicare*, which means turning someone into a participant. A passive and uninterested receiver won't let any messages over the threshold, but an active and participating one will.

How does the sender create this participation?

Tell a personal and captivating story, with a high and genuine degree of relevance, and you're halfway there. If you also decide not to tell absolutely everything, you will have got even further. The receiver has to tell the rest, fill in the gaps, participate.

And if you let the words and the pictures work together instead of just standing there yelling at each other, that's a giant leap forwards. If you also leave a little gap between the words and the pictures, the receiver can't help but fill it. Participation, again.

WORDS VS. IMAGES

But not everyone would agree. Words tear images apart, give false information and distort the grey scale of truth, claims a photographer in front of a display of photographs at an art gallery, feeling that words and pictures must be kept apart. A caption, for example, becomes the mouthpiece of the picture, speaking directly to the receiver and steering them down paths of thought that the originator perhaps never intended and never wanted. Beware of words!

A great poet gives the reader complete inner freedom. Words, and words alone, create these internal images for the reader. A drawing or a photograph next to the lines of verse would lock or freeze the words in a particular meaning and the ambiguity of metaphors, for example, would be lost. Beware of images!

ABOVE / Traffic signs are found everywhere, in every village, in every country. Many are so simple and clear that everybody will grasp their meaning.

But some may object in this instance – how are you supposed to know whether you are allowed or forbidden to drive a motorcycle or car?

In one sense, text and images are totally incompatible. They hinder each other, making it more difficult for the receiver to gain a powerful experience.

A picture says more than a thousand words. Or is that just an old wives' tale? Let's prove it wrong anyway. A picture says more than a thousand words, only as much as a thousand words say more than a picture. A thousand apples don't taste any better than a pear, and a thousand pears don't taste any better than an apple. The apple tastes different to the pear, no matter how many of them there are. A thousand words say something different to a picture.

Words and pictures clearly say different things but despite (or perhaps because of) this, they seem to be constantly drawn to one another, and then something always happens.

But what should a partnership between text and image be like in order to work? The answer lies in an in-depth look at semiotics.

SEMIOTICS

Words and images seem completely different, despite the fact that they both have the same origin, the sign. The sign is the prerequisite for all communication, all human exchanges of thoughts and ideas.

We need the sign as a means of expression in order to be able to convey and share our knowledge, ideas, insights and warnings. We also need signs in order to document these, and thus avoid keeping everything in our heads, and we need them to make logical and abstract systems out of theories. Signs enable humans to reflect, alone and together, and to view an experience from the outside.

So what is a sign? It is one letter or more, but it can also be a picture. When we build systems using signs, the opportunities are endless. What we need to do, as a tribe, a group, inhabitants of a country or a continent, is agree on what the signs stand for, otherwise communication is impossible.

All communication (other than sounds and body language) is based on these signs, which, according to the semiotic triangle, are based on the referent (the reality – a fire, for example) and on an interpreter, a person who sees and interprets the fire and its characteristics in words and pictures. The sign itself then consists of an *expression* (which shows something) and *content* (which means something) and it can be broken down into the following three components:

Icon
Index
Symbol

Icon

One component – the icon – stands for similarity, refering to a sign that depicts an object, such as a fire, a bird, a woman or a man.

Index

This stands for proximity, a part-whole relationship or indication of another characteristic of the object, such as smoke. The smoke is indirectly present in the fire (no smoke without fire), and a bird's nest gives away the existence of a bird. A lipstick leads thoughts towards a woman, a tie towards a man.

Symbol

An arbitrary agreement is a symbol, for example when letters, alone or in combination, by convention have come to mean something, for instance the letters F,I,R,E or B,I,R,D. Or in French L,E F,E,U or L',O,I,S,E,A,U.

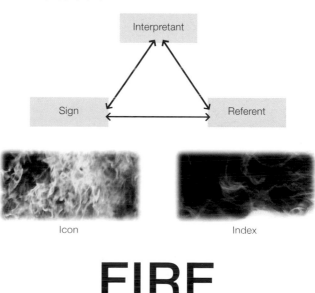

FIRE

'IF YOU SEE
SOMETHING,
SAY SOMETHING'

ABOVE / To the left we have text and to the
right a picture. There are differences between
the two, but also similarities. Placed together
they can make wonders.

Two languages
An icon lets us see something, an index gives us the chance to
work something out and the symbol is a sign which we have to
learn. Icon and index create the visual language and symbol the
verbal. The languages are equal on the level of content – in both
cases it is about fire, bird, woman and man – but on the expression level they differ. The visual language links the fire, the bird, the
woman and the man to a certain extent, while the actual letters
have no natural connection.

Do the differences mean incompatibility? No. Although the
world around us is filled with pictures, most messages are also
filled with text. It seems, in fact, as if pictures can't quite manage
on their own, and vice versa.

The third language
Text and pictures find their way to each other and this results in a
marriage, which is known as the third language, or *verbovisual
communication*, a term which encompasses all the contexts in
which a sender is seeking to inform, educate and convince with
the help of text and images. Sub-categories of this are *lexivisual
communication* in print, and *audiovisual communication* in film,
television and on the web. The combination of the two is called
multivisual communication.

The marriage between text and pictures is so strong that
some media researchers see no cause to distinguish between
them, instead giving the couple a single name, *text*, from the Latin
textere, to weave. How this affects society's view of the unnamed
image is hard to tell.

LEFT AND RIGHT
How is this third language created? Let's start inside our heads.
As we know, the human brain has two hemispheres. The left acts
like a computer – if it encounters a problem, it solves it by dividing it up into small pieces and solving them in a logical order. You
could compare it to cooking a meal, starting by looking up a
recipe in a cookery book and then following the instructions point
by point.

The right hemisphere of the brain works differently, as it sees
the whole picture and thus everything at once. This is where imagination and intuition are found and back in the kitchen, we're
cooking in a completely different way. Instead of following the
cookery book, we think about roughly how we want it to taste
(imagination is the best seasoning). We come up with an impression of the meal we want and work towards it.

Now think of a line. On the left we have text and on the far right
pictures, and in the middle of the line they form a unit. What the
sender, the art director and the designer all know is that the
receiver reads text with the left hemisphere of the brain and sees
pictures with the right.

The left-hand side of the line
Reading demands a certain amount of effort, as the text is an
abstraction which must be decoded and processed. Text stands
for common sense and critical reflection (although words do of
course set off emotions – 'summer nights', 'sunrise' …).

Reading gives the receiver good control of the message. The
reader will understand and take on board the meaning of the
words in a logical fashion – for instance in a poster intended to
combat terrorism in London, on which commuters read: 'If you
see something, say something'. To a Londoner the message is
probably clear.

But text alone lacks visual power, which is something the
image has in abundance.

The right-hand side of the line
Looking takes very little time and very little effort, and a picture
speaks straight to the emotions. The receiver can't really avoid
looking at pictures, so it goes without saying that designers will
choose a picture to dominate a poster. The picture represents
irrationality and intuition (even if a simple, direct picture of a product does not leave much to the imagination). It has strong visual
power, but its weakness is that it gives the receiver little control
over the message.

Pictures are easy to understand on one level, because they
are so similar to the 'reality' they depict, but on closer inspection
the receiver starts to experience more and more, and the associations and interpretations become very personal – too personal.
On a poster in London, travellers can now see a photograph (only
a photograph, no text) of a bus that has been blown up. The
receiver interprets the image in a way the sender might not have
intended – wrongly, in fact. What's more, another receiver will
interpret it completely differently.

In the centre of the line
How can the sender unite the two? Well, in the centre of this text
and image continuum lies the opportunity to give the message
power by combining text and image in front of the receiver's eyes
and letting them work together.

'IF YOU SEE SOMETHING, SAY SOMETHING'

ABOVE / When text and image are placed close to each other but do not say the same thing, receivers' interest is engaged, and they become participants in the message.

INTERPLAY OF TEXT AND IMAGE

A clever combination of text and image has the ability to tell an appealing tale, wildly exceeding what either of the two languages could achieve alone. Quite simply, the effect is to reinforce the message, as the intellectual, verbal element is united with the emotional, visual one. The sender thus will benefit from the similarities and dissimilarities, the strengths and weaknesses, of both of these languages.

Text and image also each have different tempos. We have a tendency to spend more time with a text than with a picture because reading is quite a lengthy process. The image, however, has the ability to go straight in and influence more layers in the viewer than words can. A good combination thus means that text and image together take on a more uniform, common tempo, which better highlights the message. The text calms down the image, which in turn speeds up the text. In London the text 'If you see something, say something' is combined with the photograph of the wreckage of the bus, and a powerful message is conveyed.

It is also the case that for most of us our visual memory is better than our verbal one, which means that combining the two helps us to learn and remember more. What remains in the memory three days later? Approximately ten per cent of what we have only read, but approximately 20 per cent of what we have looked at and a whole 70 per cent of a message that has been conveyed in text and pictures.

There are two main ways of creating an effective interplay between text and image. These methods are based on the famous French media theorist Roland Barthes's theories of *anchorage* and *relay*.

The former is about text and image being anchored in each other, saying and showing the *same* thing and so not expanding the meaning in any way. The text fixes the meaning of the image and vice versa.

In the second method we are looking at a relay which can send the flow off in different directions, becoming a metaphor for a freer interplay. Text and image say *different* things, expanding the meaning of the message. Like in cartoons in which the speech bubbles and the drawings are equally important but convey different meanings, creating a strong message. Let's take a look at these methods in more detail.

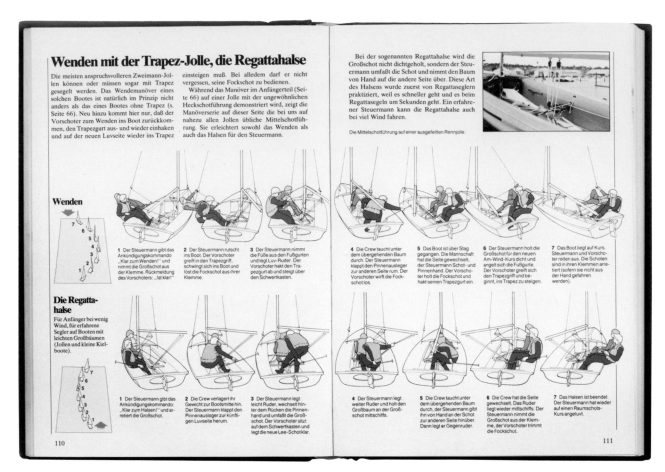

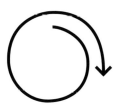

ABOVE / Harmony between text and image means that both give the same information, helping the reader to learn something – in this instance how to sail.

HARMONY

In the first method harmony prevails between text and image.

In a cookery article the text teaches the receiver how to cook a dish step by step. The pictures follow the text, finally showing what a delicious fish soup should end up looking like. In a television report what is shown in the picture is also spoken on the soundtrack. A helicopter sequence shows a major car crash accompanied by the reporter's description. The result is good, informative television journalism.

Instructions and teaching materials also require a close and harmonious interplay between text and image, otherwise it will be difficult for the receiver to understand or learn anything.

Harmony between text and image is most suitable when information, instructions and knowledge are conveyed to the receiver at a time when he or she is *motivated* to receive messages.

IRRITATING HARMONY

In other contexts where the sender wants to grab the attention of and attract the receiver, harmony won't work. This is because the receiver is *unmotivated* in the face of an invasion from a constant bombardment of messages, e.g., advertising. There has to be a different approach: disharmony.

The message becomes long-winded when text and image say the same thing. The receiver quickly puts together the over-explicit message without any effort, and that's that. Let's call this *over-communication*, which makes the receiver passive. The image of a hat is accompanied by a text saying the same thing: hat. Hat, hat. Those working in television sometimes call this

Over-communication

slightly over-explicit way of working 'orange television', as the soundtrack says 'orange' and the film sequence shows an orange. We need something more.

It should also be pointed out that saying the same thing twice (once in the text, once in the picture) isn't about clarification but irritating repetition, irritating repetition, which weakens the message. The receiver can also suspect condescension and a lack of respect on the part of the sender, who seems not to credit the receiver with the ability to understand.

DISHARMONY

The solution is disharmony. It is linked to the relay theory and means that text and image still work together but now in a contradictory manner. Text and image shouldn't say the same thing to receivers. That's a waste of resources. Instead the sender should exploit the respective strengths and unique characteristics of the verbal and visual languages. This is how a dynamic message is created.

Let's take a look at a photograph of a wheelchair with the headline 'Child seat'. The receiver is perplexed but intrigued,

'CHILD SEAT'

'INK SHOULD BE USED FOR WRITING'

'BIKE THIEVES RULE'

wanting to quickly work out and take on board the message. The receiver is forced to solve the puzzle, thereby becoming an active participant: 'Wheelchair? Child seat? A-ha. Children need to be secure in the car, otherwise ... '

This disharmony builds on an apparent lack of agreement in the intractable friction between text and image and context, a kind of breach of code or style. It is when the receiver realizes the new context that the message can be understood.

What's important is not telling as much as possible, but as little as possible. The more the sender takes away, the more the receiver adds. The receiver fills in the gaps on the basis of the limited information, possibly experiences a major 'a-ha' moment, understands the entire chain of events, draws a conclusion, has it confirmed, is rewarded and thus feels both gifted and enriched.

'Ink should be used for writing,' says a poster, whose visual element is restricted to a large picture of a fingerprint. Its aim is to get the receiver to realize the importance of education to avoid illiteracy, which in turn leads to crime and fingerprints on a police file. It's a strong message, which hits home, but also makes major demands of the receiver.

Let's call this *under-communication*. The receiver fills in what is missing, becoming an active player and participant in the message.

'Of course we can govern together' says a newspaper headline, while the picture says something completely different, with politicians going in different directions. This is intelligent interplay, and the receiver is enticed into solving the riddle and reading the article.

There has been a major increase in bike thefts in a town. A reporter has written an article on the subject and come up with the

Under-communication

following headline 'Bike thieves rule'. Now the subeditor has to find a picture to go with it.

A photo of a cyclist on one of the town's streets? No, far too boring. But a police officer giving an opinion on the reasons for the increase in thefts? Yes, that will work. A person whose bike was stolen? Yes, that works too. Powerful bolt cutters? Good. An empty cycle rack? Good. A bus with queues down the street? Even better. An out-of-work bike-shop owner with his arms folded? Very good. A woman walking towards the city in the early morning light? Fantastic.

TEST THE INTERPLAY

There is one simple way of finding out whether text and image are working together effectively. Cover the picture with your hand. Does the headline work on its own? Does it say anything to the receiver? No? Good! Now cover the headline. Does the picture work? Does it say anything to the receiver? No? Good!

Good interplay is confirmed when the receiver doesn't understand the text and image when they are encountered separately,

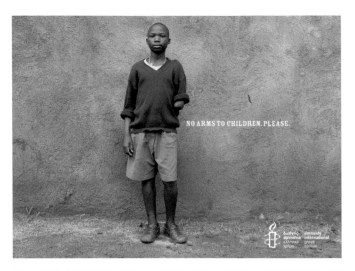

ABOVE & LEFT / Three examples of efficient disharmonious interplay between text and image. If you cover the image, and then the text, it becomes obvious that neither element can communicate on its own, but together the message is immediate and memorable.

but rather when they are placed together, and it is not until this moment that the message in all its entirety comes across. The text and image must be so closely wedded to each other that apart they are meaningless.

Poor interplay is consequently confirmed where text and image actually operate independently, as they are often saying the same over-explicit thing.

Back to the wheelchair and the 'Child seat' headline. If we took the wheelchair away, would the receiver understand anything then? No. What if we took away the headline 'Child seat'? Does the receiver understand anything then? No. Back to the heading, the picture and the whole poster. Does the receiver understand anything? Yes. Child seat and wheelchair. There's a link. A-ha, dangerous, very dangerous.

Now to a classic Volkswagen ad. The message is clear. High petrol costs are killing the economy (and you). The solution to the problem is a fuel-efficient car called a Beetle. If the picture is covered, what remains is a very cryptic headline which is not capable of conveying the message. If we now cover the headline instead, what remains is an image which is very difficult to interpret. Back to the whole ad. Together, but not separately, the text and the image convey the message. This is a sophisticated example of interplay and of the way one plus one can equal three – in other words the whole is more than the sum of its parts.

'That was a really great ad, but I can't remember what it was for!' This is a comment heard quite often, revealing that even on television, advertisers don't get it quite right. So there's a similar test for this medium too.

doing
the
sea.
in it
They're

www.frenchconnection.com

fcuk®

ABOVE / The effect of a message is increased when the user participates. Here we are required to find a meaning from a simple image and a jumble of words. Once we have made a sentence, we understand the story that the advert by clothes store French Connection (fcuk) is telling. Is it too demanding?

A commercial almost always consists of short or long filmed sequences and a concluding shot with a headline, what's known as the *pay-off* (often as a voiceover) and a logo. It is the filmed story plus the concluding presentation of the product that together make the message clear to the audience. Both parts are equally important.

The film test goes like this: Cut out the end. View the sequence without it. If this works as a separate story (whether it is funny, sad, or ...) this is evidence of poor interplay and thus of terrible advertising. The separate parts must operate in symbiosis, making the act meaningless if one part is removed, sinking all communication. It must be remembered that an isolated film sequence, which may be funny in itself, is still nothing more than an isolated funny film sequence.

A car has stopped on one of the town's sloping streets. The driver is a bowler and unloads some of his bowling balls but suddenly drops one, which starts rolling down the street towards two young men who are standing chatting. One of them notices the ball and grinning comes up with a kick worthy of David Beckham in his prime. Now the receiver is unable to follow the drama any longer but that doesn't matter, because it is clear how it ends and also how it could have been prevented. The company behind the ad is an optician, encouraging people to have their eyes checked (and buy new glasses too, of course). And it would all remain nothing but a funny sequence or sketch without the message from the optician coming in at the end.

TOO MUCH DISHARMONY

You can take disharmony and contradiction too far. As humans we are constantly seeking meaning in our surroundings and we hate feeling excluded, as we do when the message doesn't give us enough grounds for imagination and shared creativity.

We can call this type of interplay *poor communication*, which only creates confusion. Now we'll go back to the picture of a wheelchair, but with a new headline – 'Warning'. Would the receiver understand anything? Probably not. This shows very clearly how impossible it can be for the receiver to interpret poor ways of putting text and images together.

ADJUSTED DISHARMONY

Disharmony must be used with care. Having dragged a large bookcase in 13 flat-pack cardboard boxes back from an out-of-town furniture superstore, it's likely that receivers won't really appreciate a playful game with text and pictures in the assembly instructions.

Poor communication

NEWS GRAPHICS

A journalist combines text and images, photographs and drawings, with the aim of conveying information and creating an understanding of often complicated events and concepts.

This combination originated in early groundbreaking reference works in which the editors and designers operated on the basis of the following creed:

Pictures help us see reality.
Words help us understand it.
Photographs help us believe in drawings.
Drawings help us understand photographs.

Photography documents and reveals, drawing simplifies and illustrates, words explain and provide background.

News graphics have no use for separate roles. The photographers can't just concentrate on the photography, the artists can't provide only their drawings and the writers only their text. No, it's all about creating a coherent team, in which all the elements work together. This version of the third language forces them to leave their pigeonholes and start to work together on equal and effective terms, to the benefit of the receivers.

The news graphics toolkit contains: headlines, body text, captions, text in images, photographs (full or detail shots), drawings, diagrams, timelines, arrows, and other elements that, put together, help the receiver to understand.

The photographs will appear in three different contexts. In a *montage*, in which several pictures are combined into one; in a *hybrid*, where a mixture of photography and other image technology (drawn sections or speech bubbles) is created; and finally in *distortion*, in which the colours and the shapes of the photograph are changed.

This work, known as *graphic journalism*, makes a population increase comprehensible in a diagram with figures and pictures; a terrorist attack horribly real in a photographic spread with text elements; and the weather map both clearly informative and educational. All these juxtapositions and elements can be used instead of publishing tired archive pictures that have nothing to say.

Graphics are independent of time and space, which is why the receiver can be transported from a bath house in Pompeii to the innermost heart of the erupting volcano or to George Clooney, revealing his latest film plans at Cannes.

The opportunities are endless, but we should sound a note of caution. Graphics sometimes become an end in themselves. 'We have to go in with the heavy graphics guns here,' the news graphics expert must sometimes think, whether they are relevant or not. Often just one good photograph and a well-written text can be enough. If the only purpose of the graphics is to make staff happy, this will be made embarrassingly plain when there is no factual basis for the image and the end result is merely an empty echo.

Overloaded graphics tire rather than stimulate the receiver, as in some newspapers where naive and exaggerated populism threatens to trivialize important subjects.

BELOW / Two different styles of news graphics from *Die Zeit* and *Folha de S. Paulo*, illustrating efficient combinations of photographs, words and drawings.

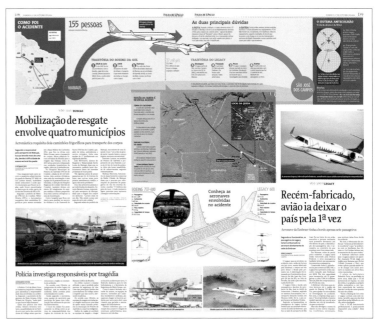

MULTIVISUAL INTERPLAY

The location of a multivisual interplay could be a news broadcast from a television studio. Here are the news anchor and presenter, the spoken word, texts, stills, film, graphics, colour, light, decor and ad breaks. With the right news angle, conveyed using the right multivisual interplay, the news broadcast could be the high point of the night's viewing for many viewers.

The location could also be a catwalk at a fashion house, an exhibition in a museum, or a show in the presence of the artist at a gallery. In these contexts the receiver meets real people of flesh and blood, not just recorded on film or in print. Important, possibly crucial, personal presence and eye contact are the result.

From a considerably larger arena, sound and light burst out around U2. Drums, bass, guitar and vocals come across loud and clear, surrounded by exuberant technical effects. The four members of the band are constantly visible on gigantic video screens above walls of speakers.

Bono starts to speak. He talks about Africa, combating poverty, cancelling Third World debt and improving trade relations. The audience hold up their mobile phones with lit displays (the lighters of today) and then key in the number of an aid fund. Bono makes the audience participants in the power of the music.

Company conferences, congresses and kick-offs are often filled with a fireworks display of media in an attempt to add drama to the annual summary of all the subsidiaries of a large international company. Presentations, interviews and visions are conveyed live and also pre-recorded using a shaky camera. Everyone is present, even those who are physically on the other side of the globe. The result is greater understanding and respect, and, we hope, better business.

But all these examples of multivisual interplay have something missing – interactivity. So far this is offered on websites, enabling a unique interplay very reminiscent of genuine two-way communication. But media trends move fast and television is merging with the internet, as we saw earlier. On a screen on the wall of the apartment, the viewer can make most things happen – check the football results, download a film or even vote in the general election.

But soon the screen won't be on the wall. It will be built into the coffee table, letting the members of the family choose their own media selection. One corner of the table is an arena for a computer game, emails are coming in just next to the coffee cups,

BELOW / U2 know how to combine different elements on stage. Light hits the stage and the members of the band, the chords start, the songs follow, and the words bring it all together to create a powerful whole.

ABOVE & RIGHT / Multivisual interplay in action at the 'Sparking Reaction' exhibition – including animated text and interactive cinema – designed by Casson Mann and Nick Bell, at the Sellafield nuclear power station in Cumbria, UK.

LEFT / Even press packs can take a step into the multivisual world. Here fashion designer John Galliano adds a DVD to his trademark newsprint and elastic band.

ABOVE / A catwalk, as the fashion house fills the air with multivisual interplay – fabrics, patterns, light, music, models, and expectation ...

the central part is for news, while the household budget is being checked in another corner. Suddenly someone stands up and leaves (the bus won't wait) taking the whole multivisual room with her in her pocket, on her mobile.

THE STRENGTH OF MULTIVISUAL INTERPLAY

The combination of all available elements is the real strength of multivisual interplay. It stimulates the receiver to use several senses simultaneously, and the chance of a powerful experience and participation increases dramatically. The receiver sees, hears, feels, and yes, in some contexts, smells and tastes too.

But this strength is also this interplay's weakness. The receiver is overwhelmed by signals and the sorting effort involved is huge. This is quite a challenge for receivers, who need time to interpret and evaluate, and relate the message to previous experiences.

What is the sender to do when the receiver seems to be both stimulated and deafened by the many means of expression? The solution is not to reduce their number (although this can sometimes be worth doing) but to reduce their simultaneous use.

In a television car advert, a faithfully filmed driving sequence, with a concluding pay-off and logo, can often be preferable to adding sales arguments on the soundtrack, and the same argument applies when scrolling text above the film. Simplicity wins, as it usually does.

In his classic *Rear Window*, director Alfred Hitchcock shows how it's done in film. First we see the sleepy, hot backyard. Then

ABOVE / 'Design your own product!'
Increasingly, we can design our own
trainers or create our own cocktails online.

the camera moves to James Stewart's sweating face, on to his plastered legs and then to a table with his broken camera and on the wall a couple of pictures of racing cars. In a single camera movement, the viewer understands where the action is taking place, who the person is, what his job is and what has happened to him. It would have been easier, but more banal, to have James Stewart tell us on the soundtrack that he had been photographing a race, that a wheel came off and injured him. But that sequence wouldn't have involved the audience in the same way.

This desired participation can be achieved without either text or image. A dissatisfied editor of a staff magazine in a large company wonders why there are so few contributions and decides to activate the staff in some way. But how? The next issue of the magazine has no text and no pictures, one page after another. The magazine is empty and white throughout, and there is no mistaking the message about the need for participation. It doesn't take long to produce results. Suddenly everyone wants to write and take photographs for the paper.

But now the sender doesn't need to manipulate receivers to turn them into participants. The consumer wants to be involved and the shift in power is clear. Nike lets visitors to nikeid.com tailor their own trainers and at absolutdrinks.com we can create the dry martini of tomorrow.

VISUAL LIVING ROOM

The interplay creates a whole, which the receiver can find attractive or can dismiss. What goes on in the head, faced with the headlines, photographs, film sequences, colours and shapes, which hold the whole thing together?

The answer possibly lies in a very ordinary context. A home. An apartment. What does this have to do with visual communication and interplay? Well, the interior designers claim that our encounter with the appearance and atmosphere of an apartment is very similar to our encounter with the media room. So let us find out what the receiver finds most attractive. Come on in.

Preference

Even as she crosses the threshold into the hall, the invited guest gains a quick and spontaneous impression of the apartment.

What are the deciding factors? Preference, what she likes and prefers over something else. A welcoming person, a hostess, a host, a smile, a fresh scent, ground coffee, Vivaldi is coming from the living room, which is bathed in evening light.

Like the introductory graphic with the accompanying music jingle for the television channel's news broadcast, where the news anchor creates expectations by saying 'Good evening' in a studio filled with promise.

Complexity

The complexity of the apartment is appealing. The hall leads to the living room, with a glimpse of the kitchen and bedroom beyond. The furniture is arranged in groups. Tarantino, Ronaldinho, Madonna perform on a plasma screen. Glass vases display cut flowers, and in one of them the guest's red tulips are placed. However the complexity should not be exaggerated or it will become cluttered. Too little, on the other hand, and the apartment will be dull.

But when it's right, it's like the inviting and attractive first page of a morning newspaper with strong headlines and pictures.

Complexity is, of course, involved in an intimate relationship with the whole.

The whole

The guest looks around and is attracted by the way the furniture and the rooms are organized. The functional proximity of certain rooms is appreciated, e.g., between the kitchen and the dining room. The group of sofas, the television and the desk are located according to personal taste, as are the oil paintings and the lithographs. Peace on earth from the CD player.

It's like a well-designed website, where general texts and images are combined with film clips and search tools in a logical, hierarchical structure that is easy to navigate.

Space

When the space is arranged so that it is possible to come in and move about without bumping into lampshades and mantelpieces, the guest feels at home. But at the same time she appreciates the cosy, enclosed space that is created when gently surrounded by bookshelves.

ABOVE / A home, an apartment, sends out
communication signals to visitors in exactly
the same way as television, newspapers,
websites, posters or adverts do.

It's like a poster which at a distance and close up attracts and
orients, opens and closes itself in its text, image, colour and
shape as well as its message.

Power

The guest seeks and finds, finally, in an impressive and tasteful
apartment a kind of power that signals assurance (never vague-
ness) and value (never superficiality). A colourful bouquet goes
with the suggestive work of art on the wall and the vase in the window adds a clear accent. Coffee? Yes please. I brought my latest
book with me, it's for you.

It's like an advert where strong visual elements in text and
image break out of the editorial framework and powerfully convey
an urgent message.

WHEN IS IT DONE?

We leave the apartment and ask the art director and designer
when in the working process they know or feel that the visual
interplay work is done? They both answer at once and their
answers are the same.

When nothing can be added. Because that would result in
boring over-explicitness, which would threaten the simplicity.

And nothing can be taken away. Because then the communication would be lost.

SUMMARY

'You have to leave something for the audience to fill in.'

INTERPLAY
The participation of the receiver is crucial to effective visual
communication. The key to this is the interplay between text
and image.

THE INTERPLAY OF TEXT AND IMAGE
Text and image work together in two ways:
In *harmony*, where the text says the same thing as the
    image, which is excellent for a motivated receiver in a
    cookery book but irritatingly over-explicit in an ad.
In *disharmony* the text and image work together in a
    contradictory manner, which can often encourage an
    unmotivated receiver to participate in the message.

MULTIVISUAL INTERPLAY
Text, typography, stills, sound, film and design are the
different means of expression that can work together in a
multivisual context, e.g., in a news broadcast in a television
studio. Interactivity makes the interplay even more powerful.

VISUAL SYSTEM
One attempt to systematize the feelings of the receiver
faced with a visual arrangement covers the following points:
preference, complexity, the whole, space and power.

234

FURTHER READING

Albers, Josef, *Interaction of Colour*, revised and expanded edition, New Haven, Connecticut: Yale University Press, 2006

Baines, Phil and Andrew Haslam, *Type and Typography*, London: Laurence King and New York: Watson-Guptill, 2002; revised edition, 2005

Baird, Russell N., Arthur T. Turnbull and Duncan McDonald, *The Graphics of Communication: Typography, Layout, and Design*, New York: Holt, Rinehart and Winston, 1987

Barry, Anne Marie Seward, *Visual Intelligence: Perception, Image and Manipulation in Visual Communication*, New York: State University of New York Press, 1997

Barthes, Roland, *Camera Lucida: Reflections on Photography*, translated by Richard Howard, New York: Hill and Wang, 1982

Berger, Arthur Asa, *Narratives in Popular Culture, Media and Everyday Life*, Thousand Oaks, California: Sage, 1997

Berger, Arthur Asa, *Ads, Fads, and Consumer Culture: Advertising's Impact on American Character and Society*, 3rd edition, Lanham, Maryland: Rowman and Littlefield, 2007

Berger, John, *Ways of Seeing,* London: Penguin and New York: Viking Press, 1972; reprinted, 1995

Bergquist, Claes, *The Creative Revolution*, Stockholm: CBC, 1997

Bergström, Bo, *Arbeta med medier*, Malmö: Liber, 2000

Bergström, Bo, *Grafisk kommunikation*, 4th edition, Malmö: Liber, 2007

Bergström, Bo, *Bild & Budskap*, 2nd edition, Stockholm: Carlssons, 2003

Bergström, Bo, *Webbdesign*, 2nd edition, Malmö: Liber, 2003

Bergström, Bo, *Titta!*, Stockholm: Carlssons, 2004

Bergström, Bo, *Effektiv visuell kommunikation*, 6th edition, Stockholm: Carlssons, 2007

Bergström, Bo, *Information och reklam*, 5th edition, Malmö: Liber, 2007

Bignell, Jonathan, *Media Semiotics: An Introduction*, Manchester: Manchester University Press, 1997

Black, Roger, *Web Sites that Work*, San José: California: Adobe Press, 1997

Boyle, Tom, *Design for Multimedia Learning*, Upper Saddle River, New Jersey: Prentice Hall, 1997

Bringhurst, Robert, *The Elements of Typographic Style*, 3rd edition, Point Roberts, Washington: Hartley and Marks, 1997

Brook, Peter, *The Empty Space,* New York: Avon, 1969

Burns, Aaron, *Typography*, New York: Reinhold, 1961

Carter, David E., *The Little Book of Layouts: Good Designs and Why They Work*, New York: Harper Design, 2003

Crowley, David, *Magazine Covers*, London: Mitchell Beazley, 2006

Dair, Carl, *Design with Type*, Toronto: University of Toronto Press, 2000

Hogbin, Stephen, *Appearance and Reality: A Visual Handbook for Artists, Designers, and Makers*, Bethel, Connecticut: Cambium Press, 2000

Hollis, Richard, *Graphic Design: A Concise History*, London and New York: Thames & Hudson, 1996

Horn, Robert E., *Visual Language: Global Communication for the 21st Century*, Bainbridge Island, Washington: MacroVU Press, 1998

Ingledew, John, *Photography*, London: Laurence King, 2005; as *The Creative Photographer: A Complete Guide to Photography*, New York: Harry N. Abrams, 2005

Itten, Johannes, *The Art of Color: The Subjective Experience and Objective Rational of Color*, revised edition, New York: John Wiley, 1997

7

Jury, David, *About Face: Reviving the Rules of Typography*, Hove, Sussex: RotoVision and Gloucester, Massachusetts: Rockport, 2002

Kao, John, *Jamming: The Art and Discipline of Business Creativity*, New York: HarperBusiness, 1997

Kepes, György, *Language of Vision*, Chicago: Paul Theobald, 1947

Klein, Naomi, *No Logo: Taking Aim at the Brand Bullies*, London: Flamingo and New York: Picador, 2000

Kress, Gunther and Theo van Leeuwen, *Reading Images: The Grammar of Visual Design*, London and New York: Routledge, 1996

Kristof, Ray and Amy Satran, *Interactivity by Design: Creating and Communicating with New Media*, Mountain View, California: Adobe Press, 1995

Laurel, Brenda, *Computers as Theatre*, Reading, Massachusetts: Addison Wesley, 1993

Lester, Paul Martin, *Visual Communication: Images with Messages*, Belmont, California: Wadsworth, 1995; reprinted, 2000

Lester, Paul Martin and Susan Dente Ross (editors), *Images that Injure: Pictorial Stereotypes in the Media*, Westport, Connecticut: Praeger, 2003

Livingston, Alan and Isabella Livingston, *The Thames and Hudson Dictionary of Graphic Design and Designers*, London and New York: Thames & Hudson, 2003

Lupton, Ellen, *Mixing Messages: Contemporary Graphic Design in America*, London and New York: Thames & Hudson, 1996

Lupton, Ellen, *Thinking with Type: A Critical Guide for Designers, Writers, Editors, & Students*, New York: Princeton Architectural Press, 2004

Messaris, Paul, *Visual 'Literacy': Image, Mind, and Reality*, Boulder, Colorado: Westview Press, 1994

Neumann, Eckhard, *Functional Graphic Design in the 20s*, New York: Reinhold, 1967

Pentagram, *Ideas on Design*, London: Faber and Faber, 1986

Poynor, Rick, *Design without Boundaries: Visual Communication in the Nineties*, London: Booth-Clibborn, 2000

Poynor, Rick, *Obey the Giant: Life in the Image World*, London: August Media and Basel: Birkhäuser, 2001

Saint-Martin, Fernande, *Semiotics of Visual Language*, Bloomington: Indiana University Press, 1990

Shaughnessy, Adrian, *How to Be a Graphic Designer Without Losing Your Soul*, London: Laurence King, and New York: Princeton Architectural Press, 2005

Shawcross, Nancy M., *Roland Barthes on Photography: The Critical Tradition in Perspective*, Gainesville: University Press of Florida, 1997

Sontag, Susan, *On Photography*, New York: Farrar Straus and Giroux, 1977; London: Allen Lane, 1978

Swann, Alan, *Graphic Design School*, London and New York: HarperCollins, 1991

Truffaut, François, *Le Cinéma selon Hitchcock*, Paris: Laffont, 1966; as *Hitchcock/Truffaut*, Paris: Gallimard, 2005

Tufte, Edward R., *Visual Explanations: Images and Quantities, Evidence and Narrative*, Cheshire, Connecticut: Graphics Press, 1997

Velande, Gilles, *Designing Exhibitions*, London: Design Council, 1988

Wilde, Richard and Judith Wilde, *Visual Literacy: A Conceptual Approach to Graphic Problem Solving*, New York: Watson-Guptill, 1991

Williamson, Judith, *Decoding Advertisements: Ideology and Meaning in Advertising*, London: Marion Boyars, 1978; reprinted, 2000

Zappaterra, Yolanda, *Editorial Design*, London: Laurence King, 2007; as *Art Direction + Editorial Design*, New York: Harry N. Abrams, 2007

PICTURE CREDITS

The publishers would like to thank all those who have supplied images and granted permission for their reproduction in this book. Every effort has been made to contact all copyright holders, but should there be any errors or omissions, Laurence King Publishing Ltd would be pleased to insert the appropriate acknowledgement in any subsequent printing of this publication.

Particular thanks go to Phil Baines and Andy Haslam for permission to reproduce the diagram, with captions, on page 101, which is taken from their book *Type & Typography*, second edition, Laurence King Publishing, 2005.

9, 10 Video Yesteryear/Photofest © Video Yesteryear
11 Photographer: the author
13 © Moemake Media Group/epa/Corbis
14 The Kobal Collection/Toho
15 Newmarket Films/Photofest © Newmarket Films
16 Image Source/Getty Images
17TL © NDP/Alamy
17TR Photographer: the author
18T © Moemake Media Group/epa/Corbis
18B © Mizzima News/epa/Corbis
19 Newmarket Films/Photofest © Newmarket Films
20L Client: HRF; Agency: Nimbus, Stockholm; Photographer: Kenneth Westerlund
20R 'Heroin Baby' advertisement. Client: Barnardo's; Agency: Bartle Bogle Hegarty; Art Director: Adrian Rossi; Copywriter: Alex Grieve; Photographer: Nick Georgiou
21T © Ed Kashi/Corbis
21B Client: Iberia Airlines; Agency: FCB/Tapsa; Creative Director: Julian Zuazo; Art Director: Antonio Botella; Copywriter: Manuel Perez de Camino
22L Sephane de Sakutin/AFP/Getty Images
22R Photo by Michael Steele/Getty Images
23T American Zoetrope/The Ronald Grant Archive
23C Courtesy Kasandra Productions
23B Campaign: Engmo Dun
24 Client: Björn Borg AB; Agency: Farfar, Stockholm
25L © Centre Pompidou
25R Courtesy Ikea
26L Poster for *MUT gegen rechte Gewalt.* Photography by Olaf Blecker
26r © Julia Fullerton-Batten/Getty Images
27 © Gareth Byrne/Alamy
29 Puma 'New Stuff' poster campaign. Photography by Andrew Zuckerman
30 © Greg Elms/Lonely Planet Images/Getty Images
31 © Stuart Franklin/Magnum Photos
32 © 2008 Digital image, The Museum of Modern Art, New York/Scala, Florence
33 Photo by Cynthia Johnson/Time Life Pictures/Getty Images
35 Copyright © BBC
36 Stills from Honda 'Cogs' commercial by Wieden+Kennedy London. Directed by Antoine Bardou-Jacquet
37 Puma 'New Stuff' poster campaign. Photography by Andrew Zuckerman
38 Arcade Fire website design by Vincent Morisset and Dominic Turmell. Illustration by Tracy Maurice. www.vincentmorisset.com
39L Art direction and design by North, London
39TR Art direction and design by Experimental Jetset
39BR Courtesy Stanley Donwood, Lazarides Gallery, London
40T Design and art direction by Farrow Design, London
40B Illustration by Jon Gray for Penguin
41L Cover of *Eye,* the international review of graphic design, issue 53, Autumn 2004. Design and art direction by Nick Bell, Nick Bell Design, London

41R *Re-Magazine.* Art direction and design by Jop van Bennekom
43 Photo by Arjen Schmitz; Courtesy Maurice Mentjens Design
44 Photo by Giuseppe Cacace/Getty Images
46 Courtesy Orla Kiely
47L Photo by Arjen Schmitz; Courtesy Maurice Mentjens Design
47R Photo courtesy Smart
48T 'For The Journey' Lloyds TSB TV commercial. Agency: RKCR/Y&R; Director: Marc Craste; Produced by Studio AKA
48B Courtesy Lloyds TSB Group plc
49 Courtesy Bang & Olufsen
50 Client: Sony Playstation; Agency: TBWA\Paris; Photography: Dimitri Daniloff. Courtesy Levine/Leavitt, New York
52 © Ahmad Fayyaz/epa/Corbis
53TL Courtesy Air France
53TR Courtesy Bayer
53BL Courtesy CNN
53BR Courtesy Kellogg's
55TL Courtesy Guardian Newspapers Ltd
55BL Courtesy *El Pais*
55R News from Baghdad, anonymous blog of US soldier in Iraq. newsfrombaghdad.blogspot.com
56L 'Absolut Obsession' poster. Client: Absolut Vodka; Agency: TWBA\Chiat\Day; Creative Director: David Page; Art Directors: Jackie End, Bill Montgomery; Photography by Serge Paulet
56R Client: Energizer; Agency: Naga DDB; Creative Director: Ted Lim; Art Director: Yip Chee Keong
57 © Diana Ninov/Alamy
59 Client: Pedestrian Council of Australia; Saatchi & Saatchi, Sydney; Creative Director: David Nobay; Art Directors: Jay Benjamin, Andy DiLallo
60 GDT/Getty Images
61 © Leonard McLane/Getty Images
62 © Rich Reid Photography.com/Getty Images
63T Client: United Nations; Agency: Saatchi & Saatchi, Sydney; Creative Director: David Nobay; Art Director: Vince Lagana; Copywriter: Luke Chess
63B Courtesy BMW Group
64L Client: Proctor & Gamble, Yes/Fairy; Agency: Grey, Stockholm; Art Director: Sten Åkerblom; Copywriter: Martin Stadhammar; Photographer: Erik Hagman
64R Client: Dyson; Director: Philip Hunt, Studio AKA; Agency: Miles Calcraft Briginshaw Duffy
65T Client: Marc Sands – Marketing Director, Guardian News & Media; Agency: Wieden+Kennedy London; Creatives: Michael Russoff, Mark Shillum, Ian Perkins, Sophie Bodoh; Planner: Lisa Conway
65B Client: Cadburys; Agency: Fallon, UK; Creative Director: Juan Cabral; Production: Blink Productions. Thanks also to Garon Michael and to Lindsay MacGowan of Stan Winston Studio
66 Robert Laberge/Getty Images for Nike
67 © Jean-Paul Gaultier Parfums
68 Courtesy Mary Boone Gallery, New York
69 Client: Pedestrian Council of Australia; Saatchi & Saatchi, Sydney; Creative Director: David Nobay; Art Directors: Jay Benjamin, Andy DiLallo
70T Client: Lego; Agency: Blattner Brunner; Executive Creative Director: Jay Giesen/Dave Kwasnick; Art Director: Derek Julin
70B Client: Clima Co., LTD; Agency: Leo Burnett, Bangkok; Executive Creative Director: Keeratie Chaimoungkalo; Creative Director: Keeratie Chaimoungkalo/Sompat Trisadikun; Copywriter: Noranit Yasopa; Art Directors: Pipat Uraporn, Sompat Trisadikun; Photographer: Chup Nokkeaw
71 Mario Tama/Getty Images
72 © Kevin Carter/Corbis/Sygma
73T Christophe Simon/AFP/Getty Images

73R Copyright © BBC
74 Rex Features
77 Tom Stoddart/Getty Images
78 Photographer: Elisabeth Zeilon
79 ACT campaign featuring Anna Friel. Client: Women's Aid; Agency: Grey London; Art Directors/Copywriters: Nicola Hawes/Andy Forest; Photographer: Rankin
80 Client: Unicef; Agency: Forsman & Bodenfors, Stockholm – Karin Frisell, John Bergdahl and Lars Jansson
81 Client: Fame Adlabs; Agency: Contract; Creative Director: Raj Nair; Art Director: Shruthi Gopalakrishnan; Copywriter: Sriram Athray; Photographer: Raj Mistry
83T © Photolibrary.com/Getty Images
83B Photographer: Åke Sandström
84TL Gloster Furniture, Ekerö Möbler
84TR © Barbara Peacock/Getty Images
84B *Morvern Callar* film poster. Client: Momentum Pictures; Design: Julian House, INTRO
87 Client: Lego; Agency: Draftfcb; Executive Creative Director: Brett Morris; Creative Team: Charles Foley/Lance Vining
88–9 Client: *The Economist*; Agency: Abbot Mead Vickers BBDO; Creatives: Paul Belford, Nigel Roberts
90T Posters for Benetton. Art direction and photography by Olivero Toscani
90B Honda 'Hate' commercial. Client: Honda; Agency: Wieden+Kennedy London; Creative Directors: Kim Papworth, Tony Davidson; Directors: Smith & Foulkes; Production: Nexus Productions
91L Courtesy KesselsKramer
91R 'Diesel Action!' campaign. Client: Diesel; Agency: KesselsKramer; Photography: Carl de Keyzer/Magnum
92 Client: Lego; Agency: Draftfcb; Executive Creative Director: Brett Morris; Creative Team: Charles Foley/Lance Vining
95 Detail from *Art in Sacred Spaces: Catherine Yass.* Design and art direction by Neville Brody Research Studios, London
96 Chris Hondros/Getty Images
97TL Poster for Beck, *The Information* – art direction and design by Big Active, London
97BL *Art in Sacred Spaces.* Design and art direction by Neville Brody Research Studios, London
97R Christoph Hein, *Das goldene Vlies*, Faber & Faber. Design: Frank Eilenberger
98TL World Press Freedom Day – World Association of Newspapers
98BL Volkswagen 'Save Fuel' campaign. Client: Volkswagen UK; Agency: DDB London; Art Director: Nick Allsop; Typographer: Spencer Lawrence; Copywriter: Simon Veksner; Illustrators: Peter Grundy, Arthur Mount, Russell Cobb; Creative Director: Jeremy Craigen; Brand Manager: Catherine Woolfe
98R *The Guardian.* Creative editor: Mark Porter
99T Central Lettering Record and the Museum & Study Collection at Central Saint Martins College of Art & Design
99C Central Lettering Record and the Museum & Study Collection at Central Saint Martins College of Art & Design. Courtesy Vatican Library, Rome
99B Central Lettering Record and the Museum & Study Collection at Central Saint Martins College of Art & Design. Courtesy Trinity College, Dublin
100T, TC Central Lettering Record and the Museum & Study Collection at Central Saint Martins College of Art & Design. Courtesy British Library, London
100BC The Trustees of the National Library of Scotland
100B Central Lettering Record and the Museum & Study Collection at Central Saint Martins College of Art & Design. Photo: Tim Marshall

101T Thanks to Stephanie Nash and Anthony Michael
101B Diagram and captions reproduced courtesy Phil Baines and Andrew Haslam, from *Type & Typography*, second edition, Laurence King Publishing, 2005
103B DaMa font, courtesy Dalton Maag
105 Book covers from the Penguin Great Ideas series, Volumes I and II. Design: David Pearson; Art direction: Jim Stoddart
108 Courtesy Trey Laird
110L Designer: Studio8
110R Invitations for Haunch of Venison, London. Design: Spin, London
111T *Viewpoint* magazine. Art direction and design by Big Active, London
111B Invitations for Haunch of Venison, London. Design: Spin, London
113 Jim and Jamie Dutcher/Getty Images
114 Extract from *City of Glass*, copyright © Paul Auster, 1985, reprinted by permission of Carol Mann Literary Agency on behalf of the author
115L *McSweeney's* Issues 2 and 3; Edited and designed by Dave Eggers
116B Courtesy Unicef
117 Image courtesy Advertising Archives. Stills from Guinness 'Horses' commercial. Client: Guinness; Agency: Bartle Bogle Hegarty; Director: Jonathan Glazer
119 Blend Images/Getty Images
120 Photographer: Mikael Öun
121T Vatican Museums, Rome
121B Nick Ut/AP/PA Photos
122L *The Guardian*. Creative editor: Mark Porter
122TR © Alexander Chadwick/AP/PA Photos
122BR Courtesy YouTube
123 Photograph by Spencer Platt/Getty Images
125TL Jerry Grayson/Helifilms Australia PTY Ltd/Getty Images
125CL James Nielsen/AFP/Getty Images
125R Marko Georgiev/Getty Images
125B Mario Tama/Getty Images
126TL Image Source/Getty Images
126TR www.photodisc.com/Alamy
126C Scanpix/Bildhuset; Photographer: Bengt af Geijerstam
126B Courtesy Volvo Group
127 © The Photolibrary Wales/Alamy
128T Getty Images
128R www.photodisc.com/Alamy
129TL © mackney/Alamy
129BL Courtesy Mercedes-Benz
129R 'Absolut Venice' poster. Client: Absolut Vodka; Agency: TWBA\Chiat\Day
130 Client: Volvo; Agency: Forsman & Bodenfors, Stockholm; Photographer: Frederik Lieberath
131 Client: Amnesty; Agency: Publicis Stockholm; Copywriter: Malin Åkersten Triumf; Art Director: Yasin Lekorchi; Account Director: Magnus Svensson; Account Manager: Maria Florell; Production Manager: Margit Blom; Final Art: Anders Modén; Photographers: Niklas Alm, Mattias Nilsson, Vostro; Retouch Artist: Sofia Cederström, Vostro; Media: Jeanette Asteborg, Zenithmedia
132T Client: Procter & Gamble; Agency: Saatchi & Saatchi, Dubai
132B Client: Volvo; Agency: Forsman & Bodenfors, Stockholm; Photographer: Frederik Lieberath
133T, TC, BC Courtesy Subaru
133B Mike Powell, Allsport Concepts/ Getty Images
134 Jerome Ferraro, Stone/Getty Images
135 'Flawed/Flawless' campaign for Dove. Client: Unilever; Agency: Ogilvy & Mather; Art Director: Dennis Lewis; Copywriter: Joerg Herzog; Photographer: Rankin
136L © Adrian Green/Getty Images
136R © Johner/Getty Images

137L ML Harris, Iconica/Getty Images
137R © So Hing-Keung/Corbis
138T © Thomas Kroeger/imagebroker/ Alamy
138BL © Jupiter Images/Brand X/Alamy
138BR © Dan Atkin/Alamy
139 Scanpix/Bildhuset. Photographer: Bruno Ehrs
140 Photographer: Peter Harron
141T © Lee Friedlander, courtesy Fraenkel Gallery, San Francisco
141BL Photographer: Åke Sandström
141BR Photographer: Per Adolphson
142 Photography by Ben Stockley at AGM for Nike
143T © Dan Atkin/Alamy
143B Photographer: Hans Bjurling
144 © Michael Jenner/Alamy
145 Photography by Robert Doisneau/ Rapho, Camera Press London
146L © Jens Lucking/Getty Images
146TC, TR Chaloner Woods/Getty Images
146CL Roger Wood/Getty Images
146CR © Vince Bevan/Alamy
146BL Bill Brandt/Picture Post/Getty Images
146BR Hulton Archive/Getty Images
147T © Andrew Carruth/Alamy
147B Photographer: The author
148T © Enigma/Alamy
148BL © PhotoAlto/Alamy
148BR Marysa Dowling/Millennium Images, UK
149 Somos/Veer/Getty Images
150 © Peter Glass/Alamy
151TL, TC, TR Blend Images/Getty Images
151C Digital Vision/Getty Images
151B Hitoshi Nishimura, Taxi Japan/Getty Images
152 ZenShui/Laurence Mouton/Getty Images
153 Courtesy Fernando Gutiérrez, Studio Fernando Gutiérrez, London (Photography of spreads by Richard Dean)
154 Client: SJ; Agency: Tempel, Stockholm
155 Photographer: Peter Harron
156 Studio photographs by Paul Statham
157L Courtesy Maria Miesenberger, Lars Bohman Gallery, Stockholm
159 © Robert Capa © 2001 By Cornell Capa/Magnum Photos
160 Photographer: Peter Harron
161 © Stockbyte/Alamy
162 'Heroin Baby' advertisement. Client: Barnardo's; Agency: Bartle Bogle Hegarty; Art Director: Adrian Rossi; Copywriter: Alex Grieve; Photographer: Nick Georgiou
165 'Builders of tomorrow' advertisement. Client: Lego; Agency: Jung von Matt, Hamburg; Photographer: Achim Lippoth
166 Photographer: Åke Sandström
167C Museum für Gestaltung, Zurich. Poster collection. Photographer: Franz Xaver Jaggy
167R Courtesy Hearst Communications (Collection of R. Roger Remington)
168T Photography of spreads by Richard Dean
168BL Cover of *The Face*, no.38, July 1983. Courtesy Neville Brody
168BR Poster for Sagmeister AIGA talk in Detroit. Design and art direction by Sagmeister, Inc.
169 Sony Bravia 'Balls' commercial. Client: Sony Bravia; Agency: Fallon, London; Creative Directors: Richard Flintham, Juan Cabral; Production: MJZ; Director: Nicolai Fuglsig; Art Buyers: Susie Morley, Sara Kavanagh; Photographer: Peter Funch
171 Spreads from *kid's wear* magazine. Published by Achim Lippoth. www.kidswear-magazine.com
172L Cover for Razorlight, *Rip it Up* CD single. Client: Mercury Records. Design: Julian House, INTRO
172R Courtesy Todd Kurnat, Circuit 73
173T Client: Nike; Agency: Ogilvy; Creative Director: Craig Smith; Art Directors: Naoki Ga, PeiPei Ng

173B Thomas Mann, *Der Tod in Venedig und andere Erzählungen*, Fischer Taschenbuch Verlag, 2004
174 Cover of *Eye*, the international review of graphic design, issue 66, Winter 2007. Design and art direction by Simon Esterson, Esterson Associates, London
175T Leo Burnett international website. Courtesy Leo Burnett, Chicago. Client: Leo Burnett Worldwide; Agency: Leo Burnett USA; Production House: Arc Worldwide Canada; Creative Directors: Mark Tutssel, Shirley Ward-Taggart; Art Directors: Peter Gomes, Charlyn Wee
175B Courtesy Mario Garcia; Art direction by Paulo Ripoll for Garcia Media and Massimo Gentile for *Folha de S. Paulo*
176TL Book covers from the Penguin Journeys series. Design: David Pearson; Art direction: Jim Stoddart. Illustration: Victoria Sawdon
176TR Re-branded promotional material for the Young Vic. Client: Young Vic Theatre Company – Re-brand. Design: Adrian Talbot, INTRO
176C Courtesy Bally; Photographer: Sølve Sundsbo
176B Photography of spreads by Richard Dean
177 Courtesy New York Review Books. Cover design: Katy Homans
178L Cover design: Hoop Design and Pentagram
178R Cover design: Roger Fawcett-Tang
179T © Lee Ross
179BL, BR Courtesy Grandpeople
180 Courtesy Fernando Gutiérrez
181 Photography of spreads by Richard Dean
182–3T Client: Orrefors, Sweden, Agency: Furturniture, Stockholm; Photographer: Pål Allan
182–3CT Courtesy *Creative Review*
182–3CB Courtesy Todd Lippy, *Esopus*; Images by David Michalek
182–3B Stills from Live Earth stings: 'Use Less Hot Water', 'Ride a Bike', Client: Live Earth; Directors: Julian House + Camella Kirk
184 Spreads from Robin Muir, *David Bailey: Chasing Rainbows*, Thames & Hudson, 2001; Art direction and design by Big Active, London
185L Courtesy *Le Monde*
185R Courtesy *Het Parool*
186 Stills from Channel 4 idents. Client: Channel 4; Agency: 4 Creative; Director: Brett Foraker; Art Director: Russell Appleford
187 Stills from MTV History of Dance idents. Client: MTV; Created by Matt Pyke; Universal Everything, with Renascent, Amsterdam. Sound by Freefarm. www.universaleverything.com
188T © Ahmed Jadallah/Reuters/ Corbis
188B © François Pugnet/Kipa/Corbis
189TL Courtesy Reuters
189CL Courtesy BBC
189BL Courtesy CNN
189B project: N!03, www.ennezerotre.it; webdesign: www.fortsetzungswerk.de
190 Client: Lego; Agency: Jung von Matt, Hamburg; Photographer: Achim Lippoth
191 *F, Fotografisk tidskrift*; Photographer: Mats Bäcker
193 Courtesy Rob Ryan. www.misterrob.co.uk
194 © 2004 David S. Holloway/All Rights Reserved/Getty Images
195 Courtesy Rob Ryan
196 Courtesy Su Blackwell
197TL Courtesy soDA – soDA #26 'Surface', front cover; ISBN 3-907868-26-9
197TR Courtesy of Walter Van Beirendonck and Paul Boudens
198B Rankin, *Fashion Stories*; Courtesy BB/Saunders
199 Web Trend Map 2008 Beta; Courtesy Information Architects

200 Nino Strohecker, *Victims 05300*, from the film *Victims* by Nino Strohecker, courtesy Designstudio S, Stockholm
201BL, BR © Richard Bryant/Arcaid/ Alamy
202TL Sony Bravia 'Paint' commercial. Client: Sony Bravia; Agency: Fallon, London; Creative Directors: Richard Flintham, Juan Cabral
202TR *The Observer*. Creative Editor: Mark Porter
202B Web Trend Map 2007 Version 2.0; Courtesy Information Architects
203 NCS-Natural Color System®© property of Scandinavian Colour Institute AB, Stockholm 2008. References to NCS®© in this publication are used with permission from the Scandinavian Colour Institute AB
204BL 'Languages for Europe' Berlin conference poster. Client: British Council, Berlin; Design: Adrian Talbot, INTRO
204R Justin Sullivan/Getty Images
205 Courtesy Philippe Apeloig; www.apeloig.com
207 Courtesy Buro X
208 Photographer: the author
209L David Paul Morris/Getty Images
209R © Iain Farley/Alamy
210T *Carlos* magazine. Client: Virgin Atlantic; Publisher: John Brown Citrus Publishing
210 Courtesy PearsonLloyd Design for Virgin Atlantic
211 Courtesy Buro X
213 © B.S.P.I./Corbis
215, 216 © Kevin Carter/Corbis/Sygma
219 © Alessandro Rizzi/Getty Images
220 Photographer: The author
221T Phillip Barker/iStockphoto
221BL © Westend61/Alamy
221BR © Educated Savage Photography/Alamy
222, 223 Dylan Martinez/AFP/Getty Images
224 Bob Bond, *The Handbook of Sailing* (German edition), Dorling Kindersley, 1980
225TL Etac, Sweden
225BL adroach/iStockphoto. Original campaign for UNESCO by Karin Frisell, John Bergdahl and Lars Jansson
225R © Alessandro Rizzi/Getty Images
226TL Client: Amnesty International; Agency Upset!, Athens; Creative Directors: Lazaros Nikiforidis, Petros Paschalidis. Photography © Gideon Mendel/Corbis
226BL Image courtesy Advertising Archives. Client: Absolut Vodka; Agency: TWBA
226R Client: Volkswagen; Agency: Doyle Dane Bernbach
227 Image courtesy Advertising Archives. FCUK campaign, Spring 2000. Client: French Connection; Agency: TBWA\London; Creative director: Trevor Beattie
228L Courtesy *Die Zeit*
228R Courtesy Mario Garcia
229 Andreas Solaro/AFP/Getty Images
230 'Sparking Reaction' exhibition, Sellafield, Cumbria, 2002. Courtesy Casson Mann and Nick Bell Design. Client: Science Museum; Lead Consultant and Exhibition Designer: Casson Mann – Team: Nick Bell Design (Graphic Design), DHA Design (Lighting Design), Immersion Studio (AV Design)
231T © Frances M. Roberts/Alamy
231B Thanks to Stephanie Nash and Anthony Michael
232L Courtesy Nike
232R Courtesy Absolut
233 Photographer: Åke Sandström

INDEX

Page numbers in *italic* refer to illustrations.